the letter
PAUL CÉZ

Alex Danchev (1955–2016)
was a historian and biographer who explored the political
and ethical force of art, and wrote a number of acclaimed
biographies, including *Cezanne: A Life* and *Georges Braque:
A Life*. A regular contributor to *The Times Literary Supplement*
and *Times Higher Education*, he was Professor of International
Relations at the University of St Andrews and held Fellowships
at the Wilson Center in Washington, DC, St Antony's
College, Oxford, and Queen Mary, London.

Ma femme, qui chargée de
soin de pourvoir à notre alimentation
journalière, fait téanie et la
souci que ça donne, ~~partage~~
prends part aux tourments de
madame Chocquet, et lui
présente ainsi que votre servite
ses plus respectueuses salutations.
Quant au petit, il est terrib.
sur toute la ligne, et nous
prépare du mal pour l'avenir

Je termine en vous souhaitant
bonne santé, ~~et je puis avec~~
reconnaissance, votre dévoué

Paul Cézanne

the letters of
PAUL CÉZANNE

Edited and translated by Alex Danchev

With 75 illustrations

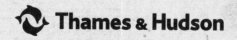

Thames & Hudson

FOR D.

Cover: Composite image.
All letter fragments, plus line drawings at top of front and back covers:
Private collection, courtesy Musée des Lettres et Manuscrits, Paris.
Front, centre: Collection of Mr and Mrs Paul Mellon, in Honor of the
50th Anniversary of the National Gallery of Art, Washington, DC.
Front periphery excluding letters and line drawings, clockwise from top left:
Wallis Foundation Fund in memory of Hal B. Wallis, Los Angeles County
Museum of Art; National Gallery, London; Musée d'Orsay, Paris;
Bridgestone Museum of Art, Ishibashi Foundation, Tokyo.
Back, top left: Brooklyn Museum, New York.
Back, top centre and bottom left: National Gallery of Art, Washington, D.C.
p. 1: Envelope addressed by Cézanne to Gustave Geffroy, 17 May 1898.
pp. 2–3: Letter to Victor Chocquet, 7 February 1879.

First published in the United Kingdom in 2013 by
Thames & Hudson Ltd, 181A High Holborn, London WC1V 7QX

First paperback edition 2019

The Letters of Paul Cézanne © 2013 and 2019 Alex Danchev

Alex Danchev has asserted his moral right under the Copyright,
Designs and Patents Act 1988 to be identified as the author of this work.

British Library Cataloguing-in-Publication Data
A catalogue record for this book is available from the British Library

ISBN 978-0-500-29517-5

Printed and bound in China by Everbest Printing Investment Ltd

To find out about all our publications, please visit
www.thamesandhudson.com. There you can subscribe
to our e-newsletter, browse or download our current
catalogue, and buy any titles that are in print.

CONTENTS

Self-Portrait with Soft Hat, c. 1890–94.
Oil on canvas, 61.2 x 50.1 cm (24⅛ x 19¾ in.).

Introduction

'PICTOR SEMPER VIRENS'

The letters of Paul Cézanne share a certain fugitive quality with their author. Occasionally, when special care had to be taken, he would draft them, in a sketchbook. He did this for business letters of various kinds, including begging letters to his father, in which he negotiated the terms of the allowance that kept him afloat until well into middle age. As a professional artist Cézanne was remarkably unsuccessful, as his father did not fail to remind him. With the partial exception of his mother, who liked the wrong things – her favourite picture was her son's faithful copy of Félix-Nicolas Frillié's melodrama, *The Kiss of the Muse* – none of his immediate family had any regard for him as an artist. All disembarrassed themselves of his paintings as soon as they decently could – in some cases sooner.

Behind his back, in 1899, his younger sister's husband sold two works by Cézanne to his dealer, Ambroise Vollard, for the derisory sum of 600 francs. His elder sister retained only one. She could hardly bear to have his paintings in the house. Immediately after Cézanne's death, in 1907, his son, who was effectively his agent and who should have known better, sold 29 for 213,000 francs, together with 187 watercolours for 62,000 francs. Regular sales and regular payments continued thereafter, subsidizing a life of indulgence and improvidence, crowned by some disastrous speculation on the stock exchange. In 1912, for example, he received 40,000 francs for *The Feast*, otherwise known as *The Orgy*; and in 1913, 100,000 francs for *The Card Players* (sold by Vollard to Albert C. Barnes for ten times that figure in 1925). Nor did he hesitate to break up his father's sketchbooks in order to sell the individual sheets, including the draft letters. He sold to the collector Paul Guillaume a sheet containing the draft of a fascinating letter to Marius Roux, author of *The Substance and the Shadow*

(1878), a novel whose central character was plainly modelled on Cézanne – as Cézanne himself had just read:

Mon cher compatriote

Although our friendly relations haven't been kept up very well, in the sense that I haven't often knocked at your hospitable door, nevertheless I do not hesitate to write to you today. I hope that you will be able to separate my small personality as Impressionist painter from the man, and that you will want only to remember the comrade. So it is not at all as the author of *L'Ombre et la proie* [sic] that I am calling on you, but as the *Aquasixtain* [man from Aix], under whose sun I too first saw the light of day, and I take the liberty of introducing you to my eminent friend and musician Cabaner. I beg you to look favourably on his request, and at the same time I commend myself to you in case the day of the Salon ever dawns for me.

In the hope that my request will be favourably received, please accept this expression of my thanks and my confraternal regards.

P. Cézanne
Pictor semper virens[1]

Here was a carefully crafted missive: at the same time an appeal for help on behalf of a friend, the eccentric Ernest Cabaner (Rimbaud's piano teacher); an indication that he had read and understood Roux's novel; and a subtle but unmistakable riposte. Cézanne's valedictions, often playful, are apt to be revealing. On another occasion, he signed off a letter to the writer and critic Gustave Geffroy with the Delphic formula, 'Paul Cézanne, painter by inclination' – a perfect example of the difficulty experienced by so many of his contemporaries in knowing how to take him.[2] Cézanne was a practised ironist, with a sharper wit and a keener intelligence than most of his fellows. He was hard to read. His speech was as difficult to interpret as his antics; Renoir remarked on the half-serious, half-joking quality of his talk. With age, he became increasingly disinhibited. His discourse might be erudite, gnomic, profane, wistful or philosophical. He had a number of comic routines: 'I who am not practical in life, I lean on my sister, who leans on her advisor, a Jesuit (those people are very strong), who leans on Rome'; 'That Gauguin! I had one little *sensation*, and he stole it from me. He took it to Brittany, Martinique, Tahiti, that's right, on all the steamships! That Gauguin!'[3] These routines had a serious undertow. Cézanne did feel that he was *faible dans la vie*, as he liked to say; he did believe in the fundamental importance of his *sensations*, or sensory experiences, especially when painting outdoors, *sur le motif*, in nature; and he did think that he had been plagiarized or misprized by Gauguin.

Cézanne's letters are a sort of serial adumbration of his world view, and they raise other difficulties of interpretation. The older Cézanne has been caricatured (or mythologized) as an unreconstructed Catholic reactionary, his nose buried in *La Croix*, his faith a rock, his church a haven, his politics an instinctual mix of blood and soil and chauvinism. That is roughly the line peddled by Vollard, who wrote the first book about him, in 1914 – a series of reminiscences masquerading as a kind of celebrity memoir. It constructs a helpless, almost childlike Cézanne, a political simpleton, a preconscious pilgrim, clinging to *le bon droit* in all its forms – the church, the state, the army – even the Boers. It seems oblivious to any contradictions, such as the lifelong insistence on *le sale bourgeois*, to say nothing of *le sale* Abbé Roux ('he's a leech'); the subversive strain, in art and life, running to a regal portrait of his dwarfish friend Achille Emperaire, and a denunciation of the real Emperor, Napoleon III ('the tyrant'); or his unshakeable loyalty to 'the humble and colossal Pissarro', an anarchist and a Jew, at a time when nationalism and anti-Semitism poisoned the land.[4] As so often, Cézanne escapes easy categorization. 'To be a Catholic,' he wrote to his son, near the end, 'I think one has to be devoid of all sense of fairness, but to keep an eye on one's own interests.' Expressions of patriotic fervour were not always to be taken straight. 'I learn with great patriotic satisfaction that the venerable statesman who presides over the political destinies of France is going to honour our country with a visit; for the people of southern France, their cup runneth over.'[5] According to Martin Heidegger – one of many philosophers and writers who drew deep inspiration from his life and work – Cézanne's philosophy was at once coherent and parsimonious: 'He said: "Life is terrifying." I have been saying just that for forty years.'[6]

Cézanne is miscast as a simpleton. Stupidity was not his forte. On the contrary, he was a thinker-painter of formidable penetration. But he could play the country bumpkin with the best of them. ('I won't offer you my hand, Monsieur

Cézanne setting out to a paint in the landscape near Auvers, c. 1874.

Manet, I haven't washed for a week.')[7] His familiars in Aix were all traditional craftsmen, such as the baker Gasquet, the locksmith Rougier and the gardener Vallier; even the sculptor Solari could be assimilated into this company. The tradition and the craft were important to him. Cézanne was a man for the *longue durée*. He admired intellectual seriousness and revelled in ideas; he also had a feeling for peasant life, and for those who lived it. 'Renoir is skilful,' he told Joachim Gasquet. 'Pissarro is a peasant.'[8] Little doubt which he preferred. He was deeply cultured and deliberately uncivilized. Salons of any sort made him squirm. Café society left him cold. 'Parisian wit bores me rigid,' he would say; 'Forgive me. I'm only a painter.'[9] At bottom was a curious mixture of pride and humility. He masked both by appearing as 'a sort of puppet figure,' Monet thought, 'testy, naive, ridiculous'.[10] Being Cézanne entailed an element of performance. In person, this was a convenient disguise. On paper, the mask drops. The intelligence shines through. The letters give the lie to the caricatures.

'Painter by inclination' ended a perky little note revealing an inclination to paint Geffroy's portrait. It was also an ironic acknowledgment of the standard criticism of his painting, with which Cézanne was only too familiar. 'Baffling imbalances,' wrote J.-K. Huysmans in the renowned collection *Certains* (1889): 'houses tilted to one side as if drunk, skewed fruit in besotted pottery, nude bathers defined by lines that are demented but throbbing'.[11] Intoxication was a staple theme. A survey of contemporary artists conducted by the prestigious *Mercure de France* in 1905 on 'Current Trends in the Plastic Arts' included the extraordinary question, 'What do you make of Cézanne?' The responses ranged from veneration to execration. 'Nothing to say about the paintings of Cézanne,' ran one that achieved a certain notoriety. 'The painting of a drunken cesspit-emptier.'[12] The painter's admirers took due note. Whenever they got together, Maurice Denis and Paul Sérusier used to raise a glass to the drunken cesspit-emptier.

'Pictor semper virens', as Cézanne styled himself to Roux, was a clever rejoinder. The message is clear: this *pictor* (painter) is *semper virens* (evergreen) – that is to say, still vigorous or still game, as he explained in another letter to his friend Numa Coste – which is precisely what his fictional alter ego was not.[13] In Roux's novel, the Cézanne character ends his days a ruined man. He is rumoured to have committed suicide (Cézanne-like figures often come to a bad end), and in the closing pages he is found lurking, deranged, in the pre-cincts of the Louvre. Thus, in more ways than one, Cézanne was contesting his fate. He was also serving notice that he was perfectly capable of recognizing and accepting his fictional selves, or distinguishing between art and life – 'separating my small personality of Impressionist painter from the man,' as he put it to Roux, leaving us to gauge the appropriate measure of irony in that self-deprecating phrase.[14]

Love letters, too, had need of special care. It is possible that Cézanne drafted only one, at the age of forty-six. It appears on the back of a landscape, acquired by the Albertina in Vienna in 1924; frustratingly, there is no provenance. It begins with a jolt of recognition – 'I saw you' – for Cézanne, the fundamental requirement. It ends abruptly at the foot of the page.

> I saw you, and you let me kiss you, from that moment I have had no peace from profound turmoil. You will forgive the liberty that a soul tormented by anxiety takes in writing to you. I do not know how to describe to you that liberty that you may find so great, but how could I remain oppressed by this dejection? Is it not better to give expression to an emotion than to conceal it?
>
> Why, I ask myself, be silent about my torment? Is it not a relief from suffering to be permitted to express it? And if physical pain seems to find some relief in the cries of the afflicted, is it not natural, Madame, that psychological suffering should seek some respite in the confession made to the object of adoration?
>
> I quite realize that this letter, sent hastily and prematurely, may appear indiscreet, has nothing to recommend me to you but the goodness of …[15]

The woman's identity has always been a mystery. Speculation has focused on a young maid at the Cézanne family home in Aix, by the name of Fanny.[16] On the face of it that is plausible, and yet highly unlikely. Fanny had left the fam-ily's service the year before. The tone of the letter does not suggest that he was writing to a young girl, and to a servant at that; and he appears to have had every expectation that its recipient would write back. Moreover, he was remarkably consistent in his attitude to domestic servants, treating them all with the utmost respect, and with a propriety bordering on prudishness. He disapproved of his father's dalliances, and of the liberties taken by his friends. Cézanne took liberties on the canvas – and sometimes on the page.

For several months after this encounter Cézanne was in such turmoil that he could hardly paint. His mental state and his movements can be tracked in the letters to his boyhood friend and comrade-in-arms, Émile Zola. For Cézanne, his relationship with Zola was unsurpassed. Theirs was one of the seminal artistic liaisons: as intimate, as complex, as fascinating and as fathomless as any in the annals of modernism. They grew up together – in the same cradle, said Zola. They loved each other, it is tempting to say, like brothers. They continued to do so, in spite of everything that came between them, even after the publication of Zola's novel *L'Œuvre* (1886) – the work that is supposed to have caused a fatal rupture, and that figures as a kind of time bomb in the letters.

On 14 April 1885 Cézanne's agitated request for help signalled his distress:

Mon cher Émile

I'm writing to ask if you would be kind enough to answer me. I should be much obliged if you would do me some service, which is I think tiny for you and vast for me. It would be to receive some letters for me, and to forward them by post to the address that I'll send you later. Either I am mad or I am sane, *Trahit sua quemque voluptas!* [Each towed by his own fancy!] I appeal to you and I beg your forgiveness, happy are the wise, don't refuse me this service, I don't know where to turn. My dear friend, warmest wishes,

Paul Cézanne

I am weak and can do you no service; as I shall leave this world before you, I will put in a good word with the Almighty to find you a good place.[17]

The quotation he reached for here was from Virgil's second *Eclogue*, which he had translated for himself some twenty years before:

A shepherd, Corydon, burned with love for his master's favourite,
Handsome Alexis. Little reason had he for hope;
But he was always going into the beech plantation
Under whose spires and shades, alone with his futile passion,

He poured forth words like these, piecemeal, to wood and hill: ...
Fierce lioness goes after wolf, wolf after goat,
The wanton goat goes after the flowering clover, and I
Go after you, Alexis – each towed by his own fancy.

The quotation and the source were absolutely characteristic. Classical reference was second nature to Cézanne, who was perhaps the best-educated painter of his generation. At the Collège Bourbon in Aix he carried off a succession of prizes for Latin and Greek translation, and almost everything else besides (except painting and drawing). 'Trahit sua quemque voluptas' was not merely schoolboy showing off or grown-up surface polish. He was steeped in Virgil, in Horace, in Lucretius. They were part of him; they shaped his world. It is hardly an exaggeration to say that they helped him to live his life.

They were also deeply embedded in his letter-writing, to his first and best friend in particular. When Zola left Aix for Paris, in 1858, Cézanne was nineteen. After five years of constant companionship, the enforced separation hit them hard. They started an intensive correspondence, by turns playful, doleful, scatological and confessional. 'Since you left Aix, *mon cher*, I've been weighed down by gloomy melancholy: I'm not lying, believe me,' Cézanne assured him lugubriously. 'I feel heavy, stupid and slow. I'd really like to see you ... but meanwhile I lament your absence.'[18] Their mutual lamentations were grounded in Virgil. The dialogue they struck up in their letters was deliberately patterned on the dialogue between two shepherds, Meliboeus and Tityrus, in the first of the *Eclogues*. By the time Cézanne appealed for help in connection with his moment of madness or saneness with the unknown woman, he had been trafficking in the classics for nearly thirty years.

Nothing came of that moment. After four months of telegraphic anguish and erratic wandering, Cézanne returned to Aix, disconsolate. 'So, for me, complete isolation,' he wrote to Zola. 'The brothel in town, or some other, but that's all. I pay, the word is dirty, but I need some peace, and at this price I ought to get it.'[19] Shaken, he sought fresh guidance on how to live. Virgil was already ringing in his ears. As he knew full well, the *Eclogues* and the *Georgics* contained awful warnings about the lengths to which any pitiable creature might be driven by sexual passion. Virgil was haunted by the theme of the destructive power of passion. Passion, he argued, must be eliminated for the sake of peaceful

Portrait of Émile Zola, 1882–83. Pencil on paper,
from a sketchbook measuring 21.7 x 12.4 cm (8½ x 4⅞ in.).

Cézanne's studio in Aix.

and ethical works and days. For Cézanne, this argument was bound to recall the tremendous denunciation of irrational sexual passion in Lucretius, whose great work *De rerum natura* (*On the Nature of Things*) was bound to appeal to an artist whose sense of connection with things was almost uncanny. Cézanne found in Lucretius a man after his own heart. 'Take my advice,' says the poet, 'and keep your fancy free.' Cézanne's confessional letter to Zola was at once a paraphrase and enactment of Lucretius's epic poem:

> For if what you love is absent, none the less
> Its images are there, and the sweet name
> Sounds in your ears. Ah, cursed images!
> Flee them you must and all the food of love
> Reject, and turn your mind away, and throw
> The pent-up fluid into other bodies,
> And let it go, not with one single love
> Straitjacketed, not storing in your heart
> The certainty of endless cares and pain.
> For feeding quickens the sore and strengthens it,
> And day by day the madness grows and woe
> Is heaped on woe, unless the first wounds by new blows
> Are deadened and while the wound's still fresh you cure it
> By wandering with Venus of the streets
> Or to some newer purpose turn your mind.[20]

~

Sometimes he meditated on a letter, or let it lie, for days at a time. He would begin it, set it aside, add to it, costively, before drawing it to a close. Whether this was ponderation or procrastination is a moot point. When he was down, he was loath to write, or loath to post the letter. All his life Cézanne was prone to mood swings and melancholia. 'I'm feeling a bit down,' he wrote to Zola at the age of twenty-seven, in 1866, after carrying the letter around in his pocket for almost a week. 'As you know, I don't know what causes it, it comes back every evening when the sun goes down, and then it rains. That brings on the gloom.' His friends used to joke about his habitual refrain of 'the sky of the future looks very black for me'.[21] Later on there was some loose talk of his going mad; Cézanne himself spoke of 'cerebral depression'. Some of the gloomy thoughts and reclusive behaviour of the last ten years of his life might suggest depressive tendencies, or simply phases of the kind that he had come to terms with thirty years before. Around 1890 he was diagnosed with diabetes. What exactly this meant for him is difficult to establish with precision. His letters offer some guidance. 'I received your letters of various dates fairly close together,' he wrote to his son during the baking hot summer of 1906:

> If I didn't reply immediately, it's because of the oppressive heat we're
> having. It fairly saps the brain and stops me from thinking. I get up early and
> it's only really between five and eight that I can lead my own life. By that
> time the heat becomes stupefying, and saps the brain so much that I can't
> even think of painting. I've had to call Doctor Guillaumont, having caught
> bronchitis, I've abandoned homeopathy for old-fashioned mixed syrups.
> I coughed a good deal, Mother Brémond applied some cotton wool
> in iodine, and that helped. I regret my advanced age, because of my
> *sensations colorantes*.[22]

The mix of the professional and the personal, the philosophical and the diurnal, the confessional and the medicinal, is typical of the profound humanity of his late letters. In the stubborn incantations of Cézanne's last words there is something of Samuel Beckett: 'You must go on, I can't go on, I'll go on.'[23] As with Cézanne becoming Cézanne, Beckett becoming Beckett was a long haul. Cézanne had a hand in that process, as Beckett's letters reveal.[24]

A few months later Cézanne sent his son a Beckettian bulletin:

> I continue to work with difficulty, but finally there is something. That's the
> important thing, I think. Since *sensations* are my stock-in-trade, I believe I'm
> impervious. So I'll let the wretch (you know who) imitate me as much as he
> likes, he's not much of a threat. ...
>
> Everything goes by with frightening speed, I'm not doing too badly.
> I look after myself, I eat well.
>
> Would you be kind enough to order me two dozen mongoose-hair
> brushes, like those we ordered last year.

Self-Portrait and a Portrait of Cézanne's Son, c. 1880–81.
Pencil on paper, from a sketchbook measuring 21.7 x 12.4 cm (8½ x 4⅞ in.).

Aix, 16 Janvier 1902,

Mon cher Monet,

Je vous remercie d'avoir
pris le soin de me
prévenir de l'arrivée —
prochaine dans la
bonne ville d'Aix, de
cet ami éclairé des ~~Arts~~.
Je le recevrai avec les égards
~~et les~~ convenances dûs à une
personne mue par le
mobile de si magnifiques
~~intentions~~. L'occasion qui
s'est présentée pour avoir de
vos nouvelles, me touche
profondément, et j'~~en~~
profite pour vous remercier

Letter to Claude Monet, 16 January 1902.

Mon cher Paul, to give you the satisfactory news you want, I would have to be twenty years younger. I repeat, I eat well, and a little boost to morale would do me a power of good, but only work can give me that. All my compatriots are arseholes [*culs*] beside me. I should have told you that I received the cocoa.[25]

Cézanne adjusted to his debilities as he adjusted to changes in the weather. As he grew older, he dug deep within himself and achieved a rare self-knowledge. Like Baudelaire, he often had the feeling that he would be better off where he was not. From the shores of Lake Annecy in the Haute-Savoie he wrote to his friend Philippe Solari: 'When I was in Aix, I had the feeling that I'd be better off somewhere else; now that I'm here, I miss Aix. For me life is becoming deadly tedious. ... To relieve my boredom, I'm painting. It's not much fun.' Contrary to popular belief, Cézanne had a sense of humour. He might even poke fun at himself and his situation. 'After much toing and froing, my family, in whose hands I find myself for the moment, have persuaded me to stay put in this spot, for the time being. It is a temperate zone. The surrounding hills are fairly high. Narrowed here by two headlands, the lake seems to lend itself to the linear exercises of young misses. It's still nature, certainly, but rather as we have learned to see it in the travel albums of young ladies.'[26]

Melancholic, diabetic, splenetic he may have been – or simply bored – but nothing would stop him painting.

~

For the most part, there was no delay in the letter-writing. He wrote them and he sent them. He wrote with feeling – very often with gusto. In writing and in speech, Cézanne was acutely sensitive to the forms of *politesse*, but he did not mince his words. On one occasion, when he visited Monet at Giverny, his host had no sooner embarked on a few gracious words of welcome than Cézanne stalked off, muttering imprecations, apparently thinking he was being made fun of, his parting shot to the assembled company ringing in their ears: 'You, too, can bugger off!'[27] A famous letter to Émile Bernard urged him to 'treat nature in terms of the cylinder, the sphere and the cone, everything put in perspective, so that each side of an object, of a plane, leads to a central point. Lines parallel to the horizon give breadth, be it a section of nature or, if you prefer, of the spectacle that Pater Omnipotens Oeterne Deus spreads before our eyes. Lines perpendicular to this horizon give depth.'[28] In this lesson on perspective the invocation of the deity was a piece of *politesse*. It was a nod to Bernard's religiosity rather than an indication of Cézanne's.

There is *politesse* aplenty in the letters, yet Cézanne was not given to dissembling or telling people what they wanted to hear. At their first meeting, in 1896, the poet Joachim Gasquet (son of Cézanne's friend Henri Gasquet) waxed lyrical about the *Mont Sainte-Victoire with Large Pine* that he had seen in a recent exhibition of the Société des Amis des Arts in Aix. Impulsively, Cézanne made him a present of it. Gasquet then received a note to the effect that he was about to leave for Paris. Shortly afterwards they bumped into each other in Aix. That evening Cézanne composed another letter, unburdening himself to his young admirer:

Cher Monsieur Gasquet,

I met you this evening at the bottom of the Cours [the main avenue in Aix], you were accompanied by Madame Gasquet. If I am not mistaken, you appeared to be extremely angry with me.

If you could but see inside me, the man within, you would not be. You do not see, then, the sad state to which I am reduced. No longer my own master, the man who does not exist. Yet you, who would be a philosopher, want to finish me off? But I curse the Geffroys and the other scoundrels who, for a fifty-franc article, have drawn the attention of the public to me. All my life, I have worked to be able to earn my living, but I thought that one could paint well without attracting attention to one's private life. Certainly an artist wishes to improve himself intellectually as much as possible, but the man should remain obscure. The pleasure must be found in the study. If it had been left to me, I should have stayed in my corner with a few friends from the studio with whom I might go out for the odd drink. I still have a good friend from that time, well, he has not been successful, which does not prevent him from being a damn sight better painter than those good-for-nothings with their medals and decorations that bring one out in a sweat. Do you expect me to believe in anything at my age? Besides, I am as good as dead. You are young, and I understand that you would like to succeed. But for me, what is there left to do in my situation but keep my head down; and if I were not so fond of the lie of the land, I should not be here.

But I have bored you enough as it is, and now that I have explained my situation, I hope that you will no longer look on me as if I had somehow threatened your safety.[29]

For all its gloom and doom and hyperbole, this letter demonstrates a strong measure of self-awareness. First of all, it was a reasonably accurate appreciation of his situation as reflected in the attitudes of society at large. In a certain sense he was neither dead nor alive, like the hunter Gracchus in Kafka's story: 'Nobody knows of me, and if anyone knew he would not know where I could be found, and if he knew where I could be found he would not know how to deal with me, he would not know how to help me.'[30] 'Cézanne appears to be a fantasy,' declared the critic André Mellerio at precisely that moment. 'Still living, he is spoken of as if he were dead.'[31] Cézanne himself may have read those words. Still living, he held his tongue.

Cézanne's letter to Gasquet discloses something more. It has a strong affinity with one of the *Odes* of Horace, most clearly evident in the letter's sense of rectitude and renunciation, deeply felt. These are in tune with Horace's fundamental rule, to maintain his own low profile, as he explained to his friend and patron Maecenas. Horace had declined an invitation from the Emperor himself, spurning privilege and cosseting in order to continue working patiently on his odes, gathering from nature 'like the bees'. Cézanne knew his Horace. His sympathetic appraisal of Zola's *Une Page d'amour* (1878) came complete with Horace's precept 'Qualis ab incepto processerit, et sibi constet' ('Let him proceed as he began, and so be consistent'), a tribute to Zola's characterization; and a number of witnesses testify to his quoting Horace by the yard.[32] The *Odes* were part of his culture. Resistance to the Emperor was something Cézanne understood only too well; being cosseted was anathema to him. He was in many ways an exemplary Horatian, learning the world's hard lessons: what cannot be had, what must be let go, the whole economy of desire and power. Was he thinking of Horace as he wrote his screed to Gasquet?

Unarmed myself, I must
Desert the moneyed ranks to join the poor
Camp of the richly satisfied,

To be a lord of more than who buys
And hoards the grain – the grain the peasant worked
So hard to cultivate – then stands alone,
A scarecrow, amid fertility.[33]

∽

Cézanne did not keep copies of the letters he sent. He did not keep the letters he received, either, with the exception of those from Zola, later returned at the latter's request, probably with an eye to publication. Cézanne's letters are widely scattered. Assembling a collection of them means tracking down the recipients and their descendants, combing archives and museums, monitoring auctions and salerooms. It was John Rewald, the founding father of Cézanne studies, who performed this labour of Hercules in the 1930s. The collection he assembled was published first in French (in 1937) and then in English (in 1941), translated by Marguerite Kay.[34] As time went by, more letters were added and piecemeal corrections made. The translation still reads as if it were stuck in the 1930s, however, as indeed it is. The idiom is consistent with that of Rewald's own translations. 'By jove!' 'He did not give a darn.' This sounds dated, while not necessarily capturing the nineteenth-century original. Register and tone are matters of some delicacy, but there is now little dispute that the Rewald collection lacks in both authenticity and vivacity. Some of the English formulations are over-literal ('the assurance of my most distinguished sentiments'). Some are more conventional, and yet distracting, perhaps even misleading. The decision to translate *mon cher* as 'my dear' throughout lends it a rather camp tone that is sometimes unfortunate ('Goodbye, my dear, goodbye'). Nevertheless, the collection was much reprinted. It is probably most familiar to English-language readers in the 'revised and enlarged' edition of 1976, republished in paperback in 1995.[35] There is also a 'new, revised and augmented' edition of 1984, translated by Seymour Hacker, published only in the United States and long out of print.[36]

These works suffered from various shortcomings. In the first place, they lost some of the flavour of the original. Cézanne was more pungent and more sapient than he appeared in English. The translations were not equal to the profundity of his thought or the individuality of his expression. His episodic philosophizing, his exasperated theorizing, his irony, his wit, his learning, his reading, his range of reference – much of this escaped them. Cézanne's personal vocabulary tolls like a bell through his letters, as Lawrence Gowing observed in a magisterial review of the 1976 edition.[37] Terms such as *sensation*, *réalisation* and *tempérament* were freighted with meaning for Cézanne – meaning not captured by simple Anglicization, or by the lifeless alternatives on offer in 1976 or 1984. *Je dois donc réaliser d'après nature.* 'I simply must produce after nature.' 'Thus, I have to work from nature.'[38] Editorial assistance was sadly lacking.

In some instances the translation was plainly inaccurate or inappropriate, and advanced, as it seems, for a purpose: to support a certain construction of Cézanne's character and behaviour. This construction was not well founded, which may perhaps explain why it was smuggled in rather than argued out. By way of example, in a moving passage in one of his last letters, written on 21 September 1906, Cézanne declares:

> *J'étudie toujours sur nature, et il me semble que je fais lents progrès. Je vous aurais voulu auprès de moi, car la solitude pèse toujours un peu. Mais je suis vieux, malade, et je me suis juré de mourir en peignant, plutôt que de sombrer dans le gâtisme avilissant, qui menace les vieillards, qui se laissent dominer par des passions abrutissantes pour leurs sens.*

In Kay's translation:

> I am always studying after nature and it seems to me that I make slow
> progress. I should have liked you near me, for solitude always weighs me
> down a bit. But I am old, ill, and I have sworn to myself to die painting,
> rather than go under in the debasing paralysis which threatens old men who
> allow themselves to be dominated by passions which coarsen their senses.

If the first part of this translation is rather pedestrian, the second is highly contentious. *Le gâtisme* is senility, not paralysis, and *abrutissant* does not mean 'coarsening', but rather 'dulling', 'exhausting' or 'stupefying'. Moreover, *passion*

Cézanne painting the Mont Sainte-Victoire, 1906.

in French does not have the same reflexive association with sexual passion as it does in English; it is associated more with enthusiasm or obsession, for such things as cars or tennis or gambling. In other words, Cézanne was not thinking about dirty old men, or revealing his fear of women, or disclosing his anxieties about sex, or evidencing any other neuroses. What is coarsening here is the translation itself, and the construction that underpins it. The psychological or psychosexual reading was part mistranslation, part misappropriation from his fictional alter ego Claude Lantier – the Cézanne character in Zola's novels – embedded and embellished in Joachim Gasquet's invaluable but unreliable witness account, first published in 1921; given a sort of biographical seal of approval in the pioneering studies of Gerstle Mack and John Rewald in the 1930s; and further elaborated by Meyer Schapiro and Theodore Reff in the 1960s, in fancifully Freudian terms. Schapiro's celebrated essay 'The Apples of Cézanne' (1968) offered a psychological interpretation of the apples, or rather the artist, that leant heavily on a battery of sexual obsession, repression, sublimation and frustration. It was replete with tropes such as 'self-chastening' and 'fear of his own impulses', to say nothing of 'the unerasable impress of the mother' and 'the child's conflicting relations to the parents'. It assumed a deeply troubled, neurotic relationship with women. It elided art and life.[39]

Such a construction may be traced back to the original characterization of Claude Lantier. Zola's account of Lantier's stunted sociability entered the biographical bloodstream, so contaminating Cézanne's psychology or pathology that it became something like received wisdom. The phobic Cézanne, the sociopath, the emotional cripple, the 'grand enfant', as Zola put it, living in dread of what life holds in store, chronically suspicious of those who want to get their hooks into him, sublimating like crazy, fearful of women (fear laced with morbid suspicion), and ceasing altogether to love his wife after the first fine, careless rapture: all that is rooted in fiction. It pertains to Lantier. It was grafted onto Cézanne. Knowingly or otherwise, the translation did its bit to reinforce the pathology.

Cézanne was more normal and less pathological than is generally allowed. The obsession, repression, sublimation and frustration have been overdone. Too much has been made of Cézanne *outlaw*, in Edmond Jaloux's phrase. Whatever the gossips might say, he was neither demented nor depressed. A more normalized version of the letter quoted above reads:

I always study from nature, and it seems to me that I'm making slow progress. I should have liked you beside me, for the loneliness always weighs on me a little. But I am old, and ill, and I have vowed to die painting rather than sink into the degrading senility that threatens old people who let themselves be ruled by passions that dull the senses.[40]

In other matters the translation was serviceable enough, though often stilted, and surprisingly inaccurate in detail. On account of the diabetes, Cézanne had trouble with his kidneys, not his ribs (nor his back, as Hacker had it).[41] Hacker's translation was more fluent and inventive, but still crucially lacking in the realm of ideas, not to mention painterly procedures; and the American idiom sometimes jars ('On May 10 I went by your place').

As a rule, the Rewald version serves to tame and to temper. The uninhibited Cézanne is reined in; the emphatic and the splenetic are toned down. The fizz evaporates, and some of the nuance. What is more, it transpires that Rewald himself was not above bowdlerizing Cézanne, moderating the language if it got too ripe. He substituted *ignares* ('ignoramuses') for *enculés* ('sods', 'buggers', 'dickheads', as some might now say) in Cézanne's periodic raillery at French intellectuals.[42] He smoothed out irregularities in the syntax and the style, making him more grammatical and less irreconcilable than he ought to be, or sought to be. The ardour is muffled, the humour muted. These suppressions and insertions are nowhere indicated in the text. A strained and self-contradictory paragraph in the preface to the French edition, avowing fidelity to the original and yet allowing changes in the interest of 'easy reading', does not figure in the English one.[43]

On the other hand, a good deal of interesting material was left untranslated. Cézanne's early letters to Zola were full of mock epics in verse, classical doggerel ('Hannibal's Dream'), literary spoofs and jokes, some ribald, some almost obscene. Almost all of this material was relegated to an appendix, 'Poems in French', and studiously ignored.[44] His Latin quotations were given short shrift (or inaccurately translated).

Less obviously, the Rewald collection suffered not only in translation but in transcription. This basic failing was recognized early on by the cognoscenti, but never rectified. Reflecting on the manifold deficiencies in the current understanding of Cézanne's 'spiritual and stylistic evolution' in the august pages of

Cézanne (centre) and Pissarro (far right) in Auvers, *c.* 1874.

the *Burlington Magazine* in 1954, Douglas Cooper lamented 'the chaotic state of the literature'. Existing biographical accounts were found wanting. The 1936 catalogue raisonné was a shambles (Cooper went so far as to speak of 'slapdash dating'). Most egregiously, 'The volume of Cézanne's letters has been badly translated into English, and in any case the transcription of the original texts in the French edition is not always accurate.'[45]

Cooper was an incorrigible controversialist. In the matter of the letters, moreover, he was an interested party. He, too, had wanted to publish a collection of Cézanne letters in the 1930s; he had corresponded with Rewald about that very project.[46] In the end it did not materialize. Cooper was thwarted, and aggrieved. But he was also a considerable authority – and he was right, as was confirmed by the publication in 2011 of fifty-three letters in French, scrupulously transcribed by Jean-Claude Lebensztejn.[47]

Taken as a whole, an examination of all extant original manuscripts reveals that the letters in the Rewald collection are riddled with textual errors and inaccuracies. Some of the mistakes are minor (punctuation, spelling, names, dates); others are more significant. Sometimes they seem to be based on a misreading of Cézanne's script. The handwriting is difficult (an intriguing reference to his *galette*, or 'taster', after Delacroix remained undeciphered), the vocabulary challenging (the little word *sherpa* eluded even Lebensztejn).[48] Sometimes they seem deliberately to ignore Cézanne's clear intentions, for instance in word-play or underlining. If there is an art of *emphasis*, Cézanne was an adept. The letters contain numerous examples of what might be called the idiosyncratic emphatic, lost in transcription.

The cumulative effect was to corrupt the text, even in the most unlikely places. In Cézanne's acknowledgment of *L'Œuvre* – the most minutely examined letter in the entire correspondence – there was a mistake in the last sentence.[49] Thus an unreliable text fed an unsatisfactory translation.

～

Douglas Cooper was not the only one to dream of a new collection. Lawrence Gowing had designs on a similar project in the 1960s, possibly a collaboration of some kind with Frances Partridge. In 1967 it was still up in the air; Gowing

Camille Pissarro, *Portrait of Cézanne*, 1874.
Etching, 52 x 35.5 cm (20½ x 14 in.).

Portrait of Ambroise Vollard, 1899.
Graphite, 45.8 x 39.8 cm (18 x 15⅞ in.).

told himself and Partridge 'it will come off eventually'.[50] Unhappily, it never did. Gowing exercised his fascination with Cézanne elsewhere, distilling a profound understanding of the man and the work into a brilliant essay, 'Cézanne: The Logic of Organized Sensations' (1977), and perhaps indulging himself a little in his appraisal of Rewald's enterprise in the *Times Literary Supplement* the same year:

> The [French] edition [of 1937], which could be found until recently,
> has nevertheless been the book on which understanding of Cézanne's
> temperament and his conception of art has depended for forty years. In 1941
> the firm of Cassirer issued an English translation under the same editorship,
> which was a remarkable feat of publishing in the circumstances of the
> time. The translation was less admirable, though successive generations of
> students have become quite attached to its awkwardnesses, and many a dull
> seminar in the past three decades has been lightened by the donnish fun to
> be had from comparison with the French at some crucial points.

After weighing the merits and demerits of the newly issued 1976 edition, Gowing concluded:

> Readers who propose to gain the meaning of these letters will still have to
> assemble the scattered French texts, now not easily found, transcribe their
> own anthologies from them, as they always have, and, very likely, compile
> their own concordances. The ground that John Rewald has gained for us
> in this collection and the apparatus that accompanies it is none the less
> extensive. The book leaves us more than ever in his debt and more eager
> for his revision of [Lionello] Venturi's catalogue [raisonné]. The truth is
> that the text of Cézanne's letters needs the kind of treatment that is given
> to a classic text in philosophy: that is perhaps the closest parallel to the
> significance that his thought and feeling hold for art.[51]

The present collection offers a new translation, founded wherever possible on a re-examination of the original manuscripts and informed by extensive archival research on the artist's life and work undertaken for a new biography.[52] For the first time, the letters are cross-referenced to the modern catalogue raisonné (eventually published in 1996) and other monuments of recent scholarship, notably the ten-volume edition of Zola's correspondence, the five-volume edition of Pissarro's correspondence, and the three-volume catalogue raisonné of Pissarro's paintings. Regrettably, all of this correspondence is available only in French.

It adds to the corpus a number of letters not previously collected or translated, among them Cézanne's exchanges with the dealer Vollard, who bought up no fewer than 678 of his paintings – over two-thirds of his lifetime production – and whose astute hoarding and animal cunning propelled him to world power status; the painter Monet, Cézanne's esteemed peer ('He is only an eye,' Cézanne said, 'but my God what an eye!'); the writer Mirbeau, who owned 13 of his paintings, and who tried and failed to obtain the Legion of Honour for him; the critic Geffroy, whose portrait he painted, whose writing he loved, and whose patronage he vehemently rejected; the young Charles Penot, an unknown acquaintance from the early years in Aix; an anonymous colour merchant; and various others.[53] In the 1976 edition there are 231 letters by Cézanne himself. In this collection there are 252.

There are also letters written by Cézanne's wife and son, and other friends and relations, Zola in particular, who often reflects on things Cézanne has said or written to him, or reviews their experiences. Only two letters in his wife's hand have come to light. Both are included here, for the first time. Hortense Cézanne née Fiquet (1850–1922) has been much maligned. Her letters serve to modify the stock character of a sulky irrelevance or a subject of convenience, casting her in an interesting new light.[54] In contrast, it is tempting to view Paul Cézanne fils (1872–1947) as a classic case of the son overmatched by the father, and by life in general. 'My son, now in Paris, is a great philosopher,' Cézanne wrote in typical fashion to the young painter Charles Camoin. 'By that I don't mean the equal or the emulator of Diderot, Voltaire or Rousseau. Would you like to honour him with a visit, 31 Rue Ballu, near the Place Clichy, near the statue of General Moncey. When I write to him, I'll tell him a little about you; he is rather touchy, incurious, but a good boy.'[55]

It may be wondered why there are so few letters from Cézanne to his son, other than the remarkable sequence from the last year of his life. At the end of every year, apparently, Cézanne fils used to dispose of unwanted papers. Given

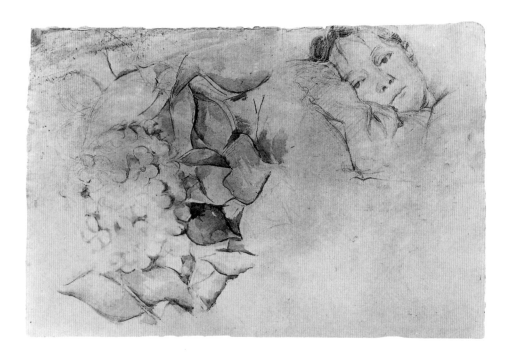

Madame Cézanne with Hortensias, c. 1885.
Pencil and watercolour, 30.5 x 46 cm (12 x 18⅛ in.).

that his father had passed away only a few weeks before, Rewald speculated that a pang of filial piety may have led him to make an exception and to preserve those of 1906.[56] If so, we should be duly grateful, for he had no compunction about disposing of everything else. Even the letters passed into private hands. Picasso kept one as a kind of talisman.[57]

This collection restores all of the juvenilia and translates it (eschewing the rhyming). Cézanne the poetaster emerges in full force. Some of the doggerel is dire; nonetheless, it is of considerable interest, for his early preoccupations, his intellectual formation, his literary tastes, and above all his immersion in the classics. Moreover, the versifying meant something to him, and continued to mean something, reluctant as he may have been to admit it. 'A man like Monet is fortunate,' he told a young visitor, forty years later; 'he reaches his beautiful destiny. Woe betide the painter who fights too much with his talent: perhaps one who composed some verses in his youth ... '.[58] In the early days Zola himself thought Cézanne might have been the better writer, or at any rate the better poet. 'Yes, *mon vieux*, more of a poet than I. My verse is perhaps purer than yours, but yours is certainly more poetic, more true; you write with the heart, I with the mind; you firmly believe what you set down, with me, often, it's only a game, a brilliant lie.'[59]

Cézanne was also a mighty reader, and a habitual rereader, reading and rereading much more widely than is generally realized. He read periodicals from across the political spectrum: *Gil Blas, Le Grognon provençal, La Revue de Paris, L'Occident, Le Voltaire*. In 1868 he wrote to Coste about Henri Rochefort's pocket-size political weekly, *La Lanterne*, whose flaming red cover announced an incendiary combination of anti-monarchical, anti-clerical and anti-bourgeois polemic, and about a new 'satirical journal of the Midi', *Le Galoubet*. In 1876 he joked with Pissarro: 'I'm reading *La Lanterne de Marseille*, and I'm about to subscribe to *La Religion laïque*. How about that!'[60]

His taste in authors ranged from the classical to the heretical. 'One who is strong is Baudelaire,' he instructed his son at the end, as if passing him on to the next generation, 'his *Art romantique* is amazing, and he makes no mistake in the artists he appreciates.'[61] *L'Art romantique* was one of Cézanne's favourite books. Among many wonderful things, it contained the famous essay 'The Painter of Modern Life' and, of greater import for Cézanne, 'The Life and Work of Eugène Delacroix'. Cézanne read and reread Baudelaire all his life. He was said to know *Les Fleurs du mal* by heart, and sometimes to take it with him for a day's work *sur le motif*. He gave a paint-spattered copy to the young poet Léo Larguier, who found on the last page an itemized list of poems, presumably the ones he valued most: 'The Beacons', 'Don Juan in Hell', 'The Giantess', *Sed non satiata* ('But not satisfied', a reference to sexual appetite), 'A Carcass', 'Cats', 'The Happy Corpse' and 'A Taste for Nothingness'.[62]

Cézanne was equally familiar with Flaubert and Stendhal – not only *Le Rouge et le noir* and *Le Chartreuse de Parme*, but also the captivating *Histoire de la peinture en Italie*. This last was a key work, which revealed to Cézanne his temperament and 'moral character': on first reading, aged thirty, choleric; on rereading, aged thirty-nine, melancholic. His bedside reading was Balzac: a well-thumbed copy of the *Études philosophiques*, including *Le Chef-d'œuvre inconnu*,

Cézanne near Aix, photographed by Émile Bernard, c. 1905.

Self-Portrait, c. 1895.
Graphite, 23.7 x 15.2 cm (9⅜ x 6 in.).

another source of self-projection. In one of the great set pieces of Cézannian idolatry, Émile Bernard's 'Memories of Paul Cézanne' (1907) relates how 'one evening, when I spoke to him of *Le Chef-d'œuvre inconnu* and Frenhofer, the hero of Balzac's tragedy, he got up from the table, stood before me and, striking his chest with his index finger, confessed wordlessly by this repeated gesture that he was the very character in the novel. He was so moved that his eyes filled with tears. One of his predecessors, who had a prophetic soul, had understood him.'[63] As Julian Barnes has noted, Cézanne 'proved that it is possible, if rare, to be a Balzacian, a Stendhalian *and* a Flaubertian all at the same time'.[64]

The reading fed the writing. Often the point of contact is a book or an article. Some of the most heartfelt passages turn on a literary allusion or association. In this respect Cézanne's late letters are at one with his late paintings: they do not surrender themselves to mere delectation, as Adorno once said.

The letters of Paul Cézanne are often moving or diverting, sometimes profound, sometimes puzzling. They afford an insight into the interior life of the exemplary artist-creator of the modern age. Picasso's remarkable tribute of 1935 testifies to his living presence:

> It is not what the artist does that counts, it is what he is. Cézanne wouldn't be of the slightest interest to me if he had lived and thought like Jacques-Émile Blanche, even if the apple he painted had been ten times as beautiful. What is of interest to us is Cézanne's *inquiétude*, that is Cézanne's lesson … that is to say, the drama of the man. The rest is false.[65]

Maurice Merleau-Ponty's celebrated essay 'Cézanne's Doubt' (1945) makes the same point in slightly different terms. Cézanne's struggle became a legend. 'The sublime little grimalkin' so marvellously evoked by D. H. Lawrence attained an unexpected grandeur.[66] If, in the final analysis, a great artist is a man who has lived greatly, then Cézanne seems to exemplify what was required. He lives again in the letters.

He was and is a revelator. It was entirely characteristic of him to write to Émile Bernard that he owed him the truth in painting, and that he would tell it to him; or to Charles Camoin that he would speak to him about painting more truly than *anyone*, and that *in art* he had nothing to hide.[67] Painting was truth-telling or it was nothing. That was his life's work and his legacy. Cézanne's doubt has dazzled us for over a century. Cézanne's truth will trouble us for the duration.

His letters show that the sublime little grimalkin was human, all too human. Cézanne himself is supposed to have remarked, 'Politicians, there are two thousand of them in every legislature, but a Cézanne, there is only one every two centuries.'[68] Who is to say that he was wrong?

1   Letter 82 in this book. See Marius Roux, *The Substance and the Shadow* [1878], trans. Dick Collins and Fiona Cox (University Park, PA: Pennsylvania University Press, 2007), a magnificent restoration by Paul Smith.

2   Letter 158.

3   Ambroise Vollard, *En Écoutant Cézanne, Degas, Renoir* [1938] (Paris: Grasset, 2005), p. 94; Denis diary, n.d. [mid-1906], in Maurice Denis, *Journal* (Paris: La Colombe, 1957–79), vol. 2, p. 46, citing Octave Mirbeau. Gustave Coquiot, *Cézanne* (Paris: Ollendorff, 1919), pp. 202–03, also citing Mirbeau, has an even more elaborate version of 'that Gauguin'.

4   Letters 253 and 260; Valabrègue to Zola, September 1865, in John Rewald, *Cézanne: Sa vie, son œuvre, son amitié pour Zola* (Paris: Albin Michel, 1939), p. 102 (hereafter *Cézanne–Zola*). The portrait of Emperaire was submitted to the Salon of 1870. Naturally, it was rejected.

5   Letters 260 and 263.

6   See Heidegger's conversation with André Masson, in Françoise Will-Levaillant (ed.), *Le Rebelle du surréalisme* (Paris: Hermann, 1976), pp. 138ff.

7   Marc Elder, *À Giverny, avec Claude Monet* (Paris: Bernheim-Jeune, 1924), p. 48.

8   Joachim Gasquet, *Cézanne* [1921], in Michael Doran (ed.), *Conversations avec Cézanne* (Paris: Macula, 1978), p. 121.

9   Vollard, *En Écoutant Cézanne*, p. 46.

10 Elder, *À Giverny*, p. 48.

11 J.-K. Huysmans, 'Paul Cézanne' [1888], in *Écrits sur l'art* (Paris: Bartillat, 2006), p. 360. I follow the translation in *Cézanne* (London: Tate, 1996), p. 27.

12 This was Victor Binet's response. See 'Enquête sur les tendances actuelles des arts plastiques', *Mercure de France*, 1 and 15 August and 1 September 1905.

13 Letter 44. Cézanne may have remembered Cicero's 'alia semper virent', but he may also have been inspired by Balzac's *Illusions perdues* (1843), of the melancholic Lucien de Rubempré.

14 With similar irony, Cézanne once told Maurice Denis: 'I should like to do decorative landscapes like Hugo d'Alési [who designed colourful posters for railway companies], yes, with my small sensibility.' Denis, *Journal*, 1906, in *Conversations avec Cézanne*, p. 94.

15 Letter 127.

16 The speculation appears to originate with Jean de Beucken, *Un Portrait de Cézanne* (Paris: Gallimard, 1955). It may reflect stories or folk memories in the family, relayed by Cézanne's son in his own old age. Like much of de Beucken's account, it is at once overheated and misdirected. The characterization of Cézanne's relationship with his wife as 'a sorry liaison there was no apparent reason to bring to an end' is equally misleading, though it has been persistently influential in the literature.

17 Letter 128, quoting Virgil, *Eclogues*, 2.65. In John Rewald's edition of Cézanne's letters the quotation is

translated 'Everyone is swept away by his passion', which is certainly arresting, and possibly apropos, but also somewhat heightened or exaggerated. The Latin verb *traho* means to draw or drag (or trail or pull); the seductive-sounding *voluptas* is more a term of endearment. I follow C. Day Lewis's translation (Oxford: World's Classics, 1999).

18 Letter 1.

19 Letter 138.

20 Lucretius, *De rerum natura*, trans. Ronald Melville as *On the Nature of the Universe* (Oxford: World's Classics, 1999), 4.1061–73.

21 Letter 38. For his friends' joking, see letter 40.

22 Letter 262.

23 Samuel Beckett, *The Unnamable* [1953] (London: Faber, 2010), p. 134, the concluding lines.

24 See e.g. Beckett to McGreevy, 8 and 16 September 1934, in *The Letters of Samuel Beckett* (London: Faber, 2009), vol. I, pp. 222 and 227.

25 Letter 275.

26 Letters 169 and 170.

27 Rewald, *Cézanne–Zola*, p. 344.

28 Letter 233. He inserted 'Oeterne Deus' [sic] as an afterthought. I follow John House's reading of this passage in 'Cézanne's letters to Émile Bernard', in Stephanie Buck et al. (eds), *The Courtauld Cézannes* (London: Courtauld, 2008), p. 149. According to Cyril Rougier, his neighbour in Aix, Cézanne would sometimes remark on how a man or a woman resembled a cylinder: see Charensol, 'Aix et Cézanne', *L'Art vivant*, 1 December 1925.

29 Letter 166. The good friend he mentions is probably Emperaire.

30 Franz Kafka, 'The Hunter Gracchus' [1931], in *Collected Short Stories* (London: Penguin, 1988), p. 230.

31 André Mellerio, *Le Mouvement idéaliste en peinture* (Paris: Floury, 1896), p. 26.

32 Letter 65. Quoting from memory, it seems, Cézanne has *incepte* rather than *incepto*. In full: 'Si quid inexpertum scaenae committis et audes personam formare nouam, seruetur ad imum qualis ab incepto processerit, et sibi constet'; from the *Ars Poetica*, 125–27. This passage was also part of the culture, deployed by Corneille and Diderot, among others. Léo Larguier and Émile Bernard both remark on Cézanne's knowledge of Horace. See *Conversations avec Cézanne*, pp. 12 and 56.

33 Horace, *Odes*, 3.16, trans. Stephen Yenser, in J. D. McClatchy (ed.), *The Odes* (Princeton: Princeton University Press, 2002), p. 205. McClatchy takes his cue from Auden, 'The Horations' (1968).

34 Paul Cézanne, *Correspondance*, ed. John Rewald (Paris: Grasset, 1937); Paul Cézanne, *Letters*, ed. John Rewald, trans. Marguerite Kay (Oxford: Cassirer, 1941).

35 *Letters* (New York: Da Capo, 1995). Subsequent references are to this edition, unless otherwise indicated.

36 *Letters* (New York: Hacker, 1984). Hereafter Hacker.

37 Lawrence Gowing, 'Making real after nature', *Times Literary Supplement*, 18 March 1977. The inadequacy of the translations was forcefully underlined by Charles Tomlinson, 'Discovering Cézanne', *Modern Painters* (Spring 1989), pp. 109–13, and by John House, who provides a kind of glossary of Cézanne's professional vocabulary, in *Courtauld Cézannes*, pp. 146–47.

38 Letter 274. Cf. *Correspondance*, p. 415; *Letters*, p. 335; Hacker, p. 327.

39 Wayne Andersen makes a similar argument in *The Youth of Cézanne and Zola* (Geneva: Fabriart, 2003), p. 439. See Gerstle Mack, *Cézanne* (New York: Knopf, 1936); Rewald, *Cézanne–Zola*; Meyer Schapiro, 'The Apples of Cézanne' [1968], in *Modern Art* (New York: Braziller, 1979), pp. 1–38; Theodore Reff, 'Cézanne's Bather with Outstretched Arms', *Gazette des Beaux-Arts* (March 1962), pp. 173–90.

40 Letter 269. This version is broadly consistent with House's translation in *Courtauld Cézannes*, p. 165. Hacker's version is an improvement on Kay's, unlike the version by Julie Lawrence Cochran in the widely used collection *Conversations with Cézanne* (Berkeley: University of California Press, 2001), p. 49.

41 Letter 261. Cf. *Correspondance*, p. 398, and *Letters*, p. 319.

42 Letter 267. Cf. *Correspondance*, p. 405, and *Letters*, p. 326.

43 Cf. *Correspondance*, p. 16, and *Letters*, p. 8.

44 Rewald was reproached for this by a number of authorities. See Meyer Schapiro, *Cézanne* [1952] (New York: Abrams, 2004), p. 23; Theodore Reff, 'Cézanne's *Dream of Hannibal*', *Art Bulletin* 45 (June 1963), pp. 148–52. Gowing made a similar point in his review of the 1976 edition. Hacker reintegrated this material into the relevant letters and translated it. Andersen also translated much of it, less systematically but sometimes more evocatively, in *The Youth of Cézanne and Zola*.

45 Douglas Cooper, 'Two Cézanne Exhibitions', *Burlington Magazine* 96/620 (November 1954), p. 345. See also his penetrating discussion of the man and the work on the occasion of an earlier exhibition at the Orangerie, Paris, in 1936 (under the pseudonym 'Douglas Lord'): *Burlington Magazine* 69/400 (July 1936), pp. 32–33.

46 The correspondence is in the Rewald Papers, 38–39, in the National Gallery of Art in Washington, DC.

47 Paul Cézanne, *Cinquante-trois lettres* (Paris: L'Échoppe, 2011), transcribed and annotated by Jean-Claude Lebensztejn (hereafter *Lettres*). Cooper's transcriptions of the letters to Émile Bernard are more accurate than Rewald's; they were first published in *Impressionnistes de la Collection Courtauld de Londres* (Paris: Musée de l'Orangerie, 1955) and then in *Conversations avec Cézanne*. That important series of letters was transcribed afresh by John House, whose translations are insightful and authoritative, if rather literal, as he acknowledged. See *Courtauld Cézannes*, pp. 146–65.

48 Letters 31 and 271. Cf. *Correspondance*, p. 411; *Letters*, p. 332; *Lettres*, pp. 89–90.

49 Letter 140. Properly, 'Tout-à-toi sous l'impression des temps écoulés'. Rewald gives 'l'impulsion'. Cf. *Correspondance*, p. 282; *Letters*, p. 223; *Lettres*, p. 32.

50 Frances Partridge diary, 28 February and 31 March 1967, in *Good Company* (London: Flamingo, 1995), pp. 11 and 16.

51 Gowing, 'Making real'. 'The Logic of Organized Sensations' is reprinted in *Conversations with Cézanne*, pp. 180–212. The revised and enlarged edition of the letters was published in French in 1978; it is still in print.

52 Alex Danchev, *Cézanne: A Life* (London: Profile, 2012).

53 Cézanne's famous characterization of Monet is in Vollard, *En Écoutant Cézanne*, p. 85.

54 Letters 150 and 254.

55 Letter 223. For letters written by the great philosopher himself, see 241, 250 and 258.

56 John Rewald, *Cézanne and America* (London: Thames & Hudson, 1989), p. 233, n. 29.

57 Letter 273, subsequently donated to the Musée Granet in Aix by Picasso's widow Jacqueline.

58 Jules Borély, 'Cézanne à Aix', in *Conversations avec Cézanne*, p. 20, from c.1903.

59 Letter 19.

60 Letters 43, 44 and 57.

61 Letter 268.

62 Léo Larguier, *Le Dimanche avec Paul Cézanne* (1925), in *Conversations avec Cézanne*, pp. 13–14. Larguier got to know Cézanne during his military service in Aix in 1900–02. The edition he mentions was a paperback published in 1899. Cézanne's taste in literature was not automatically shared, even with Zola (who was no fan of Baudelaire).

63 Émile Bernard, 'Souvenirs sur Paul Cézanne', in *Conversations avec Cézanne*, p. 30.

64 Julian Barnes, 'Bowls with souls', *Times Literary Supplement*, 21 and 28 December 2012.

65 Christian Zervos, 'Conversation avec Picasso', in Picasso, *Propos sur l'art* (Paris: Gallimard, 1998), p. 36.

66 D. H. Lawrence, 'Introduction to These Paintings' [1929], *Selected Critical Writings* (Oxford: World's Classics, 1998), p. 261.

67 Letters 255 and 223 (his emphases, highly characteristic).

68 Rewald, *Cézanne–Zola*, p. 416, citing information from Cézanne's son and his brother-in-law Maxime Conil. Larguier gives a slightly cruder variation: 'Politicians, there are over a thousand in France, and it's shit. Whereas there's only one Cézanne.'

List of abbreviations

Andersen	Wayne Andersen, *The Youth of Cézanne and Zola* (Geneva: Fabriart, 2003)
C	Adrien Chappuis, *The Drawings of Paul Cézanne: A Catalogue Raisonné* (Greenwich, CT: New York Graphic Society, 1973)
Conversations	Michael Doran (ed.), *Conversations avec Cézanne* (Paris: Macula, 1978)
Correspondance	Paul Cézanne, *Correspondance*, ed. John Rewald [1937] (Paris: Grasset, 1978)
Courtauld Cézannes	Stephanie Buck *et al.* (eds), *The Courtauld Cézannes* (London: Courtauld, 2008)
Hacker	Paul Cézanne, *Letters*, ed. John Rewald, trans. Seymour Hacker (New York: Hacker, 1984)
Letters	Paul Cézanne, *Letters*, ed. John Rewald, trans. Marguerite Kay [1941] (New York: Da Capo, 1976)
Lettres	Paul Cézanne, *Cinquante-trois lettres*, ed. Jean-Claude Lebensztejn (Paris: L'Échoppe, 2011)
Marie	Marie Cézanne (his elder sister)
P	Joachim Pissarro and Claire Durand-Ruel Snollaerts, *Pissarro: Critical Catalogue of Paintings*, 3 vols (Milan: Skira, 2005)
Paul	Paul Cézanne *fils* (his son)
Pissarro, *Correspondance*	*Correspondance de Camille Pissarro*, ed. Janine Bailly-Herzberg, 5 vols (Paris: Presses Universitaires de France, 1980–91)
R	John Rewald, *The Paintings of Paul Cézanne: A Catalogue Raisonné* (New York: Abrams, 1996)
Rose	Rose Cézanne (his younger sister)
RWC	John Rewald, *Paul Cézanne: The Watercolors* (Boston, MA: Little, Brown, 1983)
Zola, *Correspondance*	Émile Zola, *Correspondance*, ed. B. H. Bakker, 10 vols (Montreal: Presses de l'Université de Montréal/Paris: Éditions du CRNS, 1978–95)

1850s

Sketches of heads and figures, c. 1859. Pen and ink, 21 x 13 cm (8¼ x 5⅛ in.).
This page also contains the only known example of Cézanne's notes from his time
as a Law student at the University of Aix, 1858–60 (see also pp. 71, 117).

Aix, 9 April 1858

Bonjour cher Zola,

> At last I take up my pen
> and as is my wont
> I will report first of all
> on the local news:
> a heavy storm
> has struck mighty strong,
> loosing on the town
> rain that has watered
> the smiling banks of the Arc.
> So the mountain
> and our verdant countryside
> mark the coming of spring,
> for the plane trees are in bud,
> and leaves crown
> the green hawthorn with white garlands.

I've just seen Baille, this evening I'm going to his house in the country (I mean Baille the Elder),[2] so I'm writing to you,

> It is foggy
> dark and wet,
> and the pale sun
> no longer shines
> dazzling us
> with its ruby and opal fire.

Since you left Aix, *mon cher*, I've been weighed down by gloomy melancholy: I'm not lying, believe me, I feel heavy, stupid and slow. By the way, Baille told me that in a couple of weeks he will have the pleasure of placing in the hands of your most eminent Greatness a sheet of paper in which he will explain his grief and sorrow at being far away from you. I'd really like to see you, and I think that we, Baille (of course) and I, will see you in the holidays, and then we will carry out, complete, the plans we've made, but meanwhile, I lament your absence.

> Farewell, my dear Émile,
> no, on the flowing stream
> I no longer slip as gaily
> as in times gone by,
> when with agile arms
> like reptiles
> we swam together
> across the calm waters.
> Farewell, fine days
> seasoned with wine!
> Lucky fishing
> for prodigious fish!
> When in my catch,
> in the cool river
> my surly line
> caught nothing dreadful.

Do you remember the pine that stood on the bank of the Arc, lowering its leafy head over the chasm that opened at its feet? That pine that protected our bodies with its foliage from the heat of the sun, ah! May the Gods preserve it from the fatal blow of the woodcutter's axe!

We believe that you'll be coming to Aix in the holidays, and that then, hell!, then long live joy. We've planned hunts as monstrous and grotesque as our fishing-trips.

Soon, *mon cher*, we're going to hunt fish again, if the weather holds; it is magnificent today, for I'm resuming this letter on the 13th.

> In the course of his brilliant career Phoebus
> floods the whole of Aix with his streams of light.

Unpublished poem

It was deep in a wood
when I heard her ringing voice
singing and repeating three times
a charming little ditty
with the air of a mirliton,[3]

I spied a budding lass,
with a lovely mirliton,
seeing her so lovely
I felt a pleasant shiver
for a mirliton, etc.;

Her charms are marvellous
and her carriage majestic,
on her amorous lips
played an inviting smile.
Gentle mirliton, etc.;

I resolve to woo her,
I advance resolutely:
and I have this tender exchange
with that charming object:
gentle mirliton, etc.;

Did you not come,
inexpressible beauty,
from the regions of the clouds
to make me happy?
Pretty mirliton, etc.;

That goddess figure,
those eyes, that face,
the finesse of all your attractions,

everything about you seems divine.
Pretty mirliton, etc.;

Your step as light
as a butterfly's flight
easily outdistances, *ma chère*,
the gust of the north wind,
Pretty mirliton, etc.;

The imperial crown
Would not look bad on your head.
Your calf, I suspect,
Would be perfectly formed.
Pretty mirliton, etc.;

Thanks to this flattery,
she fell into a swoon,
While she is insensible,
I explore her mirliton.
Oh sweet mirliton, etc.;

Then coming back to life
Under my vigorous efforts,
She is dumbfounded
To feel me upon her.
Oh sweet mirliton, etc.;

She blushes and sighs,
Raises her languorous eyes
Which seemed to want to say
'I like this game.'
Gentle mirliton, etc.;

At the climax of her pleasure
far from saying: 'That's enough.'

Feeling that I could start again
she says to me: 'Ram it in.'
Gentle mirliton, etc.;

I withdraw my sapling
after ten or twelve thrusts
but wriggling her *derrière*:
'Why are you stopping!'
Said this mirliton, etc.

Aix, 14 April
PAUL CÉZANNE

Salve, carissime Zola

PS Let me know, when you write, if it's fine up there. I'll write very soon. I won't be so lazy in future.

(1) Note: Bernabo, Léon, with the bamboo and Alexandre are at college, I'm told, at the Lycée (I don't know what kind of contraption that is) Sainte-Barbe in Paris. As for the other aforesaid individuals, I'll find out and give you the address in a future letter. (This one is full of shit.) If you see the Bernabos, give them my regards.

(2) Note: I got your letter containing the affectionate verses that we have had the honour of singing with the bass [Gustave] Boyer and the light tenor Baille.

1 Émile Zola (1840–1902), the future writer, his best friend. Cézanne's relationship with Zola was the main axis of his emotional life, from cradle to grave. See the Introduction.

2 Baptistin Baille (1841–1918), one of the 'Inseparables' with Cézanne and Zola; later a distinguished scientist, Professor of Optics and Acoustics at the School of Physics and Chemistry of the City of Paris, an institution he helped to found. His younger brother Isidore was sometimes permitted to carry the knapsack on their rambles in the countryside.

3   A *mirliton* is a pipe or flute, or a proboscis, but also a young girl or her pudendum; the fingering, therefore, ripe for exploitation. As Cézanne would have known, there is some warrant in Virgil, whose first *Eclogue* opens seductively, 'Tityrus, here you loll, your slim reed-pipe serenading / The woodland spirit beneath a spread of sheltering beech'. In contemporary parlance, *vers de mirliton* meant very bad verse, or throwaway lines. Cézanne himself used the word in this sense in this letter, thanking Zola for 'the affectionate verses [*les affectueux mirlitons*] that we have had the honour of singing'.

2 · TO ÉMILE ZOLA

[Aix] 3 May 1858

> Dear friend who Paris keeps far from me,
> divine the mystery of a shadowy rebus.
> Is it good? I don't know; but I know for sure
> that I composed it with the aim of making it
> good, and not bad. If you can divine
> the meaning of this rebus that I'm sending you
> by post, *morbleu!* I'll know that I can claim
> that it's a very good one, and I don't wish to hear
> any contradiction on that score.
> As I'm the author, that's the reason.

[The rebus reads: *Il faut aimer les femmes*, 'One should love women.']

Are you well? I am very busy, *morbleu*, very busy. That will explain the absence of the poem you asked me for. Believe me, I feel most contrite not to be able to respond with your verve and warmth and spirit. I like the principal's 'savage mug'! (The one in your letter, I mean, not to confuse matters.) By the way, if you guess my great rebus, just for fun, let me know the solution. Do one for me, *si tempus habes*.

I gave Baille your letter. And Marguery his. Marguery is as dull as ever.[1] And now the air has suddenly turned cold. No more swimming.

> Farewell to our lovely swims
> on the laughing banks
> of the impetuous stream
> that casts upon the shore
> a wave, than which I could
> wish for nothing better.
> Red and muddy water
> now carries
> uprooted plants,
> unwanted branches
> over the muddy mire
> drifting on its current.
> Hailstones fall!
> Then they melt
> and soon they mingle
> with those blackish waters.
> Torrents of rain
> that the earth mops up
> create great floods.

These are rhymes without reason.

> *Mon cher*, you know, or perhaps you don't know,
> that I have felt the blaze of sudden passion
> you know whose charms I cherish,
> it's a sweet girl.
> Her complexion is dark, her carriage graceful,
> her feet are dainty, her delicate hand
> white-skinned,* and finally, transported,
> inspecting her divine form, I imagine

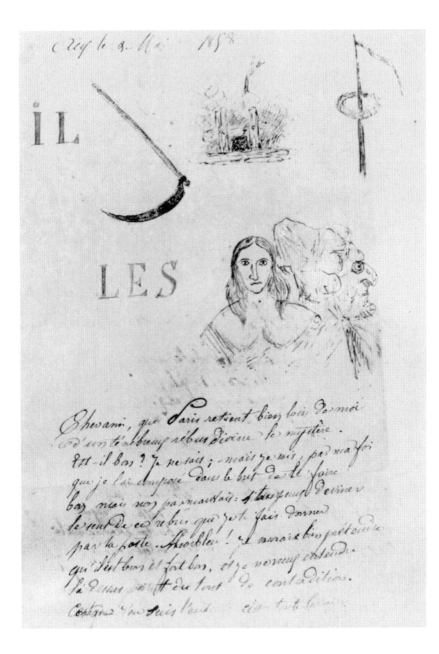

Rebus drawn on a letter to Zola, 3 May 1858.

that her lovely alabaster breasts are accommodating,
shapely for love. The wind lifting
her magnificently coloured gauze dress
revealed the charming outline of a rounded
calf ...
* For she was wearing gloves.

Just now I'm sitting opposite Boyer, at my house, on the second floor. I'm writing in his presence and I'm ordering him to add a few words to this letter in his own hand:

May your health be perfect,
May you always be happy in love,
Nothing is finer than to be in love,
That is everything I wish for you.
I warn you that when it's your turn to come and see Cézanne, you will find on the walls of his room a large collection of sayings drawn from Horace, Victor Hugo, etc.

Boyer, Gustave

Mon cher, I'm studying for the bac [baccalaureate]. Ah! If only I had the bac, you had the bac, Baille had the bac, we all had the bac. At least Baille will make it, but me: wrecked, swamped, licked, petrified, deadened, wiped out, that's what I shall be.

Mon cher, today is 5 May and it's pouring with rain. The gates of heaven are opening.

Flashes of lightning criss-cross the cloud
And the grrrowling thunderrr rrrolls all around.

There is over two feet of water in the streets. God, enraged by the crimes of man, has no doubt resolved to wash away their manifold inquities in this new flood. This frightful weather has lasted two [days]: my thermometer is at five degrees above zero and my barometer indicates heavy rain, storm and hurricane for today and the rest of the quarter. All the townsfolk are sunk in deep despair. Dismay can be read on every face. Everyone has drawn features, haggard eyes and a frightened look; they hug their arms to their chests, as though afraid of being jostled in a crowd. Everyone goes around saying prayers; at every street corner, in spite of the rain beating down, groups of young maidens – their crinolines forgotten – shout themselves hoarse, launching litanies heavenward. The town echoes to their indescribable uproar. I'm completely deafened by it. I hear nothing but *ora pro nobis* from every side. Even I followed up my impudent verses and atrocious hallelujahs with a few pious *pater nosters* or even *mea culpa, mea culpa, ter, quater, quinter mea culpa!* in the hope that my glad return would make the august Trio who reign on high forget all our past impieties.

But I notice that a change, forever sincere, has just eased the anger of the Gods. The clouds are lifting. A dazzling rainbow glows in the vault of heaven. *Adieu, adieu.*

P. CÉZANNE

---

1   Louis Marguery (1841–1881), a schoolfriend. Marguery wanted to be a writer and became a lawyer. He published some bad novels under the pseudonyms Ludovico Cyprien and Édouard de B, and some vaudeville comedies. He committed suicide by throwing himself from the gallery of the Palais de Justice in Aix.

3 • TO ÉMILE ZOLA

[Aix] 9 July 1858

Carissime Zola, Salve.
Accepi tuam litteram, inqua milis dicebas
Te cupere ut tibi rimas mitterem ad bout-rimas
Faciendas, gaude; ecce enim pulcherrimas rimas.
Lege igitur, lege, et miraberis!

[Hail, dearest Zola.
I received your letter, in which you asked me to
Send rhymes for use as as end-rhymes, so rejoice:
For here are some beautiful rhymes.
Read, therefore, read and marvel!]

Révolte	Zola	métaphore	brun
Récolte	voila	phosphore	rhum
Vert	bachique	bœuf	aveugle
Découvert	chique	veuf	beugle

Chimie	uni	borne
Infamie	bruni	corne

With regard to the above-mentioned rhymes, you have permission, *primo*, to put them in the plural, if your most serene highness sees fit; *secondo*, you can put them in any order you like; but *tertio*, I request Alexandrines; and finally *quarto*, I want – no, I do not want – I beg you to put the whole thing into verse, even Zola.

Here are some little verses of mine, which I find admirable, because they are mine – for the good reason that I am their author.

LITTLE VERSES
I see Leydet[1]
On a bidet
Spurring his donkey
As he goes singing
Triumphantly
Under a plane tree.
The famished ass
All inflamed
Stretches a very long neck
Up to the leaves
Joyful and wild
As if to pluck them.

Boyer the hunter
Full of valour
Pockets a juicy
Black white-tail
Ready for the roast.
Zola the swimmer
Strikes fearless
Through the clear water.
His sinewy arms
Stretching joyfully
Over the calm fluid.

It's very foggy today.
Look, I've just done another couplet. Here it is:

Let us celebrate the sweetness
of the divine bottle,
Its incomparable goodness
gladdens my heart.

To be sung to the tune of: Let us celebrate the grandeur of a dear mother,
etc.

Mon cher, I'm convinced that you must be sweating when you say in your
letter,

That your brow bathed in sweat
Was enveloped in the learned vapour
Given off – it even reaches me – by horrible Geometry!
(Don't take that vile abuse seriously)
If I qualify,
So much for Geometry!
In studying it I feel my whole body
Dissolve in water, under my too powerless efforts.

Mon cher, when you have sent me your end-rhymes,

> For in the end-rhymes I find you adorable
> And in the other verses truly incomparable!

I'll get busy researching other rhymes, richer and more outlandish. I'm preparing them, I'm developing them, I'm distilling them in my alembic brain. These will be new rhymes. Ahem! Rhymes such as have never yet been seen, *morbleu*, in short, accomplished rhymes.

    Mon cher, having started this letter on 9 July, it is only fitting that I finish it today, the 14th [Bastille Day], but alas! in my arid mind I cannot find even the smallest idea, and yet, with you, how many subjects I could cover, hunting, fishing and swimming, there are some subjects for you, and love (*Infandum* let's not broach that corrupting subject):

> Our soul still pure,
> Walking with timid step,
> Has not yet struck
> The edge of the precipice
> Where one so often slips;
> In this corrupting age
> I have not yet raised
> To my innocent lips
> The cup of pleasure
> From which amorous souls
> Drink their fill.

Here's a mystical tirade, ahem, look, it seems to me that I can see you read these soporific verses, I can see you (though it's a bit far) shaking your head saying: 'the poetry doesn't purr in him'.

> Letter finished on the evening of the 15th.

> Song in your honour!
> (I sing here as if we were together revelling

In all the joys of life,
It's as it were an elegy;
It's vapouring, as you'll see.)
In the evening, sitting on the mountainside
My eyes straying over the distant landscape
I said to myself, when will a companion come,
Great Gods, to deliver me from all the pain
I feel today, and comfort me in my misery?
Yes, my misery would lift, with her,
Kind as a shepherdess
With sweet charm, a fresh round chin,
Rounded arms and shapely legs,
A dainty crinoline,
A divine form,
A crimson mouth,
Digue, dinguedi, dindigue, dindon,
Oh the pretty chin.

I'll stop at last, for I see that I'm not really in the mood, alas.

Alas! Muses, weep for your nursling
Who cannot even compose a short song.
Oh the bac, the very terrible exam
Examiners, with horrid faces!
If I pass, oh indescribable joy.

Good God, I don't know what I'm doing. *Adieu, mon cher* Zola, I'm rambling as usual.

PAUL CÉZANNE

I've had an idea for a five-act tragedy that we (you and I) will call *Henry the Eighth of England*. We'll do it together, during the holidays.

I Victor Leydet (1845–1908), a schoolfriend, later senator of the Bouches du Rhône. His
son Louis (1873–1944), a painter, got to know the elderly Cézanne.

4 · TO ÉMILE ZOLA

[Aix] 26 July 1858

Mein lieber Freund,
It's Cézanne writing and Baille dictating. Muses! Descend from Helios into
our veins to celebrate my baccalaureatical triumph. (Baille is speaking and
my turn will not come until next week.)

[Baille writes:]

This bizarre originality is quite in keeping with our characters. We
were going to give you a batch of riddles to puzzle out: but fate
decided otherwise. I came to see the poetic, fantastic, bacchic,
erotic, classical, physical, geometrical friend of ours: he had already
written 26 July 1858, and was awaiting inspiration. I supplied some:
I put the title in German: he was going to write at my dictation,
and sprinkle in profusion, alongside his rhetorical figures, my
geometrical flowers (permit me this adaptation, else you might have
thought that we were going to send you triangles and suchlike).
But, *mon cher*, the love that lost Troy is still causing havoc: I have
good grounds for suspecting that he is in love. (He does not want
to admit it.)

[Cézanne writes:]

Mon cher, it's Baille who had the temerity (oh empty thought) to write those
treacherous lines, his mind never conceives of any other kind. You know
him well enough, you know his follies before he submitted to that terrible examination, and now see what has become of him? What ridiculous,

ill-formed ideas sprouted in his crafty, derisive brain. (You know, Baille is *bachelier ès sciences*, and on the 14th of next month he will sit for the *bachelier ès lettres*.) As for me, I sit on 4 August, may the all-powerful Gods keep me from breaking my nose in my coming fall. I swot, great Gods, I rack my brains over this abominable work.

I tremble, when I see all the Geography,
History, Latin, Greek, Geometry
Conspiring against me: I see them threatening,
Those examiners whose piercing gaze
Brings deep distress to the bottom of my heart.
Every moment my fear grows more intense!
And I say to myself: 'Lord, disperse these foes,
Brazenly joined in my certain downfall,
Confound the foul band.
It's true that the prayer is not so charitable!
Yet forgive me, Lord, by thy grace,
I am a devoted servant at your altar.

I honour your images with daily incense.
Ah! Lord, bring down those wicked characters.
Look at them already preparing to gather,
Rubbing their hands, ready to fail us all?
Look at them, Lord, with cruel delight
Targeting their prey?
Look, look, Lord, how carefully they pool
Their deadly numbers in their offices!
No, no, do not suffer me to fall,
An innocent victim, under the blows of their increasing wrath.
Send your sanctifying Holy Spirit!
Let it soon shed over your servant
The dazzling light of its profound knowledge.
And if you forgive me, in my final hour,
You will still hear me bellowing prayers
Which will leave all you Saints crestfallen.

Hear me, Lord, hear my prayer,
Be so good, Lord, also not to dally
(in the bestowing of thy aforesaid favours)
And may my avowals ascend to your celestial Eden:

In saecula, saeculorum, Amen!

Isn't that a preposterous digression! What do you think? Isn't it formless? Ah! If I had the time, you'd have to swallow lots more. By the way, a bit later I'll send you your end-rhymes. Send a prayer of some sort to the All-Highest for the Faculty to grant me the title so devoutly wished.

[Baille writes:]

My turn to continue: I'm not going to make you swallow more verses: I haven't got much more to tell you, other than that we're all awaiting you: Cézanne and me, me and Cézanne. Meanwhile we're swotting. Come then: only I won't be going hunting with you: let that be understood: I won't hunt but I will come with you. Enough said! We can still have some good times: I'll bring the bottle: even though it weighs the most! This letter has bored you enough already: it's made for that: I don't mean that we wrote it with that intention.
Give our regards to your mother (I say our for good reason: the Trinity is but a single person).
Our best wishes to you: this letter is from two characters.

BACÉZANLLE

Mon cher, when you come, I'll let my beard and moustache grow: I await you *ad hoc*. By the way, have you a beard and moustache?
Adieu mon cher, I don't know how I can be so stupid …

Aix, 29 [July] 1858

Mon cher,

Not only did your letter make me happy, getting it made me feel better. I'm gripped by a certain internal sadness and, my God, I dream only of that woman I told you about. I don't know who she is; I sometimes see her out in the street as I'm going to the monotonous college. I sigh, *morbleu*, but sighs that do not give themselves away, these are mental sighs.

I thoroughly enjoyed that poetic morsel you sent me, I really liked to see you remember the pine that provides shade for the riverbank of the Palette, the pine that I love, how I should like to see you here – damn everything that keeps us apart. If I didn't restrain myself, I should let off a whole string of *nom de Dieu, de Bordel de Dieu, de sacrée putain*, etc.; but what's the point of getting in a rage, that wouldn't get me any further, so I put up with it.

Yes, as you say in another piece no less poetic – though I prefer your piece about swimming – you are happy, yes you [are] happy; but I suffer in silence, my love (for it is love that I feel) will not come bursting out. A certain ennui is always with me, and when I forget my sorrow for a moment it's because I've had a drink. I've always liked wine, but now I like it more. I've got drunk, I'll get drunker, unless by chance I should succeed, my God! I despair, I despair, so I'm going to deaden the pain.

Mon cher, I reveal to your eyes a picture representing:[1]

> Cicero
> striking down Catiline,
> having uncovered the conspiracy
> of that dishonourable citizen.

> Admire, dear friend, the force of language
> With which Cicero assails that wicked person,
> Admire Cicero whose blazing eyes
> Flashed with venomous loathing,
> Overthrowing Statius that hatcher of plots
> And knocking senseless his infamous accomplices.

Mark well, dear friend, Catiline
Who falls to the ground, screaming 'Agh! Agh!'
Behold the bloody dagger, the gore-stained blade
this hellraiser carried at his side.
Behold all the spectators, overcome, terrified
At having been so nearly sacrificed!
Do you see the standard whose Roman purple
Once crushed African Carthage?
Though I am the creator of this great picture
I tremble to look on such a beautiful sight.
With each word that is spoken of Cicero
(I recoil, I tremble) as he speaks my blood boils,
And I foresee, I am quite convinced,
That you too will be deeply moved by this astonishing sight.
How can it be otherwise! Never was anything
In the Roman Empire so grand.
Do you see the cuirassiers with their waving plumes
Bobbing in the air as the wind blows?
Behold too the array of pikes
That the author of the Philippics planted there.
I think it will give you a new view
That reveals also the meaning of the phrase:
'*Senatus, Curia.*' Ingenious idea
Taken up for the first time by Cézanne!
Oh sublime spectacle to amaze the eyes
And plunge into deep astonishment.

But it's enough to have pointed out to you the incomparable beauties to be found in this admirable watercolour.

It's clearing up, I don't really know if that will last. What is certain is that I long to go:

> like an intrepid diver
> plunging through the liquid
> of the Arc

Cicero striking down Catiline, sketch on a letter to Zola, 29 July 1858.

and in that limpid water
to catch in my treacherous net
the fish that chance sends.
Amen! Amen! To these stupid verses.
they are tasteless
and stupid
and worthless.
Adieu, Zola, adieu.

I see that compared to my brush, my pen cannot say anything much, and
that today I try in vain
To sing to you of some wood nymph
I can't find a good enough voice
And the beauties of the countryside
Mock my immodest songs.
At last I'm going to stop, for I'm piling trivialities on stupidities.
So you see piled to the sky a heap of absurdities
Raised on stupidities.
Enough.

P. Cézanne

I A poem based on Cicero's *First Catiline Oration*, a popular text in Latin classes. The
poem has been interpreted in cod Freudian terms as an insight into Cézanne's predicament, such that Cicero stands for 'the righteous father whose anger he fears',
and Catiline for Cézanne himself, 'the culprit whose crime is disclosed'. This seems
unlikely.

[Aix] Wednesday 17 November 1858

Work, *mon cher*, *nam labor improbus omnia vincit* [because hard works conquers everything].[1]

Excuse, friend, excuse me! Yes, I am guilty, however forgiveness for all sins. Our letters must have crossed, let me know when you next write – no need to put yourself out for that – if you didn't receive a letter dated from my chamber, rhyming with 14 November?

I'm waiting till the end of the month for you to send me another letter when you can furnish me with the title for a *longissime* poem that I have in mind, of which I spoke in my letter of 14 November, as you'll see, if you receive it, if not I'm at a loss to understand its non-arrival, but as nothing is impossible, I've hastened to write to you. I passed the bac, but you'll know that from that same letter of the 14th, providing that it reached you.

> Damn and blast and 600,000 bombs!
> I cannot rhyme. I fall and you succumb
> To 600,000 blasts of 600,000 bombs.
> Yes it's too much wit at one blow
> I sense it (encore) I shall die young,
> For how can I keep hold of such wit?
> I'm not big enough, and cannot
> Contain the wit, so, I will expire young.

I've written to Baille, to tell him, and to announce irrevocably and definitively, that I'm a *bachelier*. Ha! Hum!

> Yes, *mon cher*, yes *mon cher*, an immense joy
> Spreads through my heart at this new title,
> I am no longer prey to Latin and Greek!
> Oh happy day, Oh happy day,
> On which this distinguished title was conferred on me;

Yes, I am *bachelier*, it's a big thing,
Yes, a person made *bachelier* may be assumed
To contain a strong dose of Greek and Latin!

Content of Latin verses set for Rhetoric and translated into French by ourself, poet.

Hannibal's Dream[2]
Annibalis Somnium

The hero of Carthage stumbled and staggered,
Leaving a banquet at which too much rum and brandy
Had been consumed.
Yes, already the great conqueror of Cannes was going
To fall asleep under the table: Oh astonishing miracle!
The remains of the feast a frightful disaster!
For with one great blow the hero struck
The tablecloth, and the wine spilled in floods.
Plates, platters and empty salad bowls
Rolled sadly in the limpid streams
Of still-warm punch, deplorable waste!
Could it be, Sirs, that Hannibal wasted
Infandum, Infandum his homeland's rum.
Oh liquor so dear to any old French soldier!
However, Zola, to commit such an outrage,
Without Jupiter avenging that dreadful evil deed?
Could it be that Hannibal so far lost his head
That he forgot you completely,
Oh rum! Let us withdraw from such a sorry spectacle!
Oh punch, you deserved an entirely different tomb!
This conqueror so fierce, why couldn't he give you
A valid passport to enter his mouth,
And go down directly to the pit of his stomach!
He left you lying on the ground, oh brandy!

But, irrevocable shame, the victor of Saguntum
Is soon lifted onto a bed by four flunkeys: Morpheus and his
     poppies
On his heavy eyes send him to sleep,
He yawns, stretches his arms, sleeps on his left side;
Our hero was snoozing after that debauchery,
When mighty swarms of fitful dreams
All of a sudden fell on his pillow.
So Hannibal slept. The oldest of the band
Disguised as Hamilcar, he had the build —
Spiky hair, prominent nose,
Extraordinarily thick moustache:
Add to his cheek a huge scar
Giving his face a misshapen look
And you have, gentlemen, the picture of Hamilcar.
His chariot was drawn by four great white horses:
He arrives, and seizes Hannibal by the ear
And gives him a good shake: Hannibal wakes up,
And already in a rage. But he calms down
Seeing Hamilcar, who turns pale
With stifled anger: 'Unworthy son, unworthy one!
Look at the state to which the pure juice of the vine
Has reduced you, my son. Blush, *corbleu*, blush
To the roots of your hair. Instead of doing battle,
you hang about aimlessly, a shameful life.
Instead of guarding the borders of your homeland,
Instead of repelling the implacable Roman,
You, the conqueror of Ticinus,
Trasimene, Cannes, instead of preparing a battle
In which the city that was always the most hostile to the Hamilcars
And the most bitter of all enemies
That saw all its citizens submit to Carthage,
Oh degenerate son, you are living it up here.
Alas! Your new doublet is stained with gravy,
Good Madeira wine and rum! It is shocking!

Come, my son, and follow instead the example of your
    ancestors.
Keep away from that brandy and those lascivious women
Who keep our captive souls under the yoke!
Forego spirits. They are most pernicious
And drink nothing but water, you'll feel better for it.'
At these words Hannibal, resting his head
On his bed, fell into another deep sleep.

Have you ever found more admirable style?
If you're not satisfied, you're unreasonable.

P. CÉZANNE

1 From a well-known line in Virgil, 'Labor omnia vincit improbus': *Georgics*, 2.145.

2 Modelled, possibly, on 'Scipio's Dream' (*Somnium Scipionis*), the concluding episode of Cicero's *Republic*. This poem, too, has fallen prey to Freudian interpretations. According to Meyer Schapiro, 'these fantasies convey something of the anxiety of the young Cézanne under the strict regime of his father. They lead us to ask whether in his lifelong preoccupation with still life there is not perhaps an unconscious impulse to restore harmony to the family table, the scene and symbol of Cézanne's conflict with his father.' For Theodore Reff, taking up where Schapiro left off, the poem 'proceeds from a profound sense of guilt'; the imagery and the language give evidence of 'a disguised sexual fantasy', centring on 'the adolescent author's remorse about masturbation and consequent fear of discovery'. It follows that 'almost the entire first stanza can in fact be read as an extended metaphor of onanism', complete with 'sustained symbolism of ejaculation'. As Wayne Andersen has pointed out, all this is completely fanciful. Reff also points acutely to the influence of Alfred de Musset, in particular a one-act play entitled *Les Marrons du feu* (1829), with a character called Annibal Desiderio, only to revert to more speculation about 'an unconscious desire to eliminate his own father as a rival and threat, an impulse which is hardly surprising when we consider his temperament and relations to his parents' – one of the more outlandish constructions of Cézanne's fabled temperament.

Aix, 7 December 1858

Mon cher,

You didn't tell me that you were seriously, very seriously ill. You should have told me; Monsieur Leclerc told me instead; but since you're well now, greetings.

Having hesitated for some time – for I must confess that this *pitot* was not to my liking – I've finally decided to show him as little pity as possible. And so I've set to work; but, heavens, I don't know my mythology; however, I will see that I get to know the exploits of Master Hercules, and convert them into the great deeds of the *pitot*, as best I can. I must tell you that my work – if it deserves to be called work rather than muddle – will be long elaborated, digested, perfected, for I have little time to devote to the adventures of the Herculean *Pitot*.[1]

> Alas, I took the tortuous path of Law.
> I took is not the word, I was forced to take
> Law, horrible Law with all equivocations
> Will make my life a misery for three years!
> Muses of Helicon, Pindus and Parnassus
> Come, I pray you, soothe my disgrace.
> Have pity on me, an unhappy mortal
> Snatched in spite of himself from your altar.
> The arid problems of the Mathematician,
> His pallid brow furrowed, his lips as white
> As the white shroud of a sullen ghost,
> I know, sisters, they seem frightful to you!
> But he who embraces the career of Law
> Forfeits your trust and Apollo's too.
> Do not cast too scornful an eye on me
> For I am less culpable than miserable.
> Hasten to my words, relieve my disgrace,
> And in eternity I will render thanks.

Didn't you say to yourself on hearing, or reading, these insipid verses that the muse of poetry had left me forever? Alas, that's what this accursed Law does.

> Oh Law who bore thee, what twisted brain
> Created to make me unhappy the deformed Digest?
> And this incongruous Code, could it not remain
> Unknown in France for another century?
> What strange furore, what stupidity and
> Folly disturbed your quivering brain,
> Oh wretched Justinian, compiler of the Pandects
> And shameless editor of the *Corpus Juris*?
> Wasn't it enough that Horace and Virgil,
> Tacitus and Lucan forced on us difficult texts
> For eight years representing the horror,
> Without adding to them, as the cause of my unhappiness!
> If hell exists, and room remains,
> God in heaven, despatch the editor of the Digest.

Find out about the competition for the Academy [the Beaux-Arts in Paris, or perhaps the Prix de Rome], because I'm sticking to the plan we had of competing come what may, provided of course that it doesn't cost anything.

> You know that Boileau's broken shoulderbone
> Was found last year in a deep ditch,
> And that digging deeper the workmen found
> All his old bones, which they took to Paris.
> There, in a museum, this king of the jungle
> Was classified as an old rhinoceros.
> Then these words were carved at the foot of his carcass:
> 'Here lies Boileau, the rector of Parnassus.'

> This tale full of truth
> Shows you his well-deserved fate
> For having overpraised with his indiscreet eloquence

The fourteenth Louis, the stupidest of our kings.
Then one hundred francs was given to reward
The keen workmen, who for this discovery
Sport a fine medal, with these words:
'They found Boileau in a deep ditch.'

One day, Hercules was sound asleep
In a wood, for the air was good, for in truth
If he had not taken refuge in a charming grove
And he had exposed himself to the glare
Of the sun, which was beating down,
Perhaps he would have had a terrible headache.
So he slept deeply. A young dryad
Passing by ... But I see that I was about to say something silly,
so I'll shut up. Permit me to end this letter as stupidly as it began.

I wish you a thousand and one good things, joys, pleasures, *adieu mon cher*, greetings to Monsieur Aubert [Zola's grandfather], and to your parents, *adieu*, I take my farewell.

Your friend   P. CÉZANNE

PS – I've just received your letter, it gave me great pleasure; but I beg you in future to use slightly thinner paper, for you've drained more blood from my purse than is good for it, Ye Gods, those post-office monsters made me pay 8 sous, I would have had enough to send you two more letters. So do use slightly thinner paper. *Adieu mon cher.*

ı   *Pitot* is Provençal for 'young man'. The figures of the *pitot* and of Hercules were deeply rooted in the culture. Hercules had traversed Provence on his way from Spain to Italy, and fought a great battle against two giants on the nearby plain of La Crau. The *pitot* was rooted also in the shared memory or mythology of the three Inseparables, Cézanne, Zola and Baille. 'You remember our swimming parties,' wrote Zola, 'that happy era when, indifferent to the future, one fine evening we devised the tragedy of the celebrated *pitot*; then the great day, there on the riverbank, the radiant sunset, the countryside that perhaps we didn't admire then, but that seems so calm and pleasant in the memory.' This particular *pitot* seems to have been a real person: judging from Zola's correspondence, a nickname for a master or supervisor at their school. Cézanne's conception was at the same time allegorical and ironical. He imagined himself as the valiant *pitot* – even as he offered a woeful account of his indenture – and as Hercules at the crossroads, with Virtue on his right and Vice on his left, an allegory familiar either from school editions of Cicero, Lucian or Xenophon, or from back numbers of the *Magasin Pittoresque*, which included 'The Choice of Hercules' from Xenophon's text, complete with suggestive illustration (the youthful Hercules, sporting an impressive club, caressed by the comely Vice). This conception allowed him to poke fun at all concerned, including himself. It also yielded a satisfying play on the word *droit*, meaning the law, the straight and narrow, the right (side), and the righteous path that he must follow: the path to Virtue.

8 · TO ÉMILE ZOLA

Aix, 17 January 1859

Dante: Tell me, *mon cher*, what are they nibbling at there?[1]
Virgil: It's a skull, *parbleu*.
Dante: *Mon Dieu*, that's horrible.
    But why are they gnawing on that detestable brain?
Virgil: Listen, and you will learn.
The father: Eat up this inhuman mortal
    Who made us go hungry for so long.
The oldest boy: Let's eat!
The youngest boy: I'm starving, give me that ear!
The third boy: For me, the nose!
The smallest boy: I want that eye!
The oldest: I'll have the teeth!
The father: Ha-ha, if you eat like that
    What will be left for tomorrow, my children!

I decided, *mon cher*, to terrify you
To give you an enormous, dreadful fright
At the monstrousness of this awful tragedy
Calculated to move the hardest of hearts.

I thought that your heart, touched by these evils,
Would exclaim: what a marvellous picture that is!
I thought that a great cry of horror would spring
From your breast, upon seeing what is only imagined
In Hell, where the sinner dying unrepentant
Suffers horribly for all eternity.

But I note, *mon cher*, that for a fortnight
Our correspondence has slackened;
Is it perchance that you are prey to boredom,
Or has some annoying cold gripped your brain
And confined you to bed, against your will, and a cough
Plagues you? Alas, that's unpleasant,
Yet better that than some other ills.
Perhaps it is love that slowly eats
Your heart? Yes? No? My word, I have no idea,
But if it's love, I should say that's fine.
For I firmly believe that love never killed anyone;
Though sometimes perhaps it causes us
Some little torment, some little sorrow,
But here today, gone tomorrow.

If, by misfortune, misfortune there be, you must say,
If you are racked by some terrible illness;
Though I don't believe that the malevolent Gods
Would have given you, for Christ's sake, some awful toothache,
Or some other terribly stupid ache
To suffer, for example, a tremendous headache
Whose torment wanders from head to toe
Making you swear bitterly to the heavens.

That would be stupid; whatever the illness may be,
To be ill is to be extremely morose;
For one loses one's appetite, and one doesn't eat;
A thousand sweet delectable dishes may pass before our eyes
In vain; our stomach rejects
The sweetest, the best foods, the sweetest
Of sauces: good wine – which I love – it is true
That at Baille's it went to our heads,
But I forgive it: for wine is a good thing
It can heal the cause of all manner of ills
So drink up, dear friend, drink up, for it is good
And what ails you will soon be cured.
For wine is really good: twice, thrice.

Did you, perchance, eat too many sweets
On New Year's Day? Why not? For an excessive dose
Would have condemned you to keep your mouth shut,
By giving you, alas, indigestion,
But enough of such shameless indulgence
In silliness: for time gnaws ceaselessly
At our lives, and our days draw to a close.
The tomb, that voracious, terrible, insatiable abyss,
Is always gaping open – virginal or not,
When our time comes, virtuous or sinful,
We shall pay tribute to that inevitable fate.

Now, it's several days since I wrote the foregoing; I said to myself something like this, I haven't anything good to tell him, so I should wait a little before sending him my letter, but now I'm worried because I've received no news at all from you. By God, *sacrebleu,* I've made up hypotheses, and even inanities, regarding this keeping silent. Perhaps, I thought, it's that he's busy with some *immensissime* work, perhaps he's dreaming up some huge poem, perhaps he's preparing some truly unsolvable riddle for me, perhaps he's even become editor of some limp rag; but all those suppositions don't really tell me *quod agis, quod vivis, quod cantas, quomodo te ipsum portas* [what

'La Mort règne en ces lieux' ('Death reigns in this place'),
drawing on a letter to Zola, 17 January 1859.

you're doing, how you're living, what you're singing, how you're behaving], etc.; I could bore you much longer and you could, in your vexation, exclaim with Cicero: *Quosque (sic!) tandem, Cézasine, abuteris patientia nostra?* [Why, Cézasine, are you trying our patience?] To which I will reply that in order not to be bored you should write to me at once, if there's no serious impediment. *Salut omnibus parentibus tuis, salut tibi quoque, salve, salve.*

PAULUS CEZASINUS

| The point of departure of this fantasia is *The Divine Comedy*. In the *Inferno*, Dante and Virgil enter the ninth circle of hell, reserved for the treacherous, who are condemned to a kind of moral and physical deep-freeze. There they come upon Count Ugolino and his mortal enemy, Archbishop Ruggieri, locked in a macabre embrace:

> We had already gone away from him,
> When I saw two so frozen in one hole
> That the head of one made headgear for the other;
> And, as in hunger people will gnaw bread,
> So the one on top fixed his teeth in the lower one,
> Just where the brain joins to the nape of the neck.

At Dante's request Ugolino tells his tale. Ruggieri treacherously imprisoned him in the Tower of Hunger in Pisa, in 1288, together with his sons and grandsons; Ugolino was compelled to watch the children starve to death. Dante leaves open the possibility that the starving father ate the flesh of his dead sons – who offered him that privilege, to relieve his suffering – as Ugolino relates:

> 'Then he died: and, as you see me now,
> I saw the three of them fall one by one,
> Between the fifth day and the sixth; then I started,
> Already blind, to grope over their bodies,
> Calling to them for two days, after they were dead:
> And, after that, grief was less strong than hunger.'

Ugolino is condemned to hell on account of his own treachery in the political infighting for control of Pisa; but he is also permitted to avenge himself on Ruggieri – whose head he gnaws.

Cézanne's version is accompanied by a crude drawing, showing father and sons at table, preparing to tuck into a severed head. Once again, it has been psychoanalysed in terms of conflict with the tyrannical father. According to Meyer Schapiro: 'Instead of devouring his children, the bald father is pictured sardonically offering them portions of his own head. One might interpret this image as an unspoken wish for the father's death which will give the young Cézanne the freedom and means for an independent career. If he addressed the letter with this text to his friend Zola, it was perhaps because Zola was a fatherless boy who could receive with sympathy the play about a grim constraining parent.' Kurt Badt constructed an even more elaborate version along similar lines, with which Schapiro may well have been familiar. Once again, this seems to be misguided. Leaving aside the obvious inconsistencies ('the bald father' is a figment of Schapiro's imagination), Cézanne and Zola were very familiar with *The Divine Comedy*; they alluded to it in their correspondence. The story of Ugolino and Ruggieri was part of the culture. In that culture Ugolino's behaviour in relation to his sons was not automatically to be condemned; on the contrary, it was often interpreted as tender and loving. Murderous feelings about the father did not arise. The head in Cézanne's reimagining could easily be Ruggieri's: that would make sense of the story. As so often in these early letters, his doggerel drama is more playful than psychological, designed to tickle Zola's fancy and tell him off for neglecting his correspondence for a whole fortnight.

9 · TO ÉMILE ZOLA

[Aix] 20 June [1859]

Mon cher,

Yes *mon cher*, it's really true, what I told you in my last letter. I tried to deceive myself, by the tithe of the Pope and his cardinals, I was very much in love with a certain Justine who is truly *very fine*; but since I don't have the honour to be *of a great beautiful*, she always turned away. When I trained my peepers on her, she lowered her eyes and blushed. Now I thought I noticed that when we were in the same street, she executed a half-turn, as one might say, and took off without a backward glance. *Quanto à della donna*, I'm not happy, and to think that I risk bumping into her three or four times a day. What is more, *mon cher*, one fine day a young man accosted me, a student in his first year, like me, [Paul] Seymard, whom you know. '*Mon cher*,' he said, taking my hand, then clinging on to my arm and continuing to walk towards the Rue d'Italie, 'I'm about to show you a sweet little thing whom I love and who loves me.' I confess that just then a cloud seemed to pass before my eyes, I had a premonition that my luck had run out, as you might say, and I was not wrong, for just as the clock struck midday, Justine came out of the dressmaker's where she works, and my word, as soon as I saw her in the distance, Seymard indicated, 'There she is.' From then on I saw no more, my head was spinning, but Seymard dragged me along, I brushed against her dress … .

Since then I have seen her nearly every day and often Seymard in her tracks. Ah! What fantasies I built, as mad as can be, but you see, it's like this: I said to myself, if she didn't despise me, we should go to Paris together, there I should become an artist, we should be happy, I dreamt of pictures, a studio on the fourth floor, you with me, how we should have laughed. I did not ask to be rich, you know how I am, me, with a few hundred francs I thought we could live happily, but by God, it was a really great dream, that, and now I'm so idle that I'm only happy when I've had a drink; I can hardly do anything, I am inert, good for nothing.

My word, *mon vieux*, your cigars are excellent, I'm smoking one as I write; they taste of caramel and barley sugar. Ah! But look, look, there she is, it's her, how she glides and sways, yes, that's my little one, how she laughs at me, she floats on the clouds of smoke, look, look, she goes up, she comes down, she frolics, she rolls, but she laughs at me. Oh Justine, tell me at least that you don't hate me; she laughs. Cruel one, you enjoy making me suffer. Justine, listen to me, but she disappears, she goes up and up and up for ever, finally she disappears. The cigar falls from my lips, straightaway I go to sleep. For a moment I thought I was going mad, but thanks to your cigar my spirit has revived, another ten days and I shall think of her no more, or else glimpse her only on the horizon of the past, as a shadow in a dream.

Ah! Yes, it would give me ineffable pleasure to see you. You know, your mother told me that you would be coming to Aix towards the end of July. You know, if I'd been a good jumper, I would have touched the ceiling,

Sketch of bathers on a letter to Zola, 20 June 1859.

I leapt so high. In fact for a moment I thought I was going mad, it was dark, evening had fallen, and I thought that I was going mad, but it was nothing, you know. Only that I'd drunk too much, then I saw phantoms in front of my eyes, fluttering around the tip of my nose, dancing and laughing and jumping fit to upset everything.

Adieu, mon cher, adieu.

P. CÉZANNE

10 · TO ÉMILE ZOLA

[Aix, 29 July 1859]

Mon cher Zola,

> Perhaps you will say: Ah! My poor Cézanne,
> What she-devil has undone your skull,
> You who I used to see walking with an even step,
> Not doing anything good, not saying anything bad?
> In what confused chaos of strange dreams
> Have you lost your way today, as if at sea?
> Have you perchance seen some young nymph,
> A performer at the Opera, dancing the polka?
> Wouldn't you have written about it, asleep under the table
> After having got as drunk as one of the Pope's deacon's,
> Or full of rococo love, *mon cher,*
> Has the vermouth gone to the head?
>
> Neither love nor wine has touched my sorbonne
> And I never believed that water alone was any good;
> This very logic should prove to you, *mon cher,*
> That, although a bit of a dreamer, I can still see very clearly.

Have you never seen in daydreams
As if through a fog some graceful forms,
Indistinct beauties whose ardent charms,
Dreamed of by night, disappear by day;
As in the morning one sees the vaporous mist
When the rising sun lights with a thousand fires
The verdant hillsides where forests rustle,
Waters sparkling with rich reflections
Of azure; then a light breeze comes
Which chases away the passing mist,
This is how ravishing creatures with angelic voices
Sometimes appear before my eyes
During the night. *Mon cher*, one might say the dawn
Wants to colour them with a fresh pure glow,
They seem to smile at me and I hold out my hand to them.
Yet as I approach, they suddenly fly away,
They ascend into the sky, borne on the breeze
Casting a tender look that seems to me to say
Farewell. I try to draw near them again;
In vain, I try to touch them, in vain,
They're gone, already the transparent veil
No longer paints the ravishing shapes of their bodies.

My dream vanished, reality returns,
And finds me recumbent, sad at heart,
And a phantom appears before me,
Terrible, monstrous, its name is Law.

I think I did more than dream, I fell asleep, and I must have bored you
rigid with my platitudes, but I dreamt that I held in my arms my *lorette*, my
grisette, my sweet, my saucy wench, that I was fondling her buttocks, and
other things besides …

Oh crass collegian! Most ignoble scabs!
Oh you who paddle along ancient paths

Despised by all for whom a little fervour
Kindles some sublime impulse in their hearts;
What mad habit impels you to criticize
Him who laughs at your feeble upheaval,
Collegian myrmidons! Dragooned admirers
Of those sorry, dull verses that Virgil left us:
A real herd of swine who move under the aegis of
A corrupt pedant, who leads you blindly,
Forcing you to admire unknowingly
Verse that you find beautiful on his word alone,
While in your midst, flowing like lava,
An unfettered poet, who breaks every shackle,
As around an eagle the cheeping of a thousand puny birds
may be heard; good for nothing but horseplay,
Oh mean-minded detractors, priests of chicanery,
You vomit over him your profane venom.
I hear you now, like a chorus of frogs,
You shout yourselves hoarse, off-key,
No, the world has never seen frogs
Like you, gentlemen, jabbering so idiotically.
So fill the air with your idiot clamour,
My friend's verses will still win out!
They will withstand all your villainy,
For they are all stamped with the seal of genius.

Baille told me that the students, your workmates, had the temerity to criticize – quite ridiculously in my opinion – your piece on the Empress. That
made my blood boil, albeit a little tardy, I toss them this apostrophe, whose
terms are too weak to describe those literary deadbeats, failed drafters,
asthmatic mockers of your genuine rhymes; if you like, you can give them
my compliments and add that if they have anything to say, I'll be here,
whenever they're ready, waiting to thump the first who comes within reach
of my fist. At eight o'clock this morning, 29 July, I saw Monsieur Leclerc,
who told me that the youngest M. daughter, and once the prettiest, was
covered in sores from head to toe, and on the point of breathing her last in

Sketches and caricatures on a letter to Zola, late September 1859.

the clutches of the hospital. Her mother who was also too loose lamented her recent failings. Finally, the elder of the two daughters, she who was once the ugliest and still is, wears a bandage, after too much badinage.

Your friend who drinks your health in vermouth, Paul Cézanne. Farewell to all your relations and also to Houchart.[1]

| Aurélien Houchart, an old schoolfriend.

II • TO ÉMILE ZOLA

[Aix, late September 1859]

Baille does not write to you, for he is afraid that his wit
Remains impenetrable to you, *cher Zola*.
Fearing therefore that you will not understand him
Today he has given me free rein to write to you,
So I am here in his room and at his desk
I write you these verses, my brainchildren.
I do not believe, *mon cher*, that anyone will claim them
For they are truly uninspired in a unique way.
However, without further ado I'm going to show you
That we have been at pains to compose
In your honour: 'Tallow' is the title of the ode
That scorns the code of the art of poetry.

ODE
Oh tallow, whose truly incomparable benefits
Mean that one should do it special honour,
To you who brighten the darkness of the night,
    Honour.
No, no, nothing is more beautiful than a fine candle
And nothing gives better light than a fine candle,
May you be hymned constantly throughout the universe

In verse.
That is why I undertake with zealous ardour
To celebrate here the immortal candle.
To immortalize you I know no words
     Too fine.
Your glory is brilliant, and brilliant too the services
You render to those who grease their thighs.
Yes, your glory inspires these sublime lines
     Well conceived.
But it is above all for the Austrian army
To pass the word and sing the song.

[Baille writes:]

Come! Come! *Mon cher,*
Cézanne has had the cheek to go off to [illegible]. He wants to spend a week
there. He left this letter on my table and I'm sending it you. Come! Come!
The trips are incredible: you can't begin to imagine them.

Adieu, à bientôt. Write to us, of your result, your departure, your arrival.

12 · TO ÉMILE ZOLA

Aix, 30 November 1859

    Mon cher, if I am late
    In giving you in rhyme
    The final result
    Of the daunting exam
    Which caused me great concern

it's because (I'm not in good form) on Friday my Law exam was postponed
until Monday the 28th; however, I've passed,

Easy to believe
With two reds and a black.
Straightaway I wanted to relieve your doubts,
As to my undecided fate.

La Provence will soon carry in its columns
Feeble Marguery's insipid tale;
Provence, you shudder at this fresh misfortune,
And the chill of death has frozen your blood.

[Jean-Baptiste] Gaut's inspirational wits, Gaut himself editing the sublime
Mémorial [d'Aix].

A WIT. Grand Master, have you read the serial novel
    That *La Provence* has just started to publish?
GAUT. It's as bad as can be.
A SECOND WIT. That's what I say, Master,
    La Provence has never published
    Anything more ridiculous.
GAUT. Who is the rogue
    Presumptuous enough to defy my fame
    And follow me (me, the beacon of the press)
    With a novel so mean-minded as to spread distress.
A WIT. Until today his name is befogged
    He wants finally to appear …
ANOTHER WIT. Heavens above, what a difference!
GAUT. And what does he think he's doing, does he have the
    audacity
    To follow in our footsteps down below,
    Dare he aspire to reach the heights
    Where I reign victorious above the crowd?
A WIT. No, Master, never, for his feeble pen
    Knows nothing of how a novel unfolds,
    How a tangled plot
    makes your readers feel faint.

ANOTHER WIT. Above all he knows nothing of that difficult art,
    That art in which you are the most adept,
    That art so precious and so difficult,
    That ambitious art with which God has endowed you,
    That art, finally, that all the world admires,
    For which no word will suffice to explain.
GAUT. Fine, I know what you mean, it's Verbology,
    Derived etymologically from the Greco-Latin.
    Under the glittering blue sky
    What *gunogène* has the audacity
    To claim to have invented something
    More beautiful than the words employed in my prose?
    My French *carmines* are much superior
    To anything a bunch of rhymsters could produce;
    And above all my novels, the field I dominate,
    And like the rising sun illuminate
    The *excelses* heights of the *virides* forests,
    Like a brilliant prism I appear to the world.
A WIT. Sovereign Master, incomparable Mind,
    Praise be to you inestimable
    Virtue.
A CHORUS OF WITS. You alone, you alone, Great Gaut,
        innovator
    Sublime, soar in the heavens with grandeur.
    The most brilliant *sidères*
    Bow their heads in shame
    Before the fire from your eyes.
    Dazzled by thy glory,
    Ceding victory,
    Crossing his weary arms
    And turning his head,
    Ludovico stopped
    And said: I shall write no more.
    Glory to you, glory to you, Gaut *Philonovostyle*,
    Great Gaut, it would be hard to equal you.

Explanatory Dictionary of the Gautian Tongue

Verbology	Sublime art invented by Gaut; this art consists in creating new words drawn from Latin and Greek.
Gunogène	From the Greek 'woman' and the Latin 'to beget'. The gunogène is thus someone born of woman, that is, man.
Carmines	From the Latin *carmina* (verse).
Excelses	From the Latin *excelsus* (lofty).
Virides	From the Latin *virides* (verdant).
Domine	*Dominus* (master).
Sidères	*Sidera* (stars).
Philonovostyle	Friend of new style.

Mon cher, now that I've bored you sufficiently, permit me to put an end to my stupid epistle, *adieu, carissime Zola, salve.* Greetings to your relatives, to everyone, from your friend

P. CÉZANNE

I'll write to you when anything new happens, up till now the usual unbroken calm continues to wrap its sullen wings round our dull town.

Ludovico [the pen name of Marguery] is still a writer full of fire, verve and imagination.

Adieu, mon cher, adieu.

[Aix, 29 December 1859]

Cher ami, cher ami, when it's verse you wish to write
The end of each line must have a rhyme;
So in this letter, if it seems unfitting
To slip in some words to complete my verse,
Don't get in a huff about a sterile rhyme,
It's only there for a purpose;
So you've been warned: I'm starting and saying
Today, 29 December, I'm writing to you.
But today, *mon cher*, I much admire myself
For I'm saying freely all I want to say;
However, let's not rejoice too soon.
The rhyme may elude me in spite of myself.
I had a visit from Baille, our friend,
And I'm writing at once to tell you about it.

But the tone I've adopted seems to me too low,
I must wend my way to Pindus' heights:
For I feel heaven's secret influence;
So I'm going to spread my poetic wings
And soon fly so impetuously high
I'm going to touch heaven's vault.
But lest you be dazzled by the brilliance of my voice,
I'll put a piece of liquorice in my mouth,
Which by blocking the vocal passage
Will not deafen you with Chinese cries.

A Horror Story
It happened during the night. Bear in mind that the night
Is dark, when no star shines in the sky.
So it was the dead of night, and pitch black,
When this dismal tale must have taken place.

It's an unknown, monstrous, extraordinary story
Such that no one has heard before.

Satan, of course, must play a part in it,
It's incredible, and yet my word
That has always been believed is given to certify
The truth of what I'm about to relate.
Listen carefully: It was midnight, the hour at which
All couples are at work in bed without light
But not without heat. It was hot. It
Was a summer night; a huge cloud stretched
Across the sky from north to south,
Like a white shroud, presaging a storm.
Now and then the moon broke through that shroud
Lighting the path where I wandered, lost and alone.
A few drops of rain fell at intervals,
Staining the ground: from the usual preliminaries
Of fearsome gusts a howling gale
Blew up furiously from south to north;
The dread *simoon* that buries cities
Under waves of sand in Africa.
Trees that thrust their branches to the sky
Spontaneously bent their bold heads.
Calm gave way to the voice of the tempest.
The whistling of the wind echoed in the forest,
Struck terror in my heart. With a great crash, terrible
Lightning shredded the veils of the night:
Vividly lit in the pale glow
I saw elves and gnomes, God help me,
Flying and sniggering in the rustling trees.
Satan was in command of them; I saw him, all my senses
Froze with fear: his fiery pupils
Burned bright red; at times a spark
Would come off them, casting a terrifying reflection.
The ring of demons went round him …

I fell; my whole body, frozen, almost lifeless,
Trembled at the touch of an enemy hand.
A cold sweat bathed my whole body,
I made vain efforts to rise and flee,
I could see Satan's diabolical band
Approaching, dancing their fantastic dance;
Frightful elves, hideous vampires,
Tumbling over each other to get to me;
Their eyes, full of menace, turned heavenward,
Competing among themselves to make faces ...
'Earth, swallow me up! Rocks, crush me!'
I wanted to scream, 'Oh place of the dead,
Receive me alive.' But the infernal band
Tightened its dreadful spiral around me:
The ghouls and the demons were already gnashing their teeth
In anticipation of their horrible feast. Contented,
They threw covetous glances at me.
It was all over for me ... when, oh sweet surprise!
Suddenly from far away there came the sound
Of neighing horses galloping at full speed.
Faint at first, the sound of their swift passage
Got nearer; the intrepid coachman
Whipped his team, urging on
The mettlesome four as they traversed the woods.
At this sound, the demons of the crestfallen band
Dispersed, as the wind does the clouds.
As for me, I rejoiced then, more dead than alive,
Hailed the coachman: the obedient team
Halted on the spot. At once a sweet, refreshing voice
Came enticingly from the barouche:
'Get in,' she said to me, 'Get in.' I leap inside:
The door closes, and I find myself
Face to face with a woman ... Oh! upon my soul I swear
That I had never seen such a beautiful woman.
Blond hair: eyes glowing with a captivating fire,

Yes, in a trice she won my heart.
I throw myself at her feet; dainty, adorable feet,
Lovely legs; emboldened, with guilty lips
I plant a kiss on her quivering bosom;
But instantly I am seized by the chill of death,
The woman in my arms, the rose-tinted woman,
All of sudden disappears and metamorphoses
Into a pale cadaver with angular frame,
Its bones rattling, its eyes hollow and empty …
It was embracing me, horror! … A dreadful shock
Wakes me, and I see the convoy is stuck …
The convoy derailed, I go on, who knows where,
But as like as not I will break my neck.

Charade

My first is a crafty end with a deceptive look,
Fearsome destroyer of the gnawing class,
Full of tricks, shamelessly taking the lion's share
Of the tastiest morsels.
My second was the great delight of our young tums
In college, along with sausages.
My third is given both for indigestion
And for good digestion; the English nation
Gorge themselves on it every night, after a good dinner.
In sum, I am a theological virtue.[1]

Your friend, who wishes you *bonam valetudinem.*

PAUL CÉZANNE

Mon cher, neither Baille nor I can solve your riddle, which is a true riddle; tell me the word in your next letter.

As for my charade, I don't think I'll need to go that far.

Greetings to your family.

P. CÉZANNE

1 Solution: *chat-riz-thé* = *charité* (charity).

14 · ÉMILE ZOLA TO PAUL CÉZANNE [extracts]
Paris, 30 December 1859

[…]

Forgive me if my thoughts are a little confused. We won't talk politics; you don't read the newspapers (something I allow myself), and you wouldn't understand what I want to say. I'll tell you only that the Pope is very troubled at the moment, and urge you to read *Le Siècle* sometimes, for these are very strange times. What can I say to end this missive on a happy note? Shall I encourage you to storm the barricades? Or shall I talk about painting and drawing? Damn the barricades, damn painting! One is trial by cannon, the other is crushed by paternal veto. When you charge the wall, your timidity tells you: 'No further!' When you pick up your brushes, your father tells you: 'Child, child, think of the future. With genius you can die, with money you can eat!' Alas, alas, my poor Cézanne, life is a ball that doesn't always roll the way the hand would like it to. …

Since you've translated Virgil's second *Eclogue*, why don't you send it to me? Thank God, I'm not a young girl, and won't be shocked.

1860s

Sketches on a letter to Charles Penot, August 1862.

Paris, 14 January 1860

[…]

[Zola copies out a passage of his letter to Cézanne:]

In one of your last letters, I find this phrase: 'Michelet's love, pure, noble, may exist, but you must admit it's very rare.'[1] Not as rare as you might think, and this is a point I forgot to mention in my last letter. There was a time when I myself said the same thing, when I scoffed if purity and fidelity were mentioned, and that was not so very long ago. But on reflection I believe I've discovered that our century is not as materialistic as it wishes to appear.

[…]

1 Apropos Jules Michelet, *L'Amour* (1858).

16 · ÉMILE ZOLA TO PAUL CÉZANNE [extracts]

Paris, 25 March 1860

Mon cher ami,

[…]

You must make your father happy by studying Law as assiduously as possible. But you must also work hard at drawing – *unguibus et rostro* [tooth and nail] – in order to become a Jean Goujon [a classical sculptor, *c.* 1510–1568], an Ary Scheffer [a sentimental painter, 1795–1858], not to be a realist, but so as to be able to illustrate a certain volume that is running around in my brain … .

As for the excuses you make, about sending engravings, or the supposed boredom your letters cause me, allow me to say that that is the height of bad taste. You don't mean what you say, and that is some consolation. I have only one complaint, that your epistles are not longer and more detailed. I await them impatiently, they make me happy for a day. And you know it: so no more excuses. I'd rather stop smoking and drinking than corresponding with you.

Then you write that you are sad: I reply that I am very sad, very sad. It's the wind of time blowing round our heads, no one is to blame, not even ourselves; the fault lies in the times in which we live. Then you add, if I understand you, that you don't understand yourself. I don't know what you mean by the word understand. This is how it is for me: I saw in you a great goodness of heart, a great imagination, the two foremost qualities before which I bow. And that's enough; from that moment on, I understood you, I judged you. Whatever your failings, whatever your errings, for me you'll always be the same … What do your apparent contradictions matter to me? I've judged you a good man and a poet, and I shall go on repeating: 'I have understood you.'

Away with sadness! Let's end with a burst of laughter. In August, we'll drink, we'll smoke, we'll sing …

[…]

Paris, 16 April 1860

[…]

I got your letter. You're right not to complain too much about your fate: for after all, as you say, with two loves at heart, one for women and one for the beautiful, one would be very wrong to despair …

You sent me some verses that breathe a sombre sorrow. The speed of life, the brevity of youth, and death, there, on the horizon: that would be enough to make us tremble, if we thought about it for a moment. But isn't it an even more sombre picture if in the course of swift life, youth, the springtime of life, is entirely missing, if at twenty we haven't yet experienced happiness, if we see age striding towards us and we don't even have memories of fine summer days to brighten those hard winter days. And that's what awaits me.

You also say that sometimes you don't have the courage to write to me. Don't be selfish: your joys and your sorrows belong to me. When you're cheerful, make me cheerful; when you're sad, darken my sky without fear: a tear is sometimes as sweet as a smile. So, write me your thoughts from day to day; as soon as a new sensation is born in your soul, put it on paper. Then, when you have four pages, send them off to me.

Another phrase in your letter pained me. It's this: 'the painting I like, although I'm unable to bring it off, etc., etc.' You! Unable to bring it off: I think you're wrong about yourself. As I've told you before: in the artist there are two men, the poet and the worker. One is born a poet, one becomes a worker. And you who have the spark, who possess something that cannot be acquired, you complain; when to bring it off you have only to move your fingers, to become a worker. I won't leave this subject without adding something else. Recently I warned you to guard against realism; now I want to point out another pitfall, commerce. The realists still make art – in their way – they work conscientiously. But the commercial artists, those who paint in the morning for their bread in the evening, they have a miserable existence. I say this for a reason: you're going to work with X [Villevieille?], you'll copy his paintings, perhaps you'll admire him. I fear for you in this path you're taking, all the more so because the one you're perhaps trying to imitate has great qualities, which he puts to pitiful use, but which does not stop his paintings seeming to be better than they are. It's pretty, it's fresh, it's well painted; but all that is only a trick of the trade and you'd be wrong to stop there. Art is more sublime than that; art isn't only the folds in a fabric, the rosy skin of a maiden. Look at Rembrandt: with one ray of light, all his subjects, even the ugliest, become poetic. So, I repeat, X is a good master to learn the trade; but I doubt whether you could learn anything else from his paintings. Being rich, no doubt you dream of creating art rather than engaging in trade.

[…]

18 · ÉMILE ZOLA TO BAPTISTIN BAILLE [extracts]

[Paris] 14 May [1860]

[…]

As I told you, I wrote to Cézanne about the coolness with which he received you. I can't do better than to copy out here, word for word, his lines to me on that subject; here they are:

'According to your last letter, you seem to fear that our friendship with Baille is weakening. Oh no! For, *morbleu*, he's a fine fellow; but you know very well that with my character the way it is, I don't always know what I'm doing, and so if I've wronged him in some way, well, let him forgive me; otherwise, you know we get on very well, but I agree with what you say, for you're right … So we're still good friends.'

[…]

Paris, 1 August 1860

Rereading your letters from last year, I came upon your little poem 'Hercules, between vice and virtue', poor lost offspring, which you have no doubt forgotten, and which also disappeared from my memory. Anyway, this reading gave me great pleasure; some passages, a few isolated lines, pleased me tremendously …

Those forgotten verses seemed to me to be better than they once did, and head in hands, I began to think. What does he lack, I ask myself, this doughty Cézanne, in order to be a great poet? Purity. He has the idea; his style is vigorous, original, but what spoils it, what spoils everything, are the Provençalisms, the barbarisms, etc. Yes, *mon vieux*, more of a poet than I. My verse is perhaps purer than yours, but yours is certainly more poetic, more true; you write with the heart, I with the mind; you firmly believe what you set down, with me, often, it's only a game, a brilliant lie. And don't think that I'm joking here; above all don't think that I'm flattering you or myself; I have observed, and I'm telling you the outcome, that's all. The poet has many ways to express himself: the pen, the brush, the scissors, the tool. You have chosen the brush, and you've chosen well: one must follow one's own bent. So I'm not about to advise you now to take up the pen … Yet permit me to shed a tear for the dying writer in you … Oh! For the great poet who has gone, give me a great painter, I beseech you. You who have guided my faltering steps towards Parnassus, you who suddenly abandoned me, make me forget the budding Lamartine for the future Raphael.

[…]

20 · ÉMILE ZOLA TO BAPTISTIN BAILLE [extract]

[Paris, end August/beginning September 1860]

[…]

A charming expression in one of Cézanne's letters: 'I'm wet-nursed with illusions.'

[…]

21 · ÉMILE ZOLA TO BAPTISTIN BAILLE AND PAUL CÉZANNE [extract]

Paris, 2 October 1860

[…]

I recall one of Cézanne's sayings. When he had money, he usually hastened to spend it before bedtime. Tackled about this prodigality [he replied]: '*Pardieu!* If I should die tonight, would you prefer my parents to inherit?'

[…]

Paris, 24 October 1860

[…]

Since Cézanne wrote to me, I should reply to him. The description of
your model [Cézanne's sister Marie?] amused me no end. [Jean-Baptiste]
Chaillan maintains that here the models are drinkable, even if they're not all
that fresh. You draw them by day and caress them by night (the word caress
is a bit weak). As for the daily pose, so for the nightly one; moreover they
are certainly very accommodating, especially during the hours of darkness.
As for the fig leaf, it is unknown in the studio; undressing there is totally
free, and the love of art veils any over-excitement at all the nudity. Come,
and you'll see.

[…]

23 · POEM¹

[1860?]

My graceful Marie,
I love you and I beg you
To keep the notes
That your friends send you.

This bonbon will slip easily
Between your lovely pink lips,
Passing over many things
Without spoiling the lipstick.

This pretty pink bonbon
So sweetly popped
Into a pink mouth
Will be happy to enter.

1   On the back of an early drawing.

24 · ÉMILE ZOLA TO PAUL CÉZANNE [extracts]

Paris, 3 March 1861

[...]

You pose an odd question. Of course one can work here, as anywhere, given the willpower. Moreover Paris has something you can't find anywhere else, museums in which you can study from the masters from eleven till four. Here is how you could organize your time. From six to eleven you'll go to an atelier and paint from the live model; you'll have lunch, then from midday till four, you'll copy the masterpiece of your choice, either in the Louvre or in the Luxembourg. That will make nine hours of work; I think that's enough and that, with such a regime, it won't be long before you do something good. You see that that leaves us all evening free, and we can do whatever we like, without impinging at all on our studies. Then on Sundays we'll take off and go to some places around Paris; there are some charming spots, and if so moved you can knock off a little canvas of the trees under which we'll have lunched ...

As for the question of money, it's true that 125 francs a month [Cézanne's allowance] won't allow you any great luxury. I'll give you an idea of what you'll have to spend: 20 francs a month for a room; 18 sous for lunch and 22 sous for dinner, making two francs a day or 60 francs a month; with 20 for the room, that's 80 francs per month. Then you've got the studio to cover; the Suisse, one of the least expensive, is 10 francs, I believe; in addition I reckon 10 francs for canvases, brushes and paints; that makes 100 francs. So that leaves you 25 francs for your laundry, light, the thousand little things that come up, your tobacco, your amusements: you see that you'll have just enough to get by …

[…]

25 • ÉMILE ZOLA TO BAPTISTIN BAILLE [extract]

Paris, 22 April 1861

[…]

I've seen Paul!!! I've seen Paul, do you understand that, you; do you understand the full melody of those three words? He came this morning, Sunday [21 April 1861], to call me several times on my stairs. I was half asleep; I opened my door trembling with joy and we embraced hard. Then he reassured me about his father's antipathy towards me; he maintained that you had exaggerated a little, doubtless over-zealous. Finally he told me that his father asked for me, I must go and see him today or tomorrow. Then we went to lunch together, smoked a good many pipes in a good many public gardens, and I left him. While his father is here, we can see each other only occasionally, but in a month we should be able to take rooms together.

[…]

Paris, 4 June 1861

Cher Huot,

Ah! Doughty Joseph, I've been neglecting you, *morbleu!* And the friends and the *bastidon* [where they used to meet] and your brother and the good wine of Provence; you know the stuff here is dreadful. I don't want to compose an elegy in these few lines, but all the same, I must confess, I'm not feeling very light-hearted. I get by in my little world, this way and that; the Suisse keeps me busy from 6 a.m. to 11. I eat well for 15 sous a meal; it's not a lot, but what can you expect? I'm not dying of hunger, after all.

I thought that when I left Aix I'd leave the *ennui* that pursues me far behind. All I've done is swap places and the *ennui* has followed me. I left my parents, my friends, some of my routines, that's all. I have to admit that I wander about aimlessly practically all day. Naive as it sounds, I've seen the Louvre and the Luxembourg and Versailles. You know the potboilers they have in those fine monuments, it's *amazing, overwhelming, breathtaking.* Don't think that I'm becoming a Parisian.

I've also seen the Salon. For a young heart, for a child born for art, who says what he thinks, I believe it's there that the best is truly to be found, because there every taste and every style meets and collides. I could give you some fine descriptions and send you to sleep. Be grateful to me for sparing you.

> I saw the stunning battle by Yvon;
> In a *chic* drawing of a moving scene Pils
> Traces the memory in his vivid painting,
> And the portraits of those who lead us on a leash;
> Big, small, medium, short, handsome or ill-favoured,
> Here a stream; there the blazing sun,
> The ascent of Phoebus, the waning moon;
> Sparkling daylight, gloomy twilight,
> The Russian climate or the African sky;
> Here, a brutal Turk with brutish face,
> There, by contrast, I see a childlike smile:

On purple cushions a pretty girl
Displays her breasts, dazzling and fresh.
Sweet little cupids fly around;
A coquette admires her pretty little face in a mirror.
Gérôme with Hamon, Glaise with Cabanel,
Müller, Courbet, Gudin, compete for the honour
Of victory …

(Here I've run out of rhymes, so I'd do well to leave off, for it would be presumptuous of me to try to give you any idea, however slight, of the *chic* of this exhibition.) There are also some magnificent Meissonniers. I've seen almost everything and I plan to go back again. For that, I treat myself.

As my regrets would be superfluous, I shan't tell you how much I regret not having you with me to see all that together, but *que diable!* That's how it is.

Monsieur [Joseph] Villevieille, where I work every day, sends you a thousand good wishes, as does our friend Bourck, whom I see from time to time. [Jean-Baptiste] Chaillan greets you very cordially. Greetings to [Philippe] Solari, Félicien, [Marius] Rambert, Lelé, Fortis. A thousand good times to all. I'd never finish this if I tried to name them all; let me know, if you can, the results of the draw for all these friends. Warm regards to your parents; to you, courage, good vermouth, not too much boredom, and goodbye.

Adieu, cher Huot, from your friend

PAUL CÉZANNE

PS: Regards, too, from [Victor] Combes, with whom I've just had supper. Villevieille has just sketched out a monster painting, 14 feet high, with figures two metres tall and more.

The great G[ustave] Doré has an amazing painting in the Salon. *Adieu encore, mon cher*, until we have the pleasure of emptying a divine bottle.

P. CÉZANNE
Rue d'Enfer 39

A thousand respects to your parents; for you, courage, good vermouth, not too much *ennui*, and *au revoir*.

1   Joseph Huot (1840–1898), boyhood friend and amateur painter; later chief architect of Marseille. See letter 76.

27 · ÉMILE ZOLA TO BAPTISTIN BAILLE [extract]

Paris, 10 June 1861

[...]

I rarely see Cézanne. *Hélas!* It's not like Aix any more, when we were eighteen, and free and without a care about the future. The pressure of life, working separately, keeps us apart now. In the mornings Paul goes to the Suisse and I stay and write in my room. We lunch at eleven, each to his own. Sometimes at midday I go to his room and he works on my portrait. Then he goes to draw for the rest of the afternoon with Villevieille; he has supper, goes to bed early, and I see him no more. Is this what I'd hoped for? Paul is still that excellent capricious youth I knew in college. As proof that he's lost nothing of his originality, I need only tell you that no sooner had he got here than he was talking of going back to Aix, after struggling for three years to make the journey and seemingly unbothered. With a character like that, in the face of such unexpected and unreasonable changes of behaviour, I admit that I hold my tongue and rein in my logic. Convincing Cézanne of something is like persuading the towers of Notre Dame to execute a quadrille.

[...]

[Paris, August 1861]

[...]

No sooner had he returned from Marcoussis [a village south of Paris] than Paul came to see me, more affectionate than ever; since then, we've been together six hours a day; our meeting place is his little room; there, he's doing my portrait, during which time I read or we chat together, then, when we've had enough of work, we usually go and smoke a pipe in the Luxembourg [gardens]. Our conversations ramble over everything, especially painting; our recollections also loom large; as for the future, we touch lightly on it, in passing, either to wish for our complete reunion [the three Inseparables] or to pose for ourselves the terrible question of success. Sometimes Cézanne gives me a lecture on the economy, and, in conclusion, forces me to go and have a beer with him. At other times, he sings an idiotic refrain for hours on end; then I openly declare my preference for the lectures on the economy. We are hardly disturbed; a few intruders come from here and there to throw themselves between us; Paul paints on relentlessly; I pose like an Egyptian sphinx; and the intruder, quite disconcerted by so much work, perches for a moment without daring to move, and then makes off with a whispered goodbye, gently closing the door. ...

[Work on the portrait began in June and continued without incident for about a month, though Cézanne was never happy with the results. He started afresh, twice, and then asked for a final sitting. Zola came round the following day to find him stuffing clothes into a suitcase.]

'I'm leaving tomorrow,' he announced calmly. 'And my portrait?' 'Your portrait,' he replied, 'I've just torn it up. I wanted to redo it this morning, and as it went from bad to worse, I destroyed it; and I'm leaving.'

[At which point lunch intervened, and after they had talked into the evening Cézanne undertook to stay, at least until September. But this was merely a postponement, as Zola realized well enough.]

If he doesn't leave this week, he'll leave the week after; you can expect to see him go at any moment. Still, I believe he does right. Paul may have the genius of a great painter; he will never have the genius to become one.

The slightest obstacle sends him into despair. I repeat, let him leave if he wants to avoid a lot of unhappiness.

[…]

Aix, around the end of August [1862?]

Mon cher Carolus, Salut,

To all your people greetings too and good health: your letter has just arrived here, I've read it, and I am replying in order not to leave you too long in the agony of uncertainty. I'll come and see you soon, when? I can't give you a definite date now, but I'll write to you again, or I'll surprise you. I shan't forget your commission, if you need anything else, just send me a quick note. I'll stock up before leaving.

Young [Numa] Coste, the bizarre biped with the problematic face, comes with me every morning to the countryside, and exhausts me with thousands of different snubs that multiply every minute. The wretch, already combining his twin calling of dauber and solicitor's clerk with the habit of composing poetry (the most ridiculous and unbearable of habits), bored me to tears with numerous couplets of his own composition, which he recited or chanted with all the oppressive weight of a Russian knout or a Chinese yoke. This unusual digression is merely to get to the point and conclude that he annoys me, and that my unlucky star will lead me into his company tomorrow, when I'll tell him about the last wishes in your letter. All my relations are well, from which you may deduce that my sister is restored.

Au revoir, mon cher Penot, au revoir.

YOUR FRIEND PAUL CÉZANNE

Paris, 5 January 1863

Mon cher,

Let this letter be for both you and Monsieur Villevieille. And first of all I should have written to you long ago, for it's already two months since I left Aix.

Shall I tell you about the fine weather? No. Though today the sun, until now hidden behind the clouds, has just peeped in through the skylight and, wanting to end this last day gloriously, casts a few pale rays on us as it fades.

I hope that this finds you all in good health. Courage, and let's try to see each other again soon.

As in the past (for it's only right that I should tell you what I've been up to), I go to the Suisse in the mornings from 8 till 1 and in the evenings from 7 till 10. I work away calmly and eat and sleep that way too.

I go fairly often to see Monsieur [Joseph] Chautard, who is kind enough to correct my studies. The day after Christmas, I dined with them and tasted the fortified wine that you had sent them, oh Monsieur Villevieille; and your youngsters, Fanny and Thérèse, are they well, I do hope so, and the rest of you as well? My respects, I beg you, to Madame Villevieille, your father, your sister, and also to you. Incidentally, the picture that I saw you sketching out, is it under way? I spoke to Monsieur Chautard about it, he praised the idea and said that you may well be on to something.

Oh Coste, Coste the younger, are you still trying the patience of the most reverend Coste the elder? Are you still painting, and how are those academic *soirées* at the school, tell me who is the wretch who is holding the pose like an X or who holds his stomach in; have you still got the two apes from last year?

[Aimable] Lombard returned to Paris about a month ago. I was distressed to learn that he's going to the Atelier Signol. That worthy gentleman makes them learn certain clichés that enable them to do what he does; it's very pretty, but hardly admirable. To think that an intelligent young man should come to Paris only to be led astray. Still, apprentice Lombard has made great progress.

I'm also fond of Félicien, table companion of *Truphémus* [Auguste Truphème].

The good fellow sees only in the manner of his most illustrious friend, and gauges only according to his colours. According to him, Truphème has dethroned Delacroix, he alone can do colour, and thanks to a certain letter he's going to the Beaux-Arts. Don't think I envy him.

I've just this moment received a letter from my father, announcing his arrival on the 13th of this month; tell Monsieur Villevieille to entrust him with anything he likes, and as for Monsieur Lambert (my address for now being Impasse Saint-Dominique d'Enfer), he can write to me or have written for me some information about what he wants, where it can be bought, the best way of sending it, I'm at his disposal; meanwhile, I miss

> The day we went to the meadows of the Torse
> To eat a good lunch, and with palette in hand
> To trace on the canvas a lush landscape:
> Those places where you nearly sprained
> Your back, when you lost your footing
> You rolled to the bottom of the moist ravine,
> And 'Black' [the dog], do you remember! But the leaves
>   yellowed
> By the breath of winter have lost their freshness.
> At the edge of the stream the plants have wilted
> And the tree, shaken by the fury of the winds,
> Swings in the air like a huge cadaver,
> Its leafless branches wrenched by the mistral.

I hope that the foregoing, which I hadn't completed straight off, finds you in good health; my regards to your parents, greetings to our friends; I clasp your hand, your friend and *confrère* in painting.

PAUL CÉZANNE

See young [Charles] Penot and say hello from me.

1 Numa Coste (1843–1907), friend from the art school in Aix, painter, critic and journalist.
Joseph Villevieille (1829–1916), painter, a kind of mentor to Cézanne in the early days.

31 • TO NUMA COSTE

Paris, 27 February 1864

Mon cher,

You'll excuse the paper on which I'm replying. I haven't got anything else at the moment ... What can I say about your unhappy lot [being called up for military service], a great calamity has befallen you and I can understand how upset you must be about it. You tell me that Jules, too, has had bad luck, and that he's going to enlist before the call-up.

Baille was with me yesterday evening when I received your letter. Supposing perchance that you would like to anticipate the call-up and you could come to Paris to join a corps here, he (Baille, I mean) might be able to put in a good word for you with the lieutenant of your corps, because (he told me) he knew a lot of those who came out of the same training school as he did, as well as from Saint-Cyr [the military academy]. What I'm telling you is only in case it occurs to you to return here, where even as a recruit you would have more advantages of all sorts, be it leave or light duties, so that you could still devote yourself to painting. It's for you to decide, and to see if perhaps it might turn out well after all, but still I'm well aware that it doesn't look pretty at all. If you can see them, say hello to stout Jules, who can't be happy, and to Penot, who really should have sent news of his family and his father.

As for me, *mon brave*, hair and beard are longer than talent. Still, no discouragement from painting, one can do one's bit, even as a soldier. Here I see some who come and attend the anatomy courses at the École des Bozards [Beaux-Arts] (which as you must know has been really shaken up and the Institute swept out). Lombard is drawing, painting and pirouetting more than ever; I haven't yet been able to go and see his drawings, with

Dante and Virgil Crossing the Styx, after Delacroix, c. 1864.
Oil on canvas, 22.5 x 33 cm (8⅞ x 13 in.).

which he tells me he's pleased. For two months I haven't been able to touch my *galette* [morsel] after Delacroix [*Dante and Virgil Crossing the Styx*, R172]. I will, however, do some retouching before leaving for Aix, which I don't think will be until July, or thereabouts, unless my father summons me. In two months, that is, in May, there will be an exhibition of paintings like the one last year [the Salon des Refusés]; if you were here we could cast an eye over it together. Let's hope for the best. Give my affectionate regards to your parents, and believe me your devoted friend.

PAUL CÉZANNE

I'll be seeing Villevieille soon, he'll have your greetings for me.

32 · TO JEAN-BAPTISTE SAINT-MARTIN[1]

[L'Estaque] 15 August 1864

Mon cher Poète,
Since I do not know what else to call you, your little book can completely justify the charming title, full of mellifluous promise.

I cannot offer a better endorsement of your book than to copy out and repeat here some of your sweetest verses.

> April flowers watered by the dawn
> Fresh perfumes, beautiful butterflies,
> Breezes full of harmony,
> Nightingale, impish songster,
> Aerial symphonies,
> Joyous morning concert,
> White jasmine to snow flowers
> The path still sodden …

Yes, *mon cher*, your little book is all that and more, and yesterday on the seashore under the dark shade of the pines I devoured more than half of it – I'll finish it today, promising myself to go back to it, for it is not something that one can put aside and instantly forget.

When I write to Zola, I shall not neglect to do as you ask, and when I leave for Paris I shall write and let you know, and you may be sure that I shall receive with the greatest pleasure whatever you would like to send.

I am still at L'Estaque, that is the reason for the delay in replying, for my father brought your book and your letter from Aix only yesterday morning, Sunday.

My warmest regards, then, and best wishes.

Paul Cézanne

1   Jean-Baptiste Saint-Martin (1840–1926) was a man of many parts: he practised as a barrister in Avignon, he became a radical socialist deputy for the Vaucluse, and he ended his career as Director of the École des Beaux-Arts and municipal archivist in Avignon. He was also something of a literary figure, writing several works of history, editing an Avignon newspaper, the *Démocratie du Midi*, contributing to various national papers, and publishing a little book of verse, *Juvenilia* (1864), to which Cézanne is responding here. Saint-Martin and Cézanne had been fellow students in the Faculty of Law of the University of Aix in 1858–60 – for Cézanne an interlude of indenture, following his father's wishes, until he upped and left, determined to try to make his way as an artist. Saint-Martin's *Juvenilia* was first published in Aix, at his own expense. It is possible that he had asked Cézanne to see if Zola could help him find a better outlet; the book was indeed reissued the following year, by the Paris publisher Tardieu.

Paris, 13 January 1865

One of my friends, a painter, who is not on the course at the École des Beaux-Arts, would like to join your classes in aesthetics. Is a pass required for entry, and if so, would you be so kind as to obtain one for me? If my request is in any way inappropriate, please ignore it.

1 Professor of Aesthetics at the École des Beaux-Arts. Nothing came of this overture.

34 · TO CAMILLE PISSARRO[1]

Paris, 15 March 1865

Monsieur Pissarro,

Forgive me for not coming to see you, but I am leaving this evening for Saint-Germain and I won't be back until Saturday with [Francisco] Oller [a fellow student at the Suisse] to take his paintings to the Salon, for he has painted, so he writes, a biblical battle picture, I think, and the large painting that you know. The large one is very fine, the other I haven't seen.

I should have liked to know whether you have done your canvases for the Salon, despite the misfortune that befell you [the death of his father]. If you ever want to see me, I spend the mornings at the Suisse and the evenings at home, but give me a rendezvous that would be convenient for you and I'll be there to say hello when I get back from Oller's. On Saturday we'll go to the shack on the Champs-Élysées [the Palais de l'Industrie], carrying our canvases, which will turn the Institute red with rage and despair. I hope that you have done a beautiful landscape. My very best wishes to you.

PAUL CÉZANNE

Camille Pissarro (1830–1903), a major figure, Cézanne's collaborator and mentor. Pissarro owned twenty-one Cézannes, half of them given to him (or left with him) by his friend, as well as a number of drawings. For two decades, from the 1860s to the 1880s, they were as close as could be, as close as any two artists in the modern era, until Braque and Picasso began to cook up Cubism together in the years before the Great War. Cézanne had no better painter friend, nor perhaps anyone who understood him so well as an artist.

Cézanne openly acknowledged Pissarro's influence, in the context of a celebrated statement on Impressionism and his own relationship to it. Reminiscing with Joachim Gasquet in the 1890s, he said: 'I too was an Impressionist, I won't hide it. Pissarro had an enormous influence on me. *But I wanted to make of Impressionism something solid and enduring like the art of museums.* ... But, listen, a green patch is enough to give us a landscape, just as a flesh tone translates into a face, or gives us a human figure. Which means that all of us perhaps come out of Pissarro. ... Already in [18]65 he had eliminated black, bitumen, sienna and the ochres [from his palette]. That's a fact. Paint only with the three primary colours and their immediate derivatives, he told me. He was the first Impressionist.'

[Aix] 23 December 1865

[…]

The undersigned begs you to accept Fortuné's invitation, you will make our auditory nerves vibrate to the noble tones of Richard Wagner. I shall beseech you to do so … please accept my sincere compliments and grant our wish by performing. I sign for Fortuné [Marion].

Your old friend   PAUL CÉZANNE

1 Heinrich Morstatt (1844–1925), a German musician, later director of a school of music in Stuttgart. Morstatt knew Cézanne's boyhood friend Fortuné Marion (1846–1900), a precocious Darwinist, brilliant palaeontologist and amateur painter, later Professor of Zoology at the University of Marseille and Director of the Museum of Natural History there. Cézanne and Marion discovered a shared excitement in the fervour of their quest, and a palaeolithic love of their native soil. Wagner was all the rage in Paris in the 1860s, but Cézanne's supposed fondness for him has been overdone. His favourite composer was Weber. As Cézanne would have known, Morstatt was an admirer of Wagner (who was in his turn an admirer of Weber). See also letter 40.

36 · TO COUNT DE NIEUWERKERKE[1]

[Paris] 19 April 1866

Monsieur,

I had the honour to write to you recently on the subject of two canvases of mine that the jury has just rejected.

Since you have not yet replied, I feel I must insist on my reasons for writing to you. Given that you have certainly received my letter, there is no need for me to repeat here the arguments that I thought necessary to submit to you. I will confine myself to reiterating that I cannot accept the illegitimate verdict of colleagues who have no authority from me to assess my work.

I am therefore writing to insist on my petition. I wish to appeal to the public and to be exhibited nonetheless. My wish does not seem to me to be at all unreasonable, and if you were to question all the artists who find themselves in my position, they would all tell you that they disavow the jury and that they would wish to take part in one way or another in an exhibition that is perforce open to all serious workers.

So let the Salon des Refusés be re-established. Even if I were the only one in it, I would still want the public to know that I have no wish to have anything to do with those gentlemen of the jury, any more than they appear to wish to have anything to do with me.

I trust, Monsieur, that you will not continue to keep silent. It seems to me that every appropriate letter deserves a reply.

Yours faithfully.

PAUL CÉZANNE
22 Rue Beautreillis

---

1 Superintendent of the Beaux-Arts. Nieuwerkerke was a fastidious man, and self-righteous. For years he had swallowed his disgust at crude painters like Courbet or Millet, who demonstrated such a conspicuous lack of taste and refinement. Democrats, he called them, who don't change their linen. Cézanne was no better – if anything, worse. Nieuwerkerke's scribbled annotation across the top of the letter left no room for doubt about the tenor of the reply: 'What he asks is impossible, everyone recognizes how inappropriate was the exhibition of the Refusés to the dignity of art, and it will not be re-established.'

[Bennecourt] 30 June 1866[1]

Mon cher Émile,

I received the two letters you sent me in which were the 60 francs, for which I thank you very much, because I'm more unhappy than ever when I'm broke. Nothing very amusing can be happening since you don't say a lot in your last letter. Impossible to get rid of the landlord. I'm not sure what day I'll be leaving, but it will be Monday or Tuesday. I haven't done much work, the fair at Gloton [the neighbouring village] was last Sunday, the 24th, and the landlord's brother-in-law arrived, thus a crowd of idiots. Dumont will be leaving with me.

The painting isn't going too badly, but time passes slowly during the day; I must buy a box of watercolours so that I can work when I can't do any more on my painting. I'm going to alter all the figures in the painting; I've already given Delphin [Calvaire-Levasseur, the young son of the black-smith] a different pose, like a horse, I think it's better like that.

I'm also going to change the other two. I've added a bit of still life next to the stool, a basket with a blue cloth and some green and black bottles. If I could work at it longer it would come very quickly, but with barely two hours a day it dries too quickly, which is very annoying.

These people should really be posing in the studio. I've started an outdoor portrait of Père Rouvel the elder, which isn't going too badly, but it needs more work, especially on the background and the clothes, on a 40 canvas [100 × 81 cm; 39 × 32 in.], a bit bigger than a 25 [81 × 65 cm; 32 × 26 in.].

On Tuesday night and again yesterday evening I went fishing with Delphin, with our hands in the holes. I caught at least 20 yesterday in a single hole. I caught 6, one after the other, and once 3 at a time, one in my right hand and two in my left; they were quite big. It's easier than painting, all that, but it doesn't go very far.

Mon cher ami, à bientôt, and my regards to Gabrielle [Meley, the future Madame Zola] as well as to you.

PAUL CÉZANNE

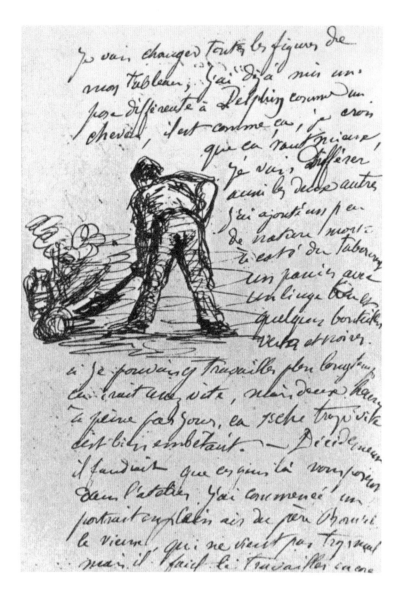

Young man working with a spade, sketch on a letter to Zola, 30 June 1866.

Sketches of planned paintings (Rose reading to her doll, and a portrait of Marion and Valabrègue) on a letter to Zola, c. 19 October 1866.

Thank Baille for me, for saving me from financial need.

The diet here is getting too meagre and trichinous, they'll end up giving me nothing more to eat than a big smile.

And hello to your mother, whom I forgot, a thousand pardons.

1   Cézanne was staying for a while with Zola and other friends in a kind of artists' colony near Nantes.

38 · TO ÉMILE ZOLA

[Aix, *c.* 19 October 1866]

Mon cher Émile,

It's been raining steadily for several days. [Antoine] Guillemet arrived on Saturday evening, he spent several days with me, and yesterday, Tuesday, he moved into a small place, nice enough, that costs him 50 francs a month, laundry included. Despite the driving rain, the countryside is superb and we've done a few studies. When the weather clears, he'll get down to serious work. For my part, idleness overwhelms me, for four or five days I've done nothing at all. I've just finished a little painting that is I think the best I've done: it shows my sister Rose reading to her doll. It's only a metre, if you'd like it, I'll give it to you; it's the same size as the [Antony] Valabrègue frame. I'll submit it to the Salon.

Guillemet's lodgings consist of a kitchen on the ground floor and a living room looking onto the garden that surrounds the country house. He has taken two rooms on the first floor with a WC. He has only the right wing of the house. It's at the beginning of the Route d'Italie, just across from the little house where you used to live, where there's a pine tree, you'll remember. It's next to Mère Constalin, who had the *guinguette* [open-air café].

You know, all the paintings done indoors, in the studio, will never be as good as the things done outdoors. In showing outdoor scenes, the contrasts between the figures and the ground are astonishing, and the landscape is magnificent. I see some superb things, and I must resolve to paint only out of doors.

I've already told you about a canvas I'm going to try, it will show Marion and Valabrègue leaving for the *motif* [1] (a landscape of course). The sketch that Guillemet thought was good, that I did from nature, puts all the rest in the shade. I do think that all the old master paintings showing things out of doors were simply done with style [*chic*], because that sort of painting doesn't seem to me to have the look of truth and above all of originality offered by nature. Père Gibert of the museum invited me to visit the Musée Bourguignon, I went with Baille, Marion, Valabrègue. I found everything bad. It's a great consolation. I'm rather bored, only work distracts me a bit, I mope less when someone else is around. I see only Valabrègue, Marion, and now Guillemet.

This will give you some idea of the morsel I'm offering you! My sister Rose is sitting in the middle, holding a little book she's reading, her doll is on a chair, she's in an armchair. Dark background, light head, blue hairnet, blue pinafore, deep yellow frock, on the left a bit of still life: a bowl, some children's toys.

Say hello to Gabrielle, as well as to Solari and Baille who must be in Paris with his *frater* [brother].

I take it that now the vexations of your disagreement with [Hippolyte de] Villemessant [editor of *L'Événement*] are over, you must be feeling better, and I hope your work isn't too overwhelming. I learned with pleasure of your introduction to the great paper [*Le Figaro*]. If you see Pissarro, give him my best wishes.

But, I repeat, I'm feeling a bit down, for no good reason. As you know, I don't know what causes it, it comes back every evening when the sun goes down, and then it rains. That brings on the gloom.

One of these days I plan to send you a sausage, but my mother will have to go and buy it, because otherwise I'd be swindled. That would be very ... annoying.

Can you believe that I hardly read any more. I don't know whether you're of the same mind, and that wouldn't change mine, but I'm beginning to realize that art for art's sake is a bad joke; this is just between ourselves.

Sketch of my forthcoming painting *en plein air*.

PS I've had this letter in my pocket for four days and I feel the need to send it to you; *adieu, mon cher*.

PAUL CÉZANNE

I   *Le motif* or *sur le motif* was Cézanne's customary way of referring to the outdoors, and to the place where he would set up his easel.

39 · TO CAMILLE PISSARRO

[Aix, 23 October 1866]

Mon cher ami,

I'm here in the bosom of my family, with the foulest people on earth, those who make up my family, excruciatingly annoying. Let's say no more about it.

I see Guillemet and his wife every day, they're fairly well set up at 43 Cours Sainte-Anne. Guillemet hasn't yet started on big paintings, he began with a few small canvases that are very good. You are quite right to speak of grey, that alone reigns in nature, but it's frighteningly difficult to capture. The countryside here is very beautiful, enormously appealing, and Guillemet did a study of it in grey weather yesterday and today that was really lovely. His studies seem to me to stand out more than those he brought back last year from Yport. I'm very taken with them. Anyway you'll be able to tell better when you see them. I've nothing more to add, except that he's going to start on a big canvas very shortly, as soon as the weather improves. In the next letter that you get, there will probably be some good news of it.

I've just posted a letter to Zola.

I'm still managing to work a little, but paints are hard to come by here and very expensive, depression, depression! Let's hope, let's hope that there's a sale. For that we would sacrifice a golden calf. You aren't sending anything to Marseille, well, neither will I. I don't want to send any more, especially as I don't have any frames, as that means more outlay that would be better spent on painting. I say that for myself, and to hell with the jury.

I think the sun will give us some more fine days. I'm very cross that Oller won't be able to return to Paris, as Guillemet told me, for he'll be very bored in Puerto Rico, and then it must be very hard to paint without any colours to hand. He also said that he might even sign on with a merchant ship coming direct to France. If you write to us again sometime, please tell me how to write to him, that is, what address to put on the letter and the correct postage in order to spare him unnecessary expense.

I send you my affectionate good wishes, and after submitting this letter for Sire Guillemet's perusal, having acquainted him with yours, I shall take this one to the post office. My respects to your family, please, to Madame Pissarro, and to your brother. I bid you good day.

PAUL CÉZANNE

[postscript written by Guillemet:]

Today 23 October year of our Lord 1866

Mon vieux Pissarro,

I was about to write to you when your letter arrived. I'm not doing too badly at the moment, likewise Alphonsine [Guillemet's wife]. I've done a few studies and I'm going to get down to my big pieces, autumn permitting. Cézanne has done some very beautiful paintings. He's lightened [the tone] and I'm sure you'll be pleased with three or four of the canvases that he'll be bringing back [to Paris]. I don't yet know exactly when I'll be returning, probably when my paintings are finished.

So there you are in Paris and I imagine that your wife prefers it to Pontoise. The little ones are well, I take it, and if you get bored, give us your news. We often speak of you and look forward to seeing you again. All the best. My wife and I send a thousand good wishes to you all.

À bientôt.

A. GUILLEMET

[Aix] Friday 2 November [1866]

[Guillemet writes:]

Mon cher Zola,

For a good month now, I've been here in Aix, this Athens of the South, and I can assure you that the time has not dragged. Fine weather, fine countryside, friends to talk painting with, and construct some theories to be demolished the next day, all that has made for a pleasurable sojourn in Aix. In his two letters Paul has spoken more about me than about himself, and I shall do the same, that is to say the opposite, and tell you a lot about the master. He is looking quite smart, his hair is long, his complexion is blooming, and his very turn-out causes a sensation in the Cours.[1] So you see all is calm on that front. Though always in turmoil, his morale shows a slight improvement, and thanks to a few solid commissions his painting promises to reward him for his efforts; in short, 'for now the sky of the future seems less black'. When he returns to Paris you'll see some paintings that you'll like a lot; among others an *Overture to Tannhäuser* that could be dedicated to Robert, for there's a splendid piano in it; then a portrait of his father in a big armchair, which comes over really well. The painting is light [in tone]; the look is very fine. The father has the air of a pope on his throne, if it weren't for the *Siècle* [the newspaper] that he's reading.[2] In short, it's coming along, and we'll soon see some very beautiful things, you may be sure.

The people of Aix still get on his nerves, they ask to come and see his painting so that they can rubbish it; and he has a good way of dealing with them: 'Bugger off,' he says to them, and the spineless ones run away, terrified. Despite or perhaps because of that, there is evidently a move in his favour, and I believe the time is coming when he'll be offered the directorship of the museum. That is devoutly to be wished, for unless I don't know him very well, I think we would then see some rather successful landscapes done with a palette knife, which have only that chance to get into any museum …

As for young Marion, whom you know by reputation, he cherishes the hope of being appointed to a Chair of Geology. He is excavating determinedly and trying to demonstrate to us from each snail fossil he finds

Louis-Auguste Cézanne, Father of the Artist, Reading 'L'Événement', 1866.
Oil on canvas, 198.5 x 119.3 cm (78⅛ x 47 in.).

that God never existed and anyone that believes in him has been hood-winked. We don't spend much time on that, because it has nothing to do with *painting*.

We received a letter from Pissarro who is well. We've often been to the dam [built by Zola's father, near Aix]. We'll be returning to Paris around the end of December.

I've added a double sheet of paper, because I think that Paul will take this opportunity to write to you; you will have all our greetings in one envelope. My best wishes to you. Your devoted friend.

A. GUILLEMET

[Cézanne continues:]

Mon cher Émile,

I'm taking advantage of Guillemet's writing to you to say hello, without having anything new to tell you. However, I can report that, just as you feared, my big painting of Valab[règue] and Marion has not worked out, and that I attempted a 'Family Soirée', which didn't come off at all. I shall persevere, nevertheless, and perhaps another shot at it will come off. We

Sugar Bowl, Pears and Blue Cup, 1865–66.
Oil on canvas, 30.2 x 41 cm (11⅞ x 16⅛ in.).

Young Girl at the Piano (Overture to Tannhäuser), c. 1868.
Oil on canvas, 57.8 x 92.5 cm (22¾ x 36⅜ in.).

went for a third walk with Guillemet, it's very beautiful. Best wishes to you
and Gabrielle.

PAUL CÉZANNE

Regards to Baille, who sent me his, in his letter to Fortuné Marion,
geologist and painter.

1　The Cours Mirabeau, the main avenue in Aix.

2　The paintings mentioned are *Young Girl at the Piano (Overture to Tannhäuser)* (R149)
　and *Louis-Auguste Cézanne, Father of the Artist, Reading 'L'Événement'* (R101). X-ray
　examination of the latter confirms that it was originally *Le Siècle*, as reported by
　Guillemet, which was indeed his father's newspaper. Cézanne's choice of *L'Événement*
　was loaded with personal significance – more than his father ever realized. It was a
　fraternal response to Zola, who launched a notorious series of Salon criticism in
　L'Événement that same year (published as a brochure, *Mon Salon*). In wider compass,

it was a response to Cézanne's own situation, at once coddled and cramped, in the bosom of his family. Switching the title was a gesture of defiance, muted and encoded, yet emblazoned on the masthead. The portrait is thus a kind of cryptogram, like those he sent to Zola. Cézanne must have relished that, and relished also the image of his father engrossed, holding in his hands the manifesto of artistic rebellion.

The portrait has another intriguing feature. In this Cézanne is another Cézanne, a painting within a painting, *Sugar Bowl, Pears and Blue Cup* (R93). That little still life is a choice example of his early *manière couillarde* (ballsy style). It hangs on the wall above his father's head, partly hidden by the papal throne, a small beacon of independence.

Too much has been made of the *Overture to Tannhäuser*. Cézanne's taste in music may or may not have run to Wagner, but it did not run very far. He cannot have been oblivious to the Paris premier of that opera in 1861, and the controversy it generated, if only because of Baudelaire's impassioned plea for the composer to 'persist in his destiny'. Wagner was de rigueur among several friends and acquaintances, but there is scant evidence of Cézanne's personal engagement. His favourite composer was in fact Weber, not Wagner. See also letter 35.

41 · TO NUMA COSTE

[Paris] Wednesday 13 May 1868

Mon cher Numa,

I've lost the address you gave me. I hope that by addressing this note to the Place Duplex (notwithstanding the wrong address) I'll have the happiness of knowing it reached you. So I beg you to come, on Thursday the 14th at 5.02 or thereabouts, to the Pont Royal, I think it is, where it enters the Place de la Concorde, and from there we shall have the pleasure of dining together, since I'm leaving for Aix on Saturday.

If you have a letter or anything else for your family, I shall be your faithful Mercury. Yours ever, your old friend

PAUL CÉZANNE

If tomorrow is not possible, make it Friday at the same time, if you like, *adieu*.

42 • TO HEINRICH MORSTATT [postscript to a letter from Fortuné Marion]

[Aix] 24 May 1868

Mon cher Morstatt,

So we shall have the pleasure of seeing you again without having to wait for the next world, since in your last letter you told us that you had come into your money. Such good fortune makes me very happy for you, for we are all striving after art without material worries disturbing the work that is so necessary to the artist. With keen sympathy I clasp the hand that need no longer soil itself in philistine labours. I had the good fortune to hear the overtures to *Tannhäuser*, *Lohengrin* and *The Flying Dutchman*.

Bonjour. Yours ever

Paul Cézanne

43 • TO NUMA COSTE

[Aix] early July [18]68

Mon cher Coste,

It's been a few days since I got your news and I should be hard put to relate anything new touching on your distant homeland.

Since my arrival I've been in the green, in the country [at the Jas de Bouffan]. On several occasions I've managed to get away; one evening, and then another, I ventured to the house of your father, who wasn't there, but one of these days, in the middle of the day, I expect to find him.

As for Paul Alexis, he was good enough to come and see me, having been apprised by the great Valab[règue] of my return from Paris. He even lent me a little review by Balzac from 1840 [on *The Charterhouse of Parma* by Stendhal]; he asked me if you were still painting, etc., you know, all the things one chats about. He promised to come again; for over a month I haven't seen him. For my part, particularly since your letter, I've been going off to the Cours in the evenings, which is a little contrary to my solitary habits. Impossible to find him. Nevertheless, impelled by a pressing desire to do my duty, I shall attempt a descent on his house. That day, however, I shall first change my shoes and shirt.

I haven't any further news of [Henri de] Rochefort, though *La Lanterne* [the radical periodical] has caused a commotion even here.

I did catch a glimpse of [Marius] Aufan, but the others seem to be in hiding and a great void seems to open around one when one has been away for some time. I shan't tell you about him. I don't know if I'm living or simply remembering, but everything makes me reminisce. I wandered alone as far as the dam and to Saint-Antonin [at the foot of the Mont Sainte-Victoire]. I slept in the miller's 'haybarn', good wine, good hospitality. I recalled our attempts at climbing. Will we ever try that again? How strange a life, that diversion, and how difficult for the three of us and the dog to go back to, how we were only a few years ago.

I have no distractions, except the family, and a few issues of *Le Siècle*, from which I garner trivial items of news. Since I'm on my own, I don't get out much to the bar. But at bottom I remain hopeful.

Did you know Penot is in Marseille. I didn't have any luck and neither did he. I was in Saint-Antonin when he came to see me in Aix. I'm going to try to go to Marseille one of these days, and we'll speak of the absent and drink to their health. In a letter, he said: 'And the beer mugs will fall.'

PS I had left this letter unfinished when, as the clock struck 12, Dethès and Alexis descended on me. You can imagine how we talked of literature, and how we refreshed ourselves, for it was a very hot day.

Alexis was good enough to read me a bit of poetry that I thought was really very good, then he recited from memory a few stanzas from another, entitled 'Symphony in A minor'. I thought those few verses more unusual, more original, and I complimented him on them. I also told him about your letter, he'll write to you, he said. Meanwhile I send his greetings, as well as those of my family, to whom I passed on your letter, for which I thank you most warmly, it's like dew amid burning sun. I've also seen Combes, who came out to the country. I send you warm greetings, yours ever from the heart.

Paul Cézanne

44 · TO NUMA COSTE

[Aix, late November 1868]

It's Monday evening.

Mon cher Numa,
I can't give you the exact date of my return [to Paris]. It will most probably be early December, around the 15th. I shan't forget to see your parents before I go and I'll bring you whatever you want.

Besides, a trunk of linen is being sent ahead by goods train, so I can take care of plenty of things.

I saw your father some time ago, and we went to see Villevieille. Telling you about it reminds me to go and see him and above all not to forget at the time of departure. But I'll make a list of all the things I should do and the people I should see, and cross them out as I do them, so that I won't forget anything. I was very happy that you wrote to me, for that rouses one from the lethargy into which one ultimately falls. The great expedition we were to have made to Sainte-Victoire fell through this summer, on account of the excessive heat, and in October on account of the rains; so you see how the comrades' willpower starts to weaken. But what can one do, that's how it is, it seems that we're not always full of life, *semper virens*, as they would say in Latin, evergreen or, rather, game.

I shan't give you any news from here, for apart from the founding of *Le Galoubet* [a satirical journal] in Marseille I don't know anything new. Yet

[Joseph] Gibert *pater*, a bad painter, refused to allow Lambert to photograph some canvases in the Musée Bourguignon, thus cutting off his work. Refused Victor Combes permission to copy, etc. Noré is an absolute dunce. They say he's doing a painting for the Salon.

All that is goitrous. For 58 months Papa Livé has been sculpting a bas-relief one metre long. He's still on the eye of Saint XXX.

It seems that the Master of Agay [Combes], that young *Fashionable* whom you know, goes to the Musée Bourguignon. And Mother Combes says to him, 'Give me your cane, Papa Gibert will have none of that.' 'I don't give a damn,' the other says. He holds on to his cane. Gibert *pater* arrives, he wants to make a scene. 'Bugger off,' shouts Agay. Truly.

Monsieur Paul Alexis, an altogether superior sort, and one might add with no airs and graces, lives on poetry and things. I saw him a few times during the fine weather. I met him again only recently and gave him your news. He's dying to leave for Paris, without paternal consent; he wants to borrow some money, secured on the paternal skull, and make off to other climes, drawn incidentally by the great Valab[règue] … who shows hardly any sign of life. So Alexis thanks you for thinking of him, he returns the compliment. I called him a little lazy, he told me that if you only knew his predicament (a poet must always be pregnant with some Iliad or rather a personal Odyssey) you would forgive him. Even if you don't give him a prize for effort or some something like that, I conclude that you must pardon him, for he read me some pieces of verse that offer proof of no mean talent. He already has in abundance the skill of the trade.

I clasp your hand from afar until I can do so from nearer, your old friend

Paul Cézanne

The word 'employee' seems ridiculous, and yet what am I to call you in the performance of your new duties?

I can't post this letter until tomorrow afternoon.

I'm still working hard on the landscape of the banks for the Arc, it's still for the next Salon, will that be 1869?

1870s

Avril 1876.

Mon Cher Pissarro

J'ai reçu il y a deux jours
une grande quantité de
catalogues et de journaux
relatifs à notre exposition de
chez Durand-Ruel —
Vous devez les avoir lus. —
J'ai vu entr'autres un long
éreintement du sieur Wolf.
C'est monsieur Choquet qui
d'avoir de ses nouvelles m'a procuré ce plaisir . —
J'ai vu aussi par lui que
la Japonaise de Monet n'
était vendue 2 mille francs.
Il paraît d'après les journaux
que le Refus au Salon de
Manet a fait beaucoup de
bruit, et qu'il s'expose chez lui.

Letter to Pissarro, April 1876.

[Paris] 7 June 1870

Mon cher Gabet,

It's a long time since I received your letter, and I've been negligent in not replying, but here I'm righting the wrong done to you. In any event, dear friend, you will have heard my news from [Achille] Emperaire, about a month ago, and lately from my uncle [Dominique?] who promised me he would see you and give you a copy of the caricature that Stock did.[2] So I was rejected as before [by the Salon], but I'm none the worse for it. Needless to say I'm still painting, and for the moment I'm fine.

I can tell you that there are some very pretty things in the exhibition, and some ugly ones too. There is the painting by Monsieur Honoré [Gibert, son of Joseph], which makes a very good impression and which is well placed. Solari has also done a very fine statue.

Please give my respects to Madame Gabet, and give little Titin a kiss from me. Remember me also to your father and father-in-law. And don't forget our friend [Louis] Gautier, the extinguisher of street lamps, and Antoine Roche.

Mon cher ami, I embrace you with all my heart, *et bon courage,* yours ever, your old friend

P. C.

Does he walk straight or still to the side, and the great Saint Y...?

1 Justin Gabet (c. 1844–1907), a boyhood friend, cabinetmaker and joiner in Aix.

2 A caricature of Cézanne and his submissions to the Salon, including his portrait of Emperaire. See illustration on p. 142.

Portrait of Achille Emperaire, 1867–68.
Oil on canvas, 201 x 121 cm (79⅛ x 47⅝ in.).

Incident du 20 mars au Palais de l'Industrie ou un succès d'antichambre avant l'ouverture du Salon

Caricature of Cézanne, from the *Album Stock*, 1870.

[Bordeaux] 4 July 1871

[…]

I was very glad to get your letter, as I was beginning to worry about you. It's now four months since we heard from one another. Around the middle of last month I wrote to you in L'Estaque, then I found out that you'd left and that my letter might have gone astray. I was having great difficulty finding you when you helped me out.

You ask for my news. Here is my story in a few words. I wrote to you, I think, just before I left for Bordeaux, promising another letter as soon as I returned to Paris. I got to Paris on 14 March. Four days later, on the 18th, the insurrection broke out, postal services were suspended, I no longer thought of giving you any sign of life. For two months I lived in the furnace: cannon fire day and night, and towards the end shells flying over my head in my garden. Finally, on 10 May, I was threatened with arrest as a hostage; with the help of a Prussian passport I fled and went to Bonnières [north-west of Paris] to spend the worst days there. Today I'm living quietly in Batignolles, as though waking from a bad dream. My pavilion is the same, my garden hasn't moved, not a single piece of furniture or plant has suffered, and I could almost believe that the two sieges were bad jokes invented to frighten the children.

What makes these bad memories more fleeting for me is that I haven't stopped working for a minute. Since I left Marseille, I've been earning a good living … I tell you this so that you won't feel sorry for me. I've never been more hopeful or keen to work. Paris is reborn. As I've often told you, our reign has begun!

My novel *La Fortune des Rougon* is being published. You wouldn't believe the pleasure I've taken once more in correcting the proofs. It's as if my first book were appearing … I do feel a little sorry to see that all the imbeciles aren't dead, but I console myself with the thought that none of us has gone. We can resume the fight.

I'm a bit rushed, I'm writing in haste only to reassure you about my situation. Another time I'll tell you at greater length. But you who have all the long day ahead of you, don't wait for months to reply. Now you know that I'm in Batignolles and your letters won't go astray, write to me without fear. Give me the details. I'm almost as alone as you, and your letters help me a lot to live.

[…]

1   This letter seems to have made a strong impression on Cézanne – an impression inter-estingly shaded. The intermission was a consequence of the Franco-Prussian War of 1870–71 – which resulted in a humiliating defeat for France – and the bloodletting of the Paris Commune (the 'insurrection' to which Zola refers). It must also have stirred memories of painting Alexis reading to Zola in that pavilion (R150) and in that garden, the writer sitting cross-legged on the grass, robed for the part of 'the morose pasha of realism', receiving the reading like a tribute (R151). When Vollard later asked him about his war, Cézanne launched immediately into a reminiscence of Zola and his letter:

> I haven't really got anything extraordinary to tell you about the years 70–71. I divided my time between the landscape and the studio. But if I didn't have any adventures during that troubled epoch, it wasn't the same at all for my friend Zola, who had all sorts of misadventures, especially after his final return to Paris from Bordeaux. He had promised me to write when he got to Paris. Only after four long months could he keep his promise!
>
> Faced with the refusal of the Bordeaux government to make use of his services, Zola decided to go back to Paris. The poor man arrived in the middle of March 1871; a few days later, the insurrection broke out. …
>
> Monsieur Vollard, I regret not having kept that letter. I would have shown you a passage where Zola lamented that all the imbeciles were not dead.
>
> Poor Zola! He would have been the first to be sorry if all the imbeciles were dead. In fact, I reminded him just recently of that phrase in his letter, for a laugh, on one of the last evenings that I saw him. He told me that he was going to dine with a big cheese to whom he'd been introduced by Monsieur Frantz Jourdain [later President of the Salon d'Automne]. All the same, I couldn't help saying, if all the imbeciles were gone, you'd be forced to eat the rest of your casserole at home, tête-à-tête with your bourgeois! Well, would you believe that our old friend looked none too happy?
>
> Surely, Monsieur Vollard, one can have a little joke when one has worn out our trousers on the same school bench. …

Zola ended his letter by urging me to return, too. 'A new Paris is in the process of being born,' he explained to me, 'it's our reign that's coming!' Our reign that's coming! I thought that Zola was exaggerating a little, at least in relation to me. But, all the same, that told me to return to Paris. It had been too long since I'd seen the Louvre! It's just that, you understand, Monsieur Vollard, at that moment I had a landscape that wasn't going well. So I stayed a while longer in Aix, to study on the *motif*.

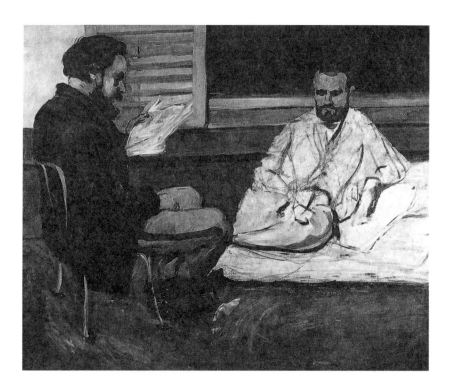

Paul Alexis Reading to Émile Zola, c. 1869–70.
Oil on canvas, 84 x 92 cm (33⅛ x 36¼ in.).

[Paris, January 1872]

Mon cher Achille,

I must ask you to be the bearer of this letter to my mother. Please forgive me for bothering you so often.

It would be a great pleasure if you were to write to me. Address your letter to 45 Rue de Jussieu – Monsieur Paul Cézanne – or care of Monsieur Zola, 14 Rue de La Condamine. I'm enclosing a 25-centime stamp, so that you won't have to run around the town for one. You need only toss into the letter-box whatever you're sending me.

Yours ever,

Paul Cézanne

If you need a few tubes [of paint], I can send them to you.

1 Achille Emperaire (1829–1898), a friend from the School of Drawing in Aix. Cézanne painted a magnificent portrait of him (R139), submitted unsuccessfully to the Salon of 1870. See illustration on p. 141.

48 • TO ACHILLE EMPERAIRE

[Paris] 26 January 1872

Mon cher Achille,

I've just seen Zola, who came to 45 Rue de Jussieu. He needs four or five more days in order to be able to give you a definite answer. He has been trying hard to obtain a [rail] pass, but has not yet managed to get one. A few more days' patience and you will have your answer. Needless to say I'd be very happy to see you. You won't be very comfortable here, but I willingly offer to share my retreat with you.

Before you leave Marseille, be good enough to send me a note in the post telling me the time of your departure and the most likely time of your arrival. I'll come and meet you with a handcart and take your luggage to my house. It's in the old Rue Saint-Victor, now called Rue de Jussieu, where I'm opposite the wine merchant, on the second floor.

In any event, I'll write to you as soon as there is any news.

Yours ever

Paul Cézanne

If you have a lot of heavy luggage, as I expect, bring what you need with you and send the rest by goods train. I must ask you to bring your own bed linen, as I have none to offer you.

49 · TO ACHILLE EMPERAIRE

Paris, 5 February 1872

Mon cher Achille,

I've got nothing from Batignolles, nor from anywhere else. If I've put off writing to you for so long, it's because until the last moment I still had some hopes. But only recently Zola told me that he was unable to obtain what I'd asked for.

If you're able to make the trip at your own expense, do. You'll find hospitality at my house.

Believe me, I tried immediately and everywhere I had any hope. But I'm sorry to say I failed.

If you're still planning to come, in spite of this disappointment, please send me a note, as I mentioned to you in my previous letter. And I'll be there to meet you at the station.

Believe me, in spite of all these problems, your devoted friend, who would like nothing more than to be somewhere other than in the fix in which he finds himself, so that he might be of assistance to you.

Paul Cézanne

I've had some bother that I'll tell you about.

50 • TO CAMILLE PISSARRO

[Pontoise, 11 December 1872]

Monsieur Pissarro,
I take up Lucien's pen, at an hour when the railway should be transporting me to my *penates* [home]. That's a roundabout way of saying that I've missed the train. Needless to add that I'm your guest until tomorrow, Wednesday.

Now then, Madame Pissarro requests that you bring back from Paris some powdered milk for little Georges. And Lucien's shirts, which are with his Aunt Felicity.

I bid you good evening.

Paul Cézanne

[Lucien adds:]

Mon cher papa,
Maman wants you to know that the door is broken so come quick because robbers could come. Please bring me a box of paints. Minette [his little sister] wants you to bring her a bathing costume. I am not writing well because I don't feel like it.

51 · LOUIS-AUGUSTE CÉZANNE TO DR PAUL GACHET[1]

Aix, 10 August 1873

Monsieur le Docteur P. F. Gachet,

I receved your sad leter of 19 July last informing me of the grivous loss of a son to your esteemed brother at the age of 19; I am much sadened and beg to beleve that I share in your sorow, you also say that Mdme your wife has just ben delivered of a child after a month of most serious ilness, but that todday she is a litle beter, I trust and hope that this leter finds her improved and fully restored, you say Mr Paul [Gachet's son] from who I received a leter todday to which I am repling behaved well towards you, he was simply doing his duty. I beg you would convay my respects to you'r honnorable family and beleve me your most humble servant.

1   Dr Gachet was a friend to many artists, including Vincent van Gogh, and apparently met Cézanne's father on a visit to Aix in 1858. He saw a good deal of Cézanne and Pissarro in the early 1870s. This translation follows Andy Millar's sympathetic rendition, with one or two minor alterations, in Bruno Ely, '*Pater Omnipotens Aeterne Deus*', in Denis Coutagne (ed.), *Jas de Bouffan* (Aix: Société Paul Cézanne, 2004), p. 26.

52 · TO ARMAND RONDEST[1] [?] [draft]

[Auvers, early 1874]

I am leaving Auvers in a few days to settle in Paris. I am therefore taking the liberty of reminding you of me.

If you would like me to sign the canvas you mentioned, would you be kind enough to send it to me care of Monsieur Pissarro, whereupon I will add my signature.

Yours sincerely

Dahlias in a Large Delft Vase,
c. 1873. Oil on canvas,
73 x 54 cm (28¾ x 21¼ in.).

The Old Road at Auvers, c. 1872–73.
Oil on canvas, 46 x 55.5 cm (18⅛ x 21⅞ in.).

1 A grocer in Pontoise, who had the sense to accept paintings as payment – at least three Cézannes, including *The Old Road at Auvers* (R191) and *Dahlias in a Large Delft Vase* (R223), and four Pissarros.

53 · TO CAMILLE PISSARRO

[Aix] 24 June 1874

Mon cher Pissarro,

I thank you for having thought of me while I was so far away, and for not being angry with me for not keeping my promise to pop in to see you at Pontoise before my departure. I started painting immediately after my arrival, which was a Saturday evening at the end of May. And I understand all the troubles you must be going through. It's really unlucky – always illness at home; however, I hope that when this letter finds you, little Georges will be well again.

But what do you think about the climate of the country you're living in? Aren't you afraid that it affects the health of the children? I'm sorry that new circumstances still keep you from your studies, for I know very well how hard it is for a painter to be unable to paint. Now that I see this country again, I believe it would satisfy you completely, for it's amazingly reminiscent of your study of the railway crossing in full sunlight in the middle of summer [*The Railway Crossing at Les Pâtis, near Pontoise*, P306].

For some weeks I had no news of my little one and I was very worried, but Valabrègue has just arrived from Paris and yesterday, Tuesday, he brought me a letter from Hortense, from which I learned that he's not doing too badly.[1]

I read in the newspapers about Guillemet's great success and the happy occasion for Groseillez, whose painting was bought by the administr[ation] after being awarded a medal. Which just goes to show that in following the path of Virtue one is always rewarded by mankind, but not by painting. I should be happy if you could give me some news of Madame Pissarro after the birth, and if you could let me know if there are any new recruits to the Société Co-op [the Société Anonyme Coopérative des Artistes Peintres …: that is, the Impressionists]. But of course you should not let this interfere in any way with your work.

When the time comes, I'll let you know about my return, and what I've been able to get out of my father, but he'll let me return to Paris. That's already quite something. Recently I saw the director of the Musée d'Aix [Gibert], who, driven by a curiosity fed by the Paris papers that mentioned the Co-op, wanted to see for himself how far Painting was under threat. However, on my assertion that seeing my efforts would not give him a very good idea of the progress of the disease, and that he should see the work of the major criminals of Paris, he said: 'I'll be able to get a good idea of the dangers run by Painting by looking at your attacks.' He arrived, without further ado, and when I told him for example that you substituted the study of tones for modelling, and that I was trying to make him understand reference to nature, he closed his eyes and turned away. But he said he understood, and we parted on good terms. But he's a decent sort, who made me promise to persevere, patience being the mother of genius, etc.

I almost forgot to tell you that mother and father have told me to pass on their affectionate greetings.

Give Lucien and Georges a kiss from me. My respects and thanks to Madame Pissarro for all the kindnesses you have shown me during our stay in Auvers. My warmest regards to you; and if wishes could make things go well, you may be sure that I would make them.

Ever yours.

Paul Cézanne

1 Cézanne met Hortense Fiquet (1850–1922) in Paris in 1869, when he was thirty and she was barely nineteen. They began to live together the following year. Soon they had a son, also christened Paul. Cézanne's relationship with Hortense was at first clandestine and then arm's-length; neither of them was cut out for joint housekeeping. For many years she was kept out of sight and hidden from his father, for fear of paternal disapproval and disinheritance. Hortense was not openly avowed, nor Paul formally legitimized, until 1886, when the couple eventually married.

Hortense was a woman of humble origins who had to fend for herself from a young age. She was plainly not his intellectual equal; she seems to have had no great regard for him as a painter; and, most seriously, she developed a taste for the good life to be found in Paris or in Switzerland, but not in Aix. It is widely believed that she and Cézanne did not have much in common, apart from their son, and that soon enough she came to mean rather little to him. Against that prejudiced account should be set at least twenty-four portraits, painted over a period of twenty years, long after they had ceased to live together all the time. Cézanne studied his wife more intently and more durably than he did anyone else, except perhaps himself, to extraordinary effect. Absent or present, no one ever took her place – certainly not the unknown woman who precipitated the emotional crisis of 1885 (see letter 128). Hortense herself was at once more 'delicate' and more resourceful than is generally allowed. She even transacted business on behalf of her husband, and she could hold her own in socializing with him (see letters 150 and 254).

Paul Cézanne junior (1872–1947) became effectively his father's agent. He had no other role in life, unless it was as a kind of guardian for his mother. Cézanne doted on him, encouraging him unstintingly by letter, though he was not blind to his shortcomings (see letter 223). After his father's death, Paul passed the time selling the paintings and gambling on the stock exchange. So dissipated his inheritance.

54 · TO HIS MOTHER[1]

[Paris] 26 November 1874

Ma chère Mère,

I must first of all thank you very much for thinking of me. For some days now the weather has been bad and very cold. But I'm not suffering in any way, and I'm making a good fire.

I shall be pleased to receive the promised parcel, you can always address it to 120 Rue de Vaugirard, I have to be there until January.

Pissarro has not been in Paris for about a month and a half, he is in Brittany, but I know that he has a good opinion of me, and I have a good opinion of myself. I am beginning to consider myself stronger than all those around me, and you know that I hold that good opinion advisedly. I have to work all the time, but not to achieve the finish that earns the admiration of imbeciles. And that thing that is so widely valued is nothing more than a workman's craft, and makes all the resulting work inartistic and common. I must strive for completion purely for the satisfaction of becoming truer and wiser. And believe you me, there always comes a time when one asserts oneself, and one has admirers much more fervent and more convinced than those who are attracted only by mere surface.

It is a very bad moment for sales, all the bourgeois baulk at parting with their sous, but that will end.

[...]

My dear Mother, remember me to my sisters.

Greetings to Monsieur and Madame Giraud and my thanks.

Ever yours, your son.

Paul Cézanne

ı This letter is known only from Gustave Coquiot's early study *Cézanne* (1914), which indicates that a few lines have been omitted (shown by [...]), perhaps because Cézanne mentioned people still alive when that book was first published. The date given by Coquiot and followed by others, 26 September, does not square with the dates of Pissarro's movements, which suggest that September is a misreading of November. It is evident from other letters that 'Girard' in Coquiot (and elsewhere) is a misreading of 'Giraud'.

[Paris, *c.* 1874?]

You ask me in your last letter why I have not yet returned to Aix. As to that, I have told you before that it is more agreeable for me to be with you than you might think, but once in Aix I am no longer free, and when I want to return to Paris there is always a struggle to be undergone; and although you may not be absolutely opposed to my return [to Paris], I am much affected by the resistance I feel on your part. I am very keen that my freedom of action should not be impeded in any way and I shall then hasten my return [to Aix] with even greater pleasure.

I ask Papa to give me 200 francs a month, that will permit me to make a long stay in Aix, and I shall be very happy to work in the Midi where the views offer such possibilities for my painting. I earnestly beg Papa to grant me this request and then I think that I will be able to make in the Midi the studies I want to pursue.

Here are the last two receipts.

[Aix] April 1876

Mon cher Pissarro,
Two days ago I received a large number of catalogues and newspapers about your exhibition at Durand-Ruel. You must have read them. Among other things I saw a long, savage attack by Sire Volf [Albert Wolff, art critic of *Le Figaro*]. It's Monsieur [Victor] Cho[c]quet who gave me the pleasure of hearing this news. I also learned from him that Monet's *La Japonaise* had been sold for 2 thousand francs. According to the papers, it seems that Manet's rejection by the Salon has caused quite a stir, and that he's doing his own exhibition at home.

Before leaving Paris, I met a certain Authier, of whom I've spoken to you. He is the fellow who signs articles on painting with the name Jean-Lubin. I told him what you had shown me about you, Monet, etc.; but (as you have no doubt heard since) he had not intended to put the word 'Imitator', but 'Initiator', which completely alters the meaning of the article. As for the rest, he told me that he felt bound, or at least it was fitting, not to say too much against the other painters at Durand's, you know why.

[Émile] Blémont's article in *Le Rappel* seems to me to be much better judged, despite too many reservations and a long preamble in which he gets a little lost. It seems to me that you're accused of Blue because of your mist effect.

We've had a very aquatic fortnight here. I'm afraid that the same weather has prevailed everywhere. Here, the frost was so severe that the fruit and vine harvests were ruined. But that's the advantage of art, painting endures.

I almost forgot to tell you that I was sent a certain rejection letter [from the Salon]. It's neither new nor surprising. I wish you fine weather and, if such a thing is possible, a good sale.

Please give my respects to Madame Pissarro, as well as greetings to Lucien and your family.

With my best wishes   Paul Cézanne

Don't forget [Armand] Guillaumin when you see him, nor Monsieur and Madame Estriel.   PC

57 · TO CAMILLE PISSARRO

L'Estaque, 2 July 1876

Mon cher Pissarro,
I'm obliged to reply to the charm of your magic pencil with an iron point (that's to say a metal pen). If I dared, I should say that your letter is imprinted

The Sea at L'Estaque, 1876.
Oil on canvas, 42 x 59 cm (16½ x 23¼ in.).

with sadness. The picture business isn't going well; I fear that your morale may be coloured a little grey, but I'm sure that it's only a passing phase.

I'd much rather not talk about the impossible, yet I'm always making plans that are very unlikely to come to fruition. I imagine that you would be delighted with the country where I am now. There are great annoyances, but I believe they're purely accidental. This year, it's rained for two days every week. That's astounding in the Midi. It's unheard of.

I must tell you that your letter surprised me in L'Estaque, by the sea. I haven't been in Aix for a month. I've started two little *motifs* of the sea, for Monsieur Chocquet, who had talked to me about it. It's like a playing card.[1] Red roofs against the blue sea. If the weather turns favourable perhaps I'll be able to finish them off. So far I've done nothing. But there are *motifs* that would need three or four months' work, which could be done, as the vegetation doesn't change here. There are the olive trees and the pines that always keep their leaves. The sun is so fierce that objects seem to be silhouetted, not only in black or white, but in blue, red, brown, violet. I may be wrong, but this seems to be the very opposite of modelling.[2] How happy the gentle landscapists of Auvers would be here, and that (insert three-letter word here) [*con*, or 'bastard'?] Guillemet. As soon as I can, I'll spend at least a month in these parts, as one must do canvases of two metres at least, like that one of yours that was sold to Fore [*The Hills at L'Hermitage*, P121, sold to the opera singer Jean-Baptiste Faure].

If we have to exhibit with Monet, I hope our cooperative's exhibition is a flop. You'll think me a swine, possibly, but our own affairs must come first. [Alfred] Meyer [the treasurer], who doesn't have any grasp of the successful elements of cooperatives, seems to be becoming totally impossible; in trying to bring forward the Impressionist exhibition, he is actually damaging its prospects. This might exhaust public opinion and lead to confusion. First, too many exhibitions one after another is a bad idea, and second, people who think they're going to see Impressionists see nothing but cooperatives: cooling off. But Meyer must be absolutely determined to damage Monet. Has he made any money? Another question – now that Monet is making money, since that exhibition was a success, why would he fall into the trap of another? As soon as he is successful, he is right. I say Monet, meaning Impressionists.

Camille Pissarro, *The Hills at L'Hermitage*, 1867.
Oil on canvas, 151.4 x 200.6 cm (59⅝ x 79 in.).

Meanwhile I rather like Monsieur Guérin's gentlemanly approach, waddling about with the riffraff of rejected cooperatives. I may be putting forward these ideas a little crudely, but I don't have much subtlety at my disposal. Don't hold it against me, we'll talk about it when I get back to Paris; we can have our cake and eat it. And if having the Impressionists as background can help me, I'll show the best I have with them, and something neutral with the others.

My dear friend, I'll end by saying, like you, that since some of us have shared views, let's hope that necessity will force us to act together, and that self-interest and success will strengthen the bond that goodwill alone so often fails to consolidate. Finally, I'm very happy that Monsieur [Ludovic] Piette [Pissarro's friend] is on our side. Remember me to him, my respects to Madame Piette, to Madame Pissarro, my very best wishes to all the family, my warmest regards to you, and fine weather. Imagine, I'm reading *La Lanterne de Marseille* and I'm going to subscribe to *La Religion laïque*. How about that!

I'm waiting for [Jules] Dufaure [President of the Council] to be laid low, but from now to the partial renewal of the Senate there's still plenty of time and plenty of traps. Yours ever. Paul Cézanne

If the looks of people round here could kill, I'd have been dead a long time ago. They don't like the look of me. PC

I'm thinking of coming back to Paris at the end of this month; if you reply before that, write to:

Paul Cézanne
Maison Giraud (dit Belle)
Place de l'Église, L'Estaque
Banlieue de Marseille.

I   This letter would become one of Cézanne's most celebrated, and the card analogy entered the culture. 'Music is not a "playing card", to adapt Cézanne's remark on painting,' wrote Pierre Boulez almost a century later; '"depth", "perspective", "relief" have an important part to play.' One of the pictures for Chocquet became *The Sea at L'Estaque* (R279).

2 'The very opposite of modelling' meant roughly that Cézanne and Pissarro would lay
   down one plane or patch of colour next to another, without any 'modelling' or shading
   between them, so that it looked as if each component part of the painting could be
   picked up from the canvas a little like a playing card from the table. In the canvas that
   made such an impact on Cézanne, *The Hills at L'Hermitage* (1867), the houses on the
   hills give just that illusion.

58 · TO HIS PARENTS [incomplete]

[Paris] Saturday 9 September 1876

Mes chers Parents,

I'm writing to give you my news and to receive yours in return. I am well
and hope you can say the same for your part.

I went to Ussy [Issy-les-Moulineux] to see my friend Guillaumin. I
tracked him down and had dinner with him last Wednesday. I learned from
him that the exhibition organized by the painters of our crew went very
well last April. The rent of the place where the exhibition was held, Rue Le
Peletier and Rue Laffitte (you go in through one door in the Rue Le Peletier
and you come out by another in the Rue Laffitte) came to 3,000 francs.
Only 1,500 francs down payment and the landlord was supposed to get the
additional 1,500 from the entrance charges. Not only were the 3,000 francs
made up, but the 1,500 francs advanced by the artists in equal shares were
reimbursed, plus a three-franc dividend, which doesn't amount to much, it's
true. So it was a good start. And already the artists from the official exhibition, hearing of this small success, have come to lease the space, but it had
already been reserved for next year by those who exhibited this year.

According to Guillaumin, I am one of the three new members who
are supposed to take part, and I was hotly defended by Monet at a reunion
dinner after the exhibition, when a certain [Vicomte?] Lepic spoke out
against my joining.

I haven't yet managed to go and see Pissarro or any of the others I know, since I got down to painting straightaway the morning after I arrived.

[…]

59 • TO DR PAUL GACHET

[Paris?] Thursday morning 5 October [1876]

Mon cher Docteur,
I'm suffering at the moment from a rather severe headache, which does not permit me to accept your invitation.

Please forgive me; Guillaumin, who you will see this evening and with whom I spent yesterday, Wednesday, at Issy, can tell you about my attack.

I would be poor company at that fine gathering in which I would have been so happy to take part, but for this rotten complication.

Please be assured of my greatest regrets.
Yours ever.

Paul Cézanne

[Paris] 24 August 1877

Mon cher Zola,

My heartfelt thanks for your kindness towards me. Please let my mother know that I don't need anything, for I'm planning to spend the winter in Marseille. Come December, if she is willing to undertake to find me a tiny two-room flat in Marseille, not expensive but in a district where there aren't too many murders, she would be doing me a great favour. She could have a bed and bedding brought there, and two chairs, which she could take from her house in L'Estaque, to avoid unnecessary expense. The weather here, I must tell you, the temperature is very often refreshed by beneficent showers (Gaut-style).

Every day I go to the park in Issy where I do some studies. And I'm not too dissatisfied, but it seems that a deep depression reigns in the Impressionist camp. They are not exactly making their fortune, and their studies are drying up on the spot. We are living in very troubled times, and I don't know when poor painting will recover a little of its lustre.

Was Marguery less unhappy than on the last excursion to Le Tholonet? And have you seen Houchart, Aurélien? Apart from two or three painters I've seen absolutely no one.

Are you going to the Cigale's *agapes* [feast]? For a month and half [Alphonse] Daudet's new novel has been appearing in *Le Temps*, yellow posters put up even in Issy told me this. I also know that Alexis will be on the bill at the Gymnase [theatre].

Is the sea bathing doing Madame Zola good, and as for you, are you cutting through the bitter waves? I send all of you my best wishes and warmest regards. Farewell then, until your return from the sun-drenched shores.

For all your kindnesses, I am the grateful painter

Paul Cézanne

[Paris] 28 August 1877

Mon cher Émile,

I turn to you once again to tell my mother not to worry. I've changed my plans. It happens that that scheme [wintering in Marseille] seems to be fraught with difficulties. I'm abandoning it.

However, I'm still planning to go to Aix in December, or rather towards the beginning of January.

My sincere thanks.

Paul Cézanne

Let me add greetings to your family.

Yesterday evening, on the way to my paint supplier [Père Tanguy] in the Rue Clauzel, I bumped into good old Emperaire.

62 · TO JULIEN TANGUY[1]

Paris, 4 March 1878

The undersigned, Paul Cézanne, *artiste peintre*, residing in Paris, 67 Rue de l'Ouest, hereby acknowledges a debt of two thousand one hundred and seventy-four francs and eighty centimes to Monsieur and Madame Tanguy, for painting materials received.

Paul Cézanne

1 Père Tanguy, Cézanne's paint supplier and informal dealer in this period. Tanguy was a Communard, lucky to escape with his life, and a true believer in progressive causes and progressive artists. Perennially impoverished, he gave Cézanne credit on painting materials – extended credit (see letter 139) – with scant prospect of recouping anything

much in the way of sales. At bottom, he was not interested in sales. Tanguy was not so much a dealer as a defender, and in his humble way a connoisseur. 'Papa Cézanne is never content with what he's done,' he would tell awed visitors avid for any scrap of information on the legendary master. 'He always stops before it's finished. When he moves, he takes care to forget the canvases in the house he's leaving; when he paints outdoors, he leaves them in the countryside. He works very slowly. The smallest thing costs him great effort. He leaves nothing to chance. Cézanne goes to the Louvre every morning.' Tanguy was a saint. He died, penniless, in February 1894. His stock contained nothing later than the mid-1880s. With Émile Bernard's assistance, he had managed to sell the portrait of Emperaire, but it seems that by accident or design he had not been entrusted with any recent work.

63 · TO ÉMILE ZOLA

[L'Estaque] 23 March 1878

Mon cher Émile,

I seem to be on the verge of having to fend for myself, if indeed I'm up to it. Relations between my father and myself are becoming very tense, and I risk losing my entire allowance. A letter from Monsieur Chocquet in which he mentioned Madame Cézanne and little Paul provided conclusive proof of my situation to my father, who by the way was already alert, full of suspicions, and who had nothing better to do than to unseal and be the first to read the letter that was sent to me, even though it was addressed to Monsieur Paul Cézanne *artiste peintre.*

So I shall appeal to your goodwill towards me to see if among your circle and through your influence you can find me something, if possible. All is not yet lost between my father and me, but I think my fate will be settled within a fortnight.

Write to me (addressing your letter to Monsieur Paul Cézanne, post restante), whatever you decide to do about my request.

I send sincere greetings to Madame Zola, and best wishes to you.

Paul Cézanne

I'm writing from L'Estaque, but returning to Aix this evening.

64 · TO ÉMILE ZOLA

[Aix] 28 March [1878]

Mon cher Émile,

Like you, I think I should not be too quick to renounce the paternal allowance.

But from the traps that have been set for me, which I've managed to escape so far, I foresee that the great debate will concern the money, and what I should do with it. As like as not I'll get only 100 [francs] from my father, though he promised me 200 when I was in Paris. So I'll have to rely on your good offices, especially since the little one has been ill for a fortnight with an attack of mucous fever.

I'm taking every precaution to ensure that my father does not obtain definitive proof.

Forgive me for making the following remark: but your notepaper and envelopes must be heavy: I had to pay 25 centimes at the post office to make up the postage – and your letter contained only one double sheet. When you write to me, would you mind using only one sheet folded in half?

If in the end my father doesn't give me enough, I'll be coming back to you again during the first week of next month, and I'll give you Hortense's address, if you would be good enough to send it there.

Greetings to Madame Zola; and my best wishes to you.

Paul Cézanne

There will probably be an Impressionist exhibition; then I'll ask you to send in the still life that you have in your dining room [*The Black Clock*, R136]. In that connection I received a letter of notification for the 25th of this month. Naturally, I wasn't there.

Has *Une Page d'amour* come out?

The Black Clock, *c.* 1870. Oil on canvas,
55.2 x 74.3 cm (21¾ x 29¼ in.).

Camille Pissarro, *Portrait of Cézanne*, c. 1874.
Oil on canvas, 73 x 59.7 cm (28¾ x 23½ in.).

[Aix] Wednesday evening [late March/early April] 1878

Mon cher Émile,

I thank you most warmly for sending me your latest book [*Une Page d'amour*] and for *the dedication*. I haven't yet read much of it. My mother is extremely ill and has been laid up for ten days, her condition is very serious. I stopped reading at the end of the description of the sun setting over Paris and the development of Hélène and Henri's mutual passion.

It's not for me to praise your book, for you can respond like Courbet that the conscious artist awards himself higher praise than that which is bestowed on him from outside.[1] Anything I say to you about it is therefore only to give you an idea of what I can grasp of the work. It seems to me that it's a picture more delicately painted than the previous one [*L'Assommoir*], but the temperament or creative force is still the same. And then, if I'm not committing a heresy, the build-up of the heroes' passion is very carefully done. Another observation I have, which also seems right to me, is that the settings are done in such a way as to become imbued with the same passion as drives the characters, forming an integral whole. They seem to come alive, as it were, and to share in the suffering of living beings. Anyway, according to the papers, it will be a literary success at least.

My best wishes to you, and please give my regards to Madame Zola.

Paul Cézanne

You'll no doubt find that my letters are not exactly answers to yours, but that's because I'm often writing before I've read yours, being unable to get to the post office regularly.

P.C.

A last-minute thought: for your characters you carefully follow Horace's precept, *Qualis ab incepte processerit, et sibi constet* [Let him proceed as he began, and so be consistent].

But you don't give a damn about that, probably, and that's another proof of how things come round again on this earth.

I A reference to Courbet's public refusal of the Legion of Honour in 1870. 'Honour is neither in a title nor a ribbon,' he instructed the Minister of Fine Arts, 'it is in the act and the motive for the act. The state is incompetent in the matter of art. I decline the honour that you believed you did me. I am fifty years old and I have always lived as a free man; let me end my days free. When I am dead, they will say of me: that man never belonged to any school, any church, any institution, any academy, above all any regime, if it was not the regime of liberty.' Cézanne and Pissarro were deeply impressed by the man and his gesture: they admired Courbet as an artist and a free spirit. When Pissarro came to paint his magnificent *Portrait of Paul Cézanne* (P326) a few years later, he included a caricature of Courbet saluting Cézanne from his vantage point in the upper right of the picture, a little like a portly conscience, or a pipe-smoking guardian angel.

66 · TO ÉMILE ZOLA

[Aix] 4 April 1878

Mon cher Émile,
Please send 60 francs to Hortense at the address below,

Madame Cézanne, 183 Rue de Rome, Marseille.

Despite the honour of treaties, I've been able to secure only 100 fr[ancs] from my father, and I was even afraid that he might not give me anything at all. He's heard from various people that I have a child, and he's trying by every means possible to catch me out. He wants to rid me of it, he says. I'll say nothing more. It would take too long to explain the good man to you, but with him appearances are deceptive, believe you me. If you could write to me when you can, you'll gladden my heart. I'm going to try and get to Marseille; I slipped off last Tuesday, a week ago, to see the little one, he's better, and I had to return to Aix on foot [a distance of some 30 km, or 19 miles], since the train shown in my timetable was wrong, and I had to be there for dinner, I was an hour late.

My respects to Madame Zola and my best wishes to you.

Paul Cézanne

67 • TO ÉMILE ZOLA

[Aix] 14 April 1878

Mon cher Émile,
I've just got back from Marseille, which will explain the long delay in reply-ing to you, I wasn't able to get your letter until last Thursday. Thank you for both dispatches. I'm writing under the paternal eye.

I was accompanied to Marseille by Monsieur Gibert. People like that see well enough, but through professors' eyes. As the train passes near Alexis's place in the country, a stunning *motif* opens up on the eastern side: Sainte-Victoire and the cliffs overlooking Beaurecueil: I said, 'What a fine *motif*'; he replied, 'The lines sway too much.' On the subject of *L'Assommoir*, of which, by the way, he was the first to speak, he said some very sensible and laudatory things, but always from the technical point of view. Then after a long pause: 'He must have studied hard,' he continued, 'to graduate from the École Normale.' I talked to him about [Jean] Richepin [author of *Les Morts bizarres* (1876) and other challenging works]: he said 'that has no future'. How thoughtless – he [Richepin] is doing fine. And yet there's no doubt that in a town of 20,000 souls he [Gibert] is the one who devotes himself most and best to art.

I'll be very good since I don't know how to be clever.

I wish you good health and my respects to Madame Zola, and thank you,

Paul Cézanne

Villevieille's pupils abuse me as I go by. I'll get my hair cut, perhaps it's too long. I'm working; little to show for it, and straying too far from the general gist.

68 · TO ÉMILE ZOLA

[Aix] May 1878

Mon cher Émile,
Since you are willing to help me out once again, would you be kind enough to send 60 francs to Hortense, at the same address, 183 Rue de Rome [Marseille].

Thank you in advance, I understand that at this very moment you must be fully occupied with your new book, but later, when you can, if you would tell me about the artistic and literary scene you would gladden my heart. In that way I will be even further from the provinces and nearer to Paris.

With my thanks, please give my regards to Madame Zola.

Paul Cézanne

69 · TO ÉMILE ZOLA

[Aix] 8 May 1878

Mon cher Émile,
Thank you for your latest dispatch. I can assure you that it's been a tremendous help to me and has eased my mind.

My mother is now out of danger, she's been getting up for two days, which is a relief to her, and means she has better nights. For a week she was exhausted. Now I'm hoping that the good weather and the care will get her back on her feet.

I didn't collect your letter until yesterday evening, Wednesday, which explains the long delay between your sending it and my reply.

Thank you for the news of my small canvas. I quite understand that it couldn't be accepted [by the Salon] on account of my starting point, which is too far removed from the end in view, that is to say, the representation of nature.

I've just finished *Une Page d'amour.* You were quite right to tell me that it couldn't be read in instalments. I hadn't begun to appreciate the connections, it seemed broken up, whereas in fact the development of the plot is handled with tremendous skill. There's a great deal of dramatic feeling in it. Nor had I noticed that the action takes place in a condensed, confined frame. It is truly a pity that a work of art isn't appreciated more and that in order to attract the public there have to be some exaggerated effects, which are not wholly appropriate, although of course they don't harm it.

I read your letter to my mother, and she joins me in sending you greetings.

My respects to all your family,

Paul Cézanne

70 · TO ÉMILE ZOLA

[Aix] 1 June 1878

Mon cher Émile,

I am back again with my monthly request to you. I hope that it's not too tiresome for you, and doesn't seem too brazen on my part. But your offer relieves me of so many problems that I'm thrown back on it again. My good family, otherwise excellent for a wretched painter who has never been able to do anything, is perhaps a little miserly; it's a minor failing, doubtless quite understandable in the provinces.

Here comes the inevitable result of such a preamble: would you be kind enough to send 60 francs to Hortense, who is otherwise none the worse for it.

I bought the illustrated *L'Assommoir* at Lambert's, the democratic bookshop. *L'Égalité* in Marseille is running it as a serial.

I'm still doing a little work. Politicians have a terrifying power. And how is Alexis?

Best wishes to you, and my regards to Madame Zola,

Paul Cézanne

71 · TO ÉMILE ZOLA

[Aix] Tuesday [early] July 1878

Mon cher Émile,

If you're still amenable, please send 60 francs to Hortense. She has moved, her address is now

12 Vieux Chemin de Rome [Marseille].

I'm planning to go to L'Estaque in ten days' time.

Giraud, known as Belle, has been released from the asylum in which he'd been interned because of temporary insanity.

It seems that they've been laying into each other quite well in Marseille. A certain Coste junior, municipal councillor, distinguished himself by taking a stick to some clerical shoulder blades.

It's beginning to be oppressively hot. Are you working at the moment? Was there a presentation of decorations on 30 May?[1] The papers here say nothing, but this evening I expect to get Monday's *Le Bien public.*

My best wishes, and beg Madame Zola to accept my greetings.

Paul Cézanne

72 · TO ÉMILE ZOLA

[L'Estaque] 16 July 1878

Mon cher Émile,

I've been in L'Estaque for about a week. Harpooned by Sire Giraud, I heard at first hand that you may have a visit from his father-in-law, who is going to Paris this Friday. We've changed house in L'Estaque, I'm now next door to Giraud, at Isnard's. If you feel like writing, drop me a line about the decoration, which I didn't see announced in *Le Petit Marseillais*. Nevertheless, I hope it's a *fait accompli*.

The heat has set in.

Thank you so much for the money you were kind enough to send to Hortense.

In the meantime I learned of the folding of *Le Bien public*, have you a new paper in which you can fight on behalf of your plays? It's a shame that paper couldn't achieve its goal.

My respects to Madame Zola, and greetings to you.

I saw Guillaumin the gardener, back from Cannes, where his boss is going to set up a nursery.

Paul Cézanne

[L'Estaque] 29 July 1878

Mon cher Émile,

Before leaving Paris, I left the key to my apartment with a certain [Antoine] Guillaume, a cobbler. This is what must have happened: because of the exhibition, this fellow must have had visitors from the provinces, and put them up at my place. My landlord, very annoyed at not being asked before-hand, sends, together with the receipt for the last period, a pretty stiff letter informing me that my apartment is occupied by strangers.

My father read the aforesaid letter and concluded that I was harbour-ing women in Paris. It's beginning to take on the air of a vaudeville farce. Otherwise all was well, I was looking for somewhere in Marseille to spend the winter, to work there, and return to Paris next spring, say in March, when it turns misty, and I thought I wouldn't be able to make such good use of my time out of doors. On the other hand I'd be in Paris during the painting exhibition.

I congratulate you on your acquisition [of a property at Médan, on the Seine, north-west of Paris], and with your permission I shall take advan-tage of it in order to get to know that area better, and if life there was not impossible for me, I would try to spend a year or two there, either at La Roche [Guyon] or Bennecourt or thereabouts, as I did at Auvers.

Please send 60 francs to Hortense as before, though I'm seriously con-sidering relieving you of this monthly tax. If I can make a trip to Paris in September or October, I will.

I passed on your good wishes to my mother, which gave her great pleas-ure, in fact I'm with her here.

Best wishes, and greetings to Madame Zola and your mother, who is no doubt with you. And good outings on the water.

Paul Cézanne

Hortense is still at: 12 Vieux Chemin de Rome, Marseille.

[L'Estaque] 27 August 1878

Mon cher Émile,

I must trespass on your kindness once again this month, if you can again send 60 francs to Hortense, at 12 Vieux Chemin de Rome until 10 September.

I haven't yet been able to find lodgings in Marseille, because I don't want anything too expensive. I plan to spend all winter there, if my father agrees to give me the money. Then I could continue some studies I'm doing in L'Estaque, where I'll stay as long as possible.

Thank you in advance, and warm greetings to you and your family.

Paul Cézanne

[L'Estaque, summer 1878]

Mon cher Émile,

Having gone to Aix, Hortense saw Achille Emperaire. His family is in dire straits, three children, winter, no money, etc., you know what it's like. In consequence, I beg you, 1 – since Achille's brother is on bad terms with his former bosses at the tobacco board, would you be kind enough to withdraw the files relating to his request, if there is nothing to be done for him soon; 2 – see if you can find or ease his passage into any kind of a job, at the docks, for example; 3 – Achille is also looking to you for a job, no matter how small.

So if you can do something for him, please try, you know how much he deserves it, fine fellow that he is, and how he endures being crushed by people and abandoned by all the clever ones. There you have it.

Besides, I wanted to write to you apart from that, for it seems to me that I haven't had any news of you for a long time. I understand that there is probably nothing very new. Give me the pleasure of writing a little, that will offer some distraction in this long series of unchanging days. My situation remains unaltered.

My respects to your wife and mother, please.
Yours ever,

Paul Cézanne

Write to me at
Madame H. Fiquet, etc.

76 • TO ÉMILE ZOLA

[L'Estaque] 14 September 1878

Mon cher Émile,
I can write to you in a more relaxed frame of mind right now, and if I've been able to get through some small misadventures without too much suffering, it's thanks to the good strong plank you've held out to me. Here is the latest blow to land on me.

Hortense's father wrote to his daughter at the Rue de l'Ouest [in Paris], under the name of Madame Cézanne. My landlord immediately forwarded the letter to the Jas de Bouffan. My father opened it and read it, you can imagine the result. I strenuously denied it, and since very luckily Hortense is not mentioned by name in the letter, I swore that it was addressed to some other woman.

I received your book of plays, I've read only five acts so far, three of *Les Héritiers Rabourdin* [1874] and two of *Le Bouton de Rose* [1878], very interesting, especially *Le Bouton de Rose*, I think. *Les Héritiers Rabourdin* has a certain family resemblance to Molière, whom I reread last winter. I'm sure you'll make a complete success of the theatre. Not having read anything of yours in that genre, I had no idea it would be so lively with such good dialogue.

I met one Huot, architect, who sang the praises of your whole Rougon-Macquart [series], and told me that it is much respected among those in the know. He asked me if I saw you: I said: sometimes – if you wrote to me: I said: recently. Stupefaction, and I rose in his estimation. He gave me his card, with an invitation to go and see him. So you see that it counts for something to have friends, and they won't say of me what the oak said to the reed, 'Now, had you the luck to be born in my shadow,' etc.[1]

My mother thanks you and is very touched by your thoughts of her. Pelouze has come back from Paris [?]: nothing is going well.

Remember me to Alexis, and tell him that commercial enterprises and artistic reputations are founded on work.

My respects to Madame Zola, and my heartfelt thanks to you.

Paul Cézanne

Nota-Bene: Papa gave me 300 francs this month. Incredible. I think he's making eyes at a charming little maid of ours in Aix; mother and I are in L'Estaque. What a turn-up.

1   A reference to the fable of 'The Oak and the Reed', by La Fontaine, in which the great oak tree offers protection (or humiliation) to the wretched reed, who politely declines:

> 'It's kind of you to be so sore chagrined
> On my account. I thank you. But, no need!
> I fear the winds far less than you, my friend.
> You see, I never break; I merely bend.'

And so it comes to pass: a great wind gets up, and arrogance gets its comeuppance.

> Oak holds ... Reed bends ... Wind blows ... Then more and more,
> Till it uproots the one who, just before,

Had risen heavenward with lofty head,
Whose feet had reached the empire of the dead.

77 · TO ÉMILE ZOLA

L'Estaque, 24 September 1878

Mon cher Émile,

I got your letter just as I was making vermicelli soup with oil, Lantier's favourite.[1] I'll be in L'Estaque throughout the winter, working.

Mother left a week ago for the grape-picking, jam-making and house-moving in Aix, they're going to live in the town behind Marguery or thereabouts. I'm on my own in L'Estaque, I go to Marseille in the evening to sleep and come back the next morning.

Marseille is the olive oil capital of France, just as Paris is the butter capital: you have no idea of the brashness of this ferocious people, they have only one instinct, that is for money; they apparently make a lot, but they're very ugly – from the outside, new modes of communication are blurring the people's distinctive features. In a few hundred years' time, living will be completely pointless, it will all be the same. But the little that remains is still very dear to the heart and the eye.

I saw Monsieur Marion from afar on the steps of the Faculty of Sciences. (Whether or not to go and see him will take me some time to decide.) He seems not to be sincere in art, in spite of himself, perhaps.

When I said that your play *Les Héritiers Rabourdin* reminded me of Molière, I hadn't read the preface. For that matter, perhaps it put me in mind more of [Jean-François] Regnard.

If I can get hold of [Florent] Dancourt, I'll read him. I've almost finished reading *Thérèse Raquin* [Zola's adaptation of his own early novel]. Probably the day you get hold of the background of a very personal and characteristic subject, success will follow, as with the novel *L'Assommoir*. In fact people are hardly fair on you, for even if they don't like the plays as plays, they might recognize the power and the bond between the characters and the flow of the plot.

Best wishes and many thanks to you, my respects to Madame Zola and Alexis.

Paul Cézanne

Think of Darnagas and the rabbit's tail.[2]

1 *L'Assommoir* features Auguste and Gervaise, the parents of Claude Lantier, Zola's Cézanne figure. Auguste wears a trademark black felt hat. He is small, dark and good-looking. He likes his food, though he is no gourmet. He has a signature dish. 'His great treat was a certain soup, very thick, of vermicelli boiled in water, into which he tipped half a bottle of oil. Only he and Gervaise would eat this, because the others, the Parisians, had been sick as dogs when they'd risked trying it one day.' The vermicelli became an in-joke between them. Given that Claude Lantier had already been introduced to the world, it is further evidence that Cézanne was perfectly capable of recognizing and accepting his fictional selves, and their families. He went so far as to borrow their recipes. See also letter 233, n.3.

2 In Provençal slang, *darnagas* means something like 'stupid' or 'foolish', after the bird said to be so.

78 · TO ÉMILE ZOLA

[L'Estaque] 4 November 1878

Mon cher Émile,
I'm sending this letter to Paris, thinking that you have made your return to town.

Here is what prompts my letter: Hortense is in Paris on urgent business, I beg you to send her 100 francs, if you can advance me that much, I'm in a real mess but I hope to get out of it.

Let me know if you can do me this further service; if it is difficult, I'll try to find a way out. Either way, I'm grateful to you, and if you write to me, tell me a little about art. I'm still thinking of returning to Paris for a few months next year, around February or March.

I've just seen in *Le Petit Journal* that they're going to perform *L'Assommoir*. Who did the adaptation, for I don't think it could be you?

Here is where you should send the money, if you can
Monsieur Antoine Guillaume, 105 Rue de Vaugirard, who will pass it on to Hortense.

My best wishes to you and to Madame Zola and Alexis,

Paul Cézanne

79 · TO GUSTAVE CAILLEBOTTE[1]

L'Estaque, 13 November 1878

Mon cher Confrère,
When you realize that I am a long way from Paris, you will forgive me for having failed in the duty incumbent upon me, when you were struck again by misfortune. It is about nine months since I left Paris, and your letter reached me at the far end of France, after lengthy detours and a considerable delay.

In your affliction allow me to voice my gratitude for the great assistance you have given to our cause, and rest assured that I share in your sorrow, though I did not know your mother at all I know very well the painful emptiness left by the death of those we love. *Mon cher* Caillebotte, I send you my best wishes and beg you to give your time and attention to painting, that being the surest way to dispel our sorrow.

Please remember me to your father and take heart if you can.

Paul Cézanne

1   Gustave Caillebotte (1848–1894), painter and collector. On his death, Caillebotte left
    his magnificent collection of modern art to the state, but the state did not want it.
    After prolonged negotiations, the Director of the Beaux-Arts, Henri Roujon, and the
    Curator of the Luxembourg, Léonce Bénédite, eventually accepted around half the
    works – despite Caillebotte's stated wish that the collection should be kept whole: two
    out of four Manets, eight out of sixteen Monets, seven out of eighteen Pissarros, six
    out of eight Renoirs, and, at the very bottom of the barrel, two out of five Cézannes.
    As one of Caillebotte's executors, it fell to Renoir to negotiate with Roujon, a dis-
    piriting experience: 'The only canvas of mine that he was prepared to accept without
    question was *Moulin de la Galette*, because [Henri] Gervex was in it. He regarded the
    presence of a member of the Institute among the models as a kind of moral guarantee.
    For the rest, without going overboard, he was somewhat inclined to sample Monet,
    Sisley and Pissaro, who had begun to accepted by the "*amateurs*". But when he got
    to the Cézannes! Those *Landscapes* that have the balance of Poussin's, those paintings
    of *Bathers* in which the colours seem to have been taken from ancient earthenware, in
    a word all that supremely wise art. ... I can still hear Roujon: "That one, for example,
    he had no idea what painting was!"'

    Of the Cézannes, the two accepted were *Farmyard* (R389) and *The Gulf of Marseille
    seen from L'Estaque* (R390); the three rejected, *The Lake Shore* (R244), *The Rococo
    Vase* (R265) and *Bathers at Rest* (R261) – one of his most important early works on that
    subject.

Farmyard, c. 1879. Oil on canvas, 65 x 54.4 cm (25⅝ x 21⅜ in.).

The Gulf of Marseille seen from L'Estaque, 1878–79.
Oil on canvas, 59.5 x 73 cm (23⅜ x 28¾ in.).

The Lake Shore, c. 1877–79. Oil on canvas, 47 x 56.2 cm (18½ x 22⅛ in.).

The Rococo Vase, c. 1876. Oil on canvas,
73 x 59.8 cm (28¾ x 23½ in.).

Bathers at Rest, 1876–77. Oil on canvas, 82 x 101.3 cm (32¼ x 39⅞ in.).

L'Estaque, 20 November [1878]

Mon cher Émile,

It's some time now since I received news from Paris telling me that you'd been kind enough to advance me the 100 francs I'd asked you for. Since then a week has passed and I've had no further news from Paris. I have the little one with me in L'Estaque, but the weather has been terrible for some days. No doubt you are chock-a-block with things to do, I'm waiting until the weather clears to continue with my researches in painting.

I bought a very strange book, a tissue of observations of a subtlety that often escapes me, I feel, but what anecdotes and true stories! And the *comme il faut* call the author paradoxical. It's a book by Stendhal: *Histoire de la peinture en Italie*, I expect you've read it, but if you haven't allow me to draw it to your attention.[1] I'd read it in 1869, but I'd read it badly, I'm rereading it for the third time. I've just finished buying the illustrated *L'Assommoir*. However, the publisher would probably not have been better served by better illustrations. When I can talk to you face-to-face, I'll ask you if your opinion is the same as mine on painting as a means of expressing feeling. I ask you to remember me, I'm still in L'Estaque.

Don't forget my greetings to Madame Zola, and best wishes to you and Alexis,

Paul Cézanne

1   One of Cézanne's favourite books, and a key work in his life. See the Introduction.

[L'Estaque] 19 December 1878

Mon cher Émile,

I probably forgot to tell you that I moved in September from the Rue du Vieux Chemin de Rome. I'm now living, or at least Hortense is, at 32 Rue Ferrari [Marseille]. As for me, I'm still in L'Estaque, where I received your last letter.

Hortense came back from Paris four days ago, which is a something of a relief, for I've got the little one with me and my father could have surprised us. It almost seems as if there's a kind of conspiracy to reveal my situation to my father, and my bastard of a landlord is poking his nose in as well. So it's over a month since Hortense got the money that I asked you to send her and I thank you for it, she had real need of it. She had a small adventure in Paris, I shan't put it in writing, I'll tell you about it when I get back, besides it's nothing much.

Finally, I think I'll stay another few months here, and leave for Paris towards the beginning of March. Here I thought that I'd find the utmost peace, on the contrary the lack of understanding between me and the parental authority disturbs me all the more. The author of my days is obsessed with the idea of liberating me [from Hortense]. There's only one good way of doing it, that would be to give me two or three thousand francs more a year, and not to wait until after my death to make me his heir, for I shall surely expire before him.

As you say, there are some very beautiful views here. The thing is to capture them, that's hardly my forte, I began to see nature a little late, which doesn't at all mean that it isn't full of interest for me.

I wish you all a happy Christmas. I'll be going to Aix for a few days next Tuesday.

You didn't tell me anything about your hunting exploits, is it that your enthusiasm and that of your weapon didn't last long? My best wishes to you.

Paul Cézanne

When you feel like writing to me, still to L'Estaque, please.

[1878–79]

Mon cher compatriote,
Although our friendly relations haven't been kept up very well, in the sense that I haven't often knocked at your hospitable door, nevertheless I do not hesitate to write to you today. I hope that you will be able to separate my small personality as Impressionist painter from the man, and that you will want only to remember the comrade. So it is not at all as the author of *L'Ombre et la proie* [*sic*] that I am calling on you, but as the *Aquasixtain* [man from Aix], under whose sun I too first saw the light of day, and I take the liberty of introducing you to my eminent friend and musician [Ernest] Cabaner. I beg you to look favourably on his request, and at the same time I commend myself to you in case the day of the Salon ever dawns for me.

In the hope that my request will be favourably received, please accept this expression of my thanks and my confraternal regards.

P. Cézanne

*Pictor semper virens*²

Although I do not have [missing phrase], may I add my humble respects to Madame Roux?

1 Marius Roux (1838–1906), journalist and writer, associated with *Le Petit Journal*. Germain Rambert, the chief protagonist of his novel *La Proie et l'ombre* (*The Substance and the Shadow*, 1878), was based on Cézanne.

2 Literally, 'painter still vigorous' (or 'still game') – a calculated riposte. See the Introduction.

Rough draft of a letter to Marius Roux, with studies of bathers, 1878–79.

L'Estaque, 28 [January] 1879

Mon cher Monsieur Chocquet,

I am taking advantage of your kindness in order to obtain some information. This is what it's about. Of course, this is only if you can obtain the aforesaid information without too much trouble and inconvenience, otherwise I shall write to the good Tanguy, which I would have done had I not thought, correctly I believe, that I would receive more satisfaction and greater clarification from you. Thus to the point. I should like to know how one would go about getting a painting to the administration of the Beaux-Arts with the aim of submitting it for consideration by the jury, and then, if, as I fear, the painting is rejected, whether the kind administration undertakes to return the aforesaid work to its author, the author being in the provinces? Needless to add that the artist is not unaware of the fact that the sending and return of his work must be at his own expense.

I take the liberty of writing to you in order to be of service to one of my compatriots. It is not for me, for I shall be returning to Paris with my little caravan around the beginning of March this year.

The weather has been very aquatic this year but very mild for a fortnight in our region.

Monsieur Chocquet, please accept my apologies, and give my respects to Madame [Marie] Chocquet; my wife and child send their greetings.

Your humble servant,

Paul Cézanne

1 Victor Chocquet (1821–1891) was a customs official and, in his own quiet way, one of the most important private collectors of the nineteenth century. Cézanne and Chocquet struck up a wonderful friendship. Renoir introduced them, but it was Delacroix who brought them together. 'Renoir tells me that you like Delacroix?' hazarded Cézanne. 'I adore Delacroix,' replied Chocquet. 'We'll look together at what I have of him.' What he had eventually amounted to over eighty paintings, drawings and watercolours. They met in 1876: it was love at first sight. Indeed, even before. In the ramshackle back room of Père Tanguy's paint shop the previous year, Chocquet had picked up a small

Cézanne, *Three Bathers* (R258), for fifty francs. He was delighted with his purchase. 'How well it will go between a Delacroix and a Courbet!'

84 · TO VICTOR CHOCQUET

L'Estaque, 7 February 1879

Monsieur Chocquet,

Thank you, albeit rather belatedly, for your kindness in sending me the information in connection with the matter of my last letter.

I think that my friend will have every reason to be satisfied with the peremptory and printed attitude of the higher administration towards its subordinates.

I am happy to learn of [Auguste] Renoir's great success [commissions for portraits] and let us hope that some particular circumstance, not too unfortunate for him, is what has kept him away from you of late.

My wife, charged with the task of providing our daily bread, knows the trouble and worry that entails, and shares the torments of Madame Chocquet and sends her most respectful greetings, as does your humble servant. As for the little one, he is an all-round terror and promises worse to come.

I close wishing you good health and I am gratefully your devoted

Paul Cézanne

L'Estaque, February 1879

Mon cher Émile,

I should have written to you some time ago, for I learned from *Le Figaro* and *Le Petit Journal* of the great success of *L'Assommoir* in the theatre, and I wanted to congratulate you. I think I'll spend only another fortnight in L'Estaque, after which I'll go to Aix and from there to Paris. If you need anything from these parts, I'm at your service, for any errand.

Mother joins me in sending greetings to you, as well as to Madame Zola and your mother.

Best wishes,

Paul Cézanne

[Paris] 1 April 1879

Mon cher Pissarro,

I think that in the midst of the difficulties arising from my submission to the Salon, it would be much better for me not to take part in the Impressionist Exhibition.

At the same time, I'll be able to avoid the bother of transporting my few canvases. Besides, I'm leaving Paris in a few days.

My best wishes, until I can come and greet you in person,

Paul Cézanne

Melun, 3 June 1879

Mon cher Émile,

It's now June, and should I come and see you, as you recently suggested, more or less? I'm going to Paris on the 8th of this month, and if you write to me before that, I'll take the opportunity to come and seek you out in your country house at Médan. If, on the other hand, you think I should put off this little excursion, let me know all the same.

On 10 May I went to your house in the Rue de Boulogne, but I was told that you had left for the country a few days before.

Perhaps you know that I paid an insinuating little call on friend Guillemet, who apparently spoke up for me on the [Salon] jury, alas without any effect on those hard-hearted judges.

I take this opportunity to thank you for having sent me your pamphlet on *La République et l'art*. It so happens that Cabaner told me similar but sadder things about the situation. Anyway, I'm sending the pamphlet to Guillaumin, who wanted to read it.

Will we have some fine days, the weather doesn't seem very promising. I tested the water, and yet it didn't seem too cold.

Warmest regards to Madame Zola, as well as to yourself. I get news of what you're doing and what you've done from *Le Petit Journal* and *La Lanterne*.

Best wishes,

Paul Cézanne

[Melun] 5 June 1879

Mon cher Émile,
So it's set for Tuesday between 4 and 4.30.

I'll go to Paris during the day on Monday, and I'll come and find you in the Rue de Boulogne the next day.

Best wishes,

Paul Cézanne

Melun, 23 June 1879

Mon cher Émile,
I arrived unspattered at Triel station, and my arm, waving out of the window as I passed your castle, must surely have told you I was on the train, which I managed not to miss. I've since received, on Friday, I think, the letter that was addressed to me care of you; I thank you, it was a letter from Hortense.

During my absence, your volume of *Mes Haines* [a new edition] arrived here, and today I've just bought the issue of *Le Voltaire* in order to read your piece on [Jules] Vallès.[1]

I've just read it and thought it magnificent. The book about Jacques Vingtras made me feel very warmly towards the author. I hope he'll be happy.

Please give my respects to Madame Zola your mother, and also to your wife my sincere thanks,
A handshake,
And good health.

Paul Cézanne

If Alexis is with you, greetings.

When the opportunity arises, let me know how deep the water in the well turned out to be.

1   *Jacques Vingtras* was an autobiographical novel (eventually a trilogy, 1879–86) by the insurrectionary Jules Vallès, of a young provincial with abusive yet loving parents, who reached the metropolis a few years before Cézanne. 'Paris, 5 am. We've arrived. What silence! Everything looks pale in the bleak light of morning, and there is a villagey loneliness in this sleeping Paris. It's as melancholy as desertion. Dawn-cold, and the last star blinking stupidly in the bleached blue sky. I'm scared like a Robinson wrecked on an empty shore, in a country without green trees and red fruit. The houses are tall, mournful, like blind men with their closed shutters and lowered curtains. The porters hustle the luggage. Here's mine.'

90 · TO ÉMILE ZOLA

[Melun] 24 September 1879

Mon cher Émile,

Here is what prompts me to write, for nothing has happened since I left you in June that could have led me to write a letter, even though you were kind enough to say last time that I should give you my news. Today and tomorrow are so like yesterday that I didn't know what to tell you. But here is what I'd like: to go and see *L'Assommoir*. Can I ask you for three seats? But that's not all, there's another issue, and that is the exact date that I'm asking for, namely 6 October. Please see if what I'm asking doesn't raise too many difficulties. Because in the first place you're not in Paris. I'm not going there either, and I'm afraid that it won't be easy to match the time I'll be going to Paris with the obtaining of the tickets. So, if there's a problem, let me know, and don't worry about saying no, for I quite understand that you must have been deluged with similar requests.

I learned from *Le Petit Journal* that Alexis had been staged successfully.

I'm still trying to find my way, pictorially. Nature presents me with the greatest problems. But I'm not getting on too badly, after an attack of bronchitis, the same as in '77, which took a month to shake off. I hope you're well out of any such troubles. I trust that this letter find you and yours in good health. My father lost his partner [Joseph Cabassol] some time ago [in 1873], but fortunately they themselves are well.

I send you a handshake and beg you to give my sincere greetings to Madame Zola your wife and to your mother.

Your devoted,

Paul Cézanne

91 • TO ÉMILE ZOLA

[Melun] 27 September 1879

Mon cher Émile,
Heartfelt thanks. Send the tickets to me at Melun. I'm not going to Paris until the morning of the 6th.

I gladly accept your invitation for Médan, above all for this time of year when the countryside is truly astonishing. It seems that there is more silence. These are *sensations* that I can't express, it's better to feel them.

Greetings to all and my thanks, a handshake,
Your devoted

Paul Cézanne

Melun, 9 October 1879

Mon cher Émile,

I'm very glad I went to see *L'Assommoir.*

I couldn't have had a better seat, and I didn't fall asleep once, even though I usually go to bed just after 8. Interest never flags, but having seen this play, I dare say that the actors, who seemed to me remarkable, must be able to make a success of lots of plays that are plays in name only. Literary form must be unnecessary for them. The end of Coupeau is truly extraordinary, and the actress who played Gervaise is captivating. But they all act very well.

What is striking is the need to make a melodramatic traitress out of the great Virginia, that obligatory concession that must have appeased the shades of Bouchardie, who would otherwise have never known what was going on.

I saw the forthcoming appearance of *Nana* advertised for the 15th, on a huge canvas that covers the entire curtain.

Hearty thanks, and when my colleagues with the big brushes have finished, write to me.

Please give my respects to Madame Zola, and your mother and yourself.

Best wishes,

Paul Cézanne

Melun, 18 December 1879

Mon cher Émile,

I received your last two letters, one telling me about the snow piling up, the other about the complete lack of any thaw. I can well believe it. When it comes to cold, we're in the same boat. On Wednesday it got to minus 25 here. And what is even less amusing, I can't get hold of any fuel.

I shall probably have run out of coal by Saturday, and be forced to seek refuge in Paris. It's quite a winter. I have some difficulty casting my mind back to July, the cold brings you back to reality.

So it's set for January, if that really doesn't put you out. If I go to Paris, I'll give you my address.

My best wishes to you, and please give my respects to Madame Zola and your mother,

Paul Cézanne

1880

94 • February 1880
95 • 25 February 1880
96 • 1 April 1880
97 • 10 May 1880
98 • 19 June 1880
99 • 4 July 1880
100 • October? 1880
101 • 28 October 1880

1881

102 • April 1881
103 • 12 April 1881
104 • April 1881
105 • 7 May 1881
106 • 16 May 1881
107 • 20 May 1881
108 • June 1881
109 • July 1881
110 • 5 August 1881
111 • 15 October 1881

1882

112 • 15 February 1882
113 • 28 February 1882
114 • 2 March 1882
115 • 2 September 1882
116 • 14 November 1882
117 • 27 November 1882

1883

118 • 6 January 1883
119 • 10 March 1883
120 • 19 May 1883
121 • 24 May 1883
122 • 10 July 1883
123 • 26 November 1883

1884

124 • 23 February 1884
125 • 27 November 1884

1885

126 • 11 March 1885
127 • spring 1885
128 • 14 May 1885
129 • 15 June 1885
130 • 27 June 1885
131 • 3 July 1885
132 • 6 July 1885
133 • 11 July 1885
134 • 13 July 1885
135 • 15 July 1885
136 • 19 July 1885
137 • 20 August 1885
138 • 25 August 1885
139 • 31 August 1885

1886

140 • 4 April 1886
141 • April 1886?
142 • 11 May 1886

1887

143 • 9 November 1887

1889

144 • 30 June 1889
145 • 7 July 1889
146 • 27 November 1889
147 • 18 December 1889
148 • 21 December 1889

1880s

Gardanne 11 Mai 1886.

Monsieur Chocquet

Touché de votre dernière lettre,
je voulais répondre assez vite,
mais toujours, quoique peu
occupé, car ou la santé faiblissante
ou désériés de temps intempestif
me remet au lendemain.

Donc, je ne voudrais pas
m'appesantir lourdement sur
vous, j'entends au moral; mais
enfin, puisque Delacroix a
servi d'intermédiaire entre vous
et moi, je me permettrai de
dire ceci : que j'aurai désiré
avoir cet équilibre intellectuel
que vous caractérise, et vous
permet d'atteindre sûrement le
but proposé. Votre bonne lettre
ajoutée à celle de Madame
Chocquet,

Letter to Victor Chocquet, 11 May 1886.

[Melun, February 1880]

Mon cher Émile,

I'm a little late in thanking you for the last volume you sent me. But drawn
by the novelty I fell on it, and yesterday I finished reading *Nana*. It's a magnificent book, but I fear that by prior agreement the newspapers haven't
mentioned it at all, in fact I haven't seen a single article or announcement
in any of the three little papers I take. That discovery annoyed me a little,
because it seems to be an indication of too great an indifference to artistic
matters or a sign of a prudish and deliberate reticence not felt for certain
other subjects.

Now, perhaps the uproar that must have been made by the publication of *Nana* hasn't reached me, which would be the fault of our dreadful
papers, which would be some consolation.

My respects to Madame Zola, and my thanks to you, I'll come and see you
in March.

Paul Cézanne

Melun, 25 February 1880

Mon cher Émile,

This morning I received the book that Alexis has just brought out [*Le Fin de
Lucie Pellegrin*]. I want to thank him, and since I don't know his address, I'm
relying on you to be good enough to let him know that I'm very touched
by the mark of friendship he has shown me. This book adds to the literary collection you have made for me, and I have enough to keep me busy
for some time and to fill my winter evenings. Besides, I hope to see Alexis
when I return to Paris and thank him myself.

Our friend Antony Valabrègue has published a charming volume, *Petits poèmes parisiens*, with Lemerre. You must have a copy, my newspaper speaks well of it.

But it appears that Mademoiselle de Reismes [Maria Deraismes, a pioneer campaigner for women's rights], of Pontoise or thereabouts, has treated you very roughly. Pons, in Sainte-Beuve, would say that she'd be better off knitting stockings.

Best wishes to you, and I hope that Madame Zola will accept my respectful greetings.

Your devoted friend

Paul Cézanne

~~~

96 · TO ÉMILE ZOLA

[Paris] 1 April 1880

Mon cher Émile,

Having received your letter this morning, 1 April, enclosing Guillemet's, I land in Paris, I learn at Guillaumin's that the Impressionists are open. I race over. Alexis falls into my arms, Doctor Gachet invites us to dinner, I prevent Alexis from paying his respects to you. Can I take the liberty of inviting us to dinner on Saturday evening? If that's impossible, please be good enough to let me know. I'm staying at 32 Rue de l'Ouest, Plaisance. I remain your grateful former classmate of 1854.

Please give my respects to Madame Zola.

Paul Cézanne

~~~

[Paris] 10 May 1880

Mon cher Émile,

I'm enclosing a copy of a letter that Renoir and Monet are going to send to the Ministre des Beaux-Arts, to protest against their poor hanging [in the Salon] and to demand an exhibition of the group of pure Impressionists next year. Here's what I've been asked to beg you to do.

That would be to get this letter published in *Le Voltaire*, with a brief foreword or afterword on the group's previous shows. The few words would be designed to demonstrate the importance of the Impressionists and the wave of real interest they have prompted. I needn't add that whatever decision you decide to take with regard to this request will in no way influence your warm feelings towards me, or the good relationship that you have always encouraged between us. For I have more than once made demands on you that may have been a nuisance. I'm acting as go-between and nothing more.

I learned yesterday of the very unhappy news of Flaubert's death. So I fear that this letter may land on you in the midst of a lot of other cares.

My sincere respects to Madame Zola and your mother.
My warmest wishes to you,

Paul Cézanne

[Paris] Saturday 19 June 1880

Mon cher Émile,

I should have thanked you for the next-to-last letter you wrote to me on the subject of what I asked you to do for Monet and Renoir. Partly through negligence and the month of June getting on, I didn't reply. Finally, your last letter arrived only today. That's because the address wasn't quite right. It's 32 Rue de l'Ouest, not 12. I'm most grateful to you. I managed to get hold of the issue dated the 19th. I'll go to *Le Voltaire* and get hold of the issue of the 18th of this month.

Monet has a very fine exhibition on now at [the publisher] Monsieur [Georges] Charpentier's at *La Vie Moderne*.

I'm not sure if it's going to get really hot, but whenever I won't disturb you, write to me, I'll come to Médan with pleasure. And if you're not afraid of the length of time I'm liable to take, I'll presume to bring a small canvas and do something there, providing all this is no inconvenience to you.

Many thanks to Madame Zola for the great pile of rags she gave me, which I'm putting to use. I'm going into the countryside every day to paint a little.

I saw the most excellent Solari. Tomorrow I'm going to see him, he came to the house three times, and I was always out. Tomorrow, Sunday, I'll be able to greet him in person. Nothing is going right for him. He can't seem to get luck on his side. How many lucky devils succeed with less effort, but that is man's lot, and for my part I thank God for having an eternal father.

Please remember me to Madame Zola, as well as your mother.
Best wishes.

Paul Cézanne

[Paris, 4 July 1880]

Mon cher Émile,

I replied on 19 June to the letter you wrote to me on the 16th.

I asked you if I could come to you, to do some painting, it's true. But of course I didn't want to be a nuisance. Since then I've had no more news of you, and now that almost two weeks have gone by I take the liberty of asking you to send me a word to keep me au fait. If you'd like me to pop in, I will, but if you tell me otherwise, I won't come yet. I've read the articles that you've been publishing in *Le Voltaire*, beginning with number II. And I thank you on my own behalf and on behalf of my colleagues.[1]

According to what I've heard, Monet has sold some of the canvases exhibited at Monsieur Charpentier's, and Renoir has got several good portrait commissions.

I wish you good health, and please give my sincere respects to Madame Zola and your mother,

I am, with gratitude, your devoted

Paul Cézanne

My address is: 32 Rue de l'Ouest, and not 12 as you mistakenly put it.

---

1 Number II contains a single reference to Cézanne himself, brief and guarded: 'M. Paul Cézanne, a temperament of a great painter still preoccupied with studies in facture, remains closer to Courbet and Delacroix.'

[Paris] Saturday [October?] 1880

Mon cher Émile,

I've just received the copy you sent me [*Les Soirées de Médan*].[1] I'm going to make it my treat during the quiet hours of the evening. Please pass on the artistic fellow-feeling that binds all sensitive people – despite their different means of expression – to your colleagues when you see them, and thank them for joining you to offer me this volume that I sense is going to be both substantial and nourishing.

Yours from the heart, the Provençal for whom old age has come before maturity. I mustn't forget to offer my respects to Madame and to beg her to consider me her humble servant.

Paul Cézanne

---

1   A collection of short stories by the members of Zola's gang, *le groupe de Médan*, among whom were Paul Alexis, Henry Céard, Léon Hennique and Joris-Karl Huysmans. It included, most famously, Guy de Maupassant's 'Boule de Suif'.

[Paris] 28 October 1880

Mon cher Émile,

This morning Solari brought me the letter you sent me. I learned from *Le Journal* that you'd lost your mother, and that you would be going to Aix, that's why I didn't come to Médan. I was going to write to ask you whether you were coming to Paris next month, but since you tell me that you'll be coming sometime later, I'll wait until then, unless you would like me to come and see you, I'm at your service for anything I can do.

I well understand all the sadness of your situation, and I hope nonetheless that your health has been affected as little as possible, as well as your wife's.

Please accept my sincere greetings and warm good wishes.

Paul Cézanne

102 • TO JORIS-KARL HUYSMANS

[Paris?] Wednesday April 1881

Monsieur Huysmans,
I received the day before yesterday the book you were kind enough to send me [*En ménage*]. My hearty thanks for that kind thought.

Along with your gift, I found one from Monsieur [Henry] Céard. Since I carelessly failed to note his address, I must ask you to give him my thanks for the token of his esteem for my qualities of mind.

I am, with gratitude, your devoted

Paul Cézanne

[Paris?] 12 April 1881

Mon cher Émile,

The Cabaner sale is due to take place in a few days' time.[1] Here, then, is what I'd like to ask you: whether you would be good enough to undertake to write a short announcement, as you did for the Duranty sale [the year before]. For there's no doubt that the backing of your name alone would be a great draw for the public, to bring in art lovers and promote the sale.

Here is a list of the some of the artists who have offered their works:

[Édouard] Manet
[Edgar] Degas
[Pierre] Frank Lamy [Franc-Lamy]
[Camille] Pissarro
[Jean] Bérand
[Henri] Gervex
[Antoine] Guillemet
[Charles Henri] Pille
[Frédéric] Cordey; etc;
and your humble servant.

As one of your oldest acquaintances, I was the one entrusted with making this request.

Warmest good wishes, and please give my respects to Madame Zola.

Yours ever,

Paul Cézanne

1 Ernest Cabaner (1833–1881), musician and metaphysician, as Cézanne described him. He came from Perpignan to study at the Paris Conservatoire and never left, claiming that he was allergic to the countryside. He lived, after a fashion, by playing bar-room piano for soldiers and prostitutes. In his spare time he collected old shoes to use as flowerpots. He had come to the notice of the Prefect of Police, who kept a file on him: 'Eccentric

musician, mad composer, one of the most fervent devotees of the caste' (a euphemism for homosexuals). As an eccentric, he out-Cézanned Cézanne. He was cadaverous, lugubrious, consumptive. He seemed to be permanently in the final stages of tuberculosis, surviving on a diet of milk, honey, rice, kippers and alcohol. Verlaine described him as 'Jesus Christ after ten years of absinthe and two weeks in the grave'. He was also a close friend of Arthur Rimbaud. Friendship with Rimbaud was not easy to sustain. In Cabaner's case it lasted until the great poet's final disappearance from Paris, despite Rimbaud's periodic chants of 'Cabaner must be killed!' and various other torments and provocations. One winter, Cabaner moved into a freezing hovel: Rimbaud removed all the window panes with a glass cutter. On another occasion, when Cabaner was out, Rimbaud found his daily glass of milk and neatly ejaculated into it.

104 · TO THÉODORE DURET[1] [?]

[Paris, April 1881]

Here is the very kind letter that Zola wrote to me.

Would you for your part please send him the necessary notes.

Believe me, respectfully, your humble servant,

Paul Cézanne

[Cézanne's note appears on the back of Zola's letter, replying to Cézanne's request:]

Mon cher Paul,

I'd be happy to write the short announcement you ask for; but I absolutely must have some details.

I have to speak of Cabaner; but in what terms? Should I say that he is ill, that he is in the Midi, that the sale is being held to assist him? In a word, should I speak of his troubles? I don't know him at all well and don't want to hurt him. Let me know quickly what you think and if we can rouse the public to pity him for his plight, while speaking of his artistic struggle and his talent. I think that would strike the right note. But I'd like the organizers of the sale to give me permission to say that.

I await your letter in order to do the announcement.
Yours,

Émile Zola

1   It is not absolutely certain that this note was addressed to Théodore Duret (1838–1927), a cultivated republican of progressive tastes and deep pockets, who combined the lives of critic and collector. But Duret had his ear to the ground, and by this time he was a convert to Cézanne's artistic achievements. As early as 1870 he wrote to Zola: 'I hear tell of a painter called Cézanne, I think, or something like that, apparently from Aix and whose paintings have been rejected by the jury [of the Salon]. I seem to remember that you have spoken to me in the past of a painter from Aix who is completely eccentric. Would he be this year's reject? If so, would you be kind enough to give me his address and a word of recommendation, so that I may go and make the acquaintance of the painter and his painting?' To this exquisite overture Zola replied by return: 'I cannot give you the address of the painter of whom you speak. He is very much withdrawn, he is going through a period of experimentation, and, to my mind, he is right not to allow anyone into his studio. Wait until he is able to find himself.'
    Three years later Duret tried again, addressing himself this time to Pissarro. 'In painting,' he wrote, 'I'm looking more than ever for the five-legged sheep.' The approach was well judged. Pissarro responded: 'If it's five-legged sheep you're after, I believe Cézanne will appeal to you, for he has some extremely strange studies and views of a unique kind.' So it proved. Duret acquired a small number of works, and after omitting Cézanne from his early *Histoire des peintres impressionistes* (1878) he devoted a whole chapter to him in subsequent editions. Duret's Cézanne was an anarchist in art and a capitalist in life: that, too, appealed to him.

[Pontoise] 7 May 1881

Mon cher Émile,

I've been in Pontoise for two days. Since you were kind enough to write and let me know that you would undertake to write the legend of Cabaner, I haven't seen Frank Lamy, who I believe is one of the organizers of the sale on behalf of the hapless musician.

So could you let me know whether you have received the notes you need to work from and if you have concocted a short announcement, as I was entrusted to ask.

I received from Huysmans and [Henry] Céard, as well as from you, your latest volumes when they appeared, and I've been enchanted with them. I think that Céard will have a great deal of popularity [with *Une belle journée*], because to me it seems very amusing, to say nothing of the great quality of insight and observation contained in his book.

Thank you very much for enabling me to make the acquaintance of these very remarkable persons and please give my respects to Madame Zola as well as to you yourself.

Hearty greetings

Paul Cézanne

I'm now living at

31 Quai du Pothuis
at Pontoise (Seine-et-Oise).

At the last moment, I've just heard that Madame [Édouard] Béliard is very ill, it's always painful to learn that fate weighs heavy on nice people.

Pontoise, 16 May [1]881

Monsieur Chocquet,

Having learnt that the [size] 40 canvas that Monsieur Tanguy must have delivered to you [*Snow Melting at Fontainebleau*, R413] did not have a frame, I should be much obliged if you would be kind enough to have the frame of said painting brought to you. I thank you in advance and beg you to accept my apologies for the further inconvenience I have just caused you.

Monsieur Chocquet, we are all in good form, and since our arrival we are revelling in all the atmospheric variations that the sky is pleased to bestow upon us. Monsieur Pissarro, whom we saw yesterday, gave us your news, and we are happy to hear that you are in good health.

My wife and Paul junior have instructed me to send you their most affectionate good wishes. Allow me to offer you the homage of my sincere greetings and to share them with Madame Chocquet, not forgetting, on behalf of my family, Mademoiselle Lisbeth [Chocquet's adopted daughter].

My warmest wishes and best regards.

Paul Cézanne

Snow Melting at Fontainebleau, 1879–80.
Oil on canvas, 73.5 x 100.6 cm (29 x 39⅝ in.).

Pontoise, 20 May 1881

Mon cher Émile,

Since you were kind enough to reply to me the sale for Cabaner's benefit has taken place. As you say, I did think that Frank Lamy must have got in touch with you, and I thank you for the preface you wrote about the metaphysician, who should really have written some conspicuous work, for he has some truly bizarre and paradoxical notions that are not without a certain spice.

A mild torture is in store for me. My sister [Rose] and brother-in-law [Maxim Conil] are coming to Paris, accompanied I believe by their sister Marie Conil. You can just see me piloting them round the Louvre and other pictorial locales.

Of course, as you say, my stay in Pontoise will not prevent me from coming to see you, on the contrary I'm plotting to come to Médan overland [a distance of 15 km, or 9 miles] and on shanks's pony and under my own steam. I don't think that task is beyond me.

I see Pissarro fairly often, I lent him Huysmans's book [*En ménage*], which he's gobbling up.

I have several studies on the go, on grey days and sunny days. I hope you soon get back to normal in your work, which is, I think, despite all alternatives, the only refuge where one can find true self-satisfaction.

Please give my respects to Madame Zola, and warmest wishes to you,
Yours ever,

Paul Cézanne

Remember me to my compatriot Alexis, whom I have not seen for some time and whom you will surely see before I shall.

[Pontoise] Tuesday June 1881

Mon cher Émile,

I wanted to thank you for sending me your latest volume [*Les Romanciers naturalistes*], but continually putting it off I could have let a long time go by had I not found myself awake before four o'clock this morning. I started reading it but haven't quite finished, although I've read a good deal, since it is in sections, now one essay, now another. The one on Stendhal strikes me as very fine.

Having gone to Paris, I found at my lodging the book [Édouard] Rod was kind enough to send me [*Palmyre Veulard*], which is an easy read. I skimmed through it. I didn't know his address and haven't been able to thank him for the copy he sent. If you happen to think of writing me a few lines, give me his address so that I can do my duty by him.

My sister and brother-in-law came to spend a few days in Paris. On Sunday morning, since my sister was unwell, I had to send them back to Aix. On the first Sunday of the month, I accompanied them to Versailles, city of the great king, to see the great fountains.

I wish you good health, that being the most precious thing, especially when one is also comfortably placed.

I take the liberty of sending my respects to Madame Zola, and best wishes to you.

Paul Cézanne

I'm working a little, plodding along.

[Pontoise] Monday [July] 1881

Mon cher Émile,

On the way to Auvers I heard that Alexis had been wounded in a duel [with the author of a defamatory article], in which, as always, the affronted party was injured. If it isn't too much trouble, you would be doing me a great favour by giving me the latest on my gallant compatriot.

I can't go to Paris until early August, when I'll enquire into his health.

I happened to hear earlier about the discussion prompted by Wolff on the subject of the article you wrote about Maupassant and Alexis.

Please convey my greetings to Madame Zola, and in the midst of all these troubles I hope you'll keep in good health; and if Alexis should happen to be with you, since I'm still hoping that his wound isn't very serious, send him my fraternal greetings.

Your old friend

Paul Cézanne

[Pontoise] 5 August 1881

Mon cher Émile,

While I was with Alexis on Tuesday morning, your letter reached me in Pontoise. So I heard from both sides that the *affaire Alexis* had been settled in a way that was not too vexing for him. I found my compatriot completely restored, and he showed me the articles that preceded and followed his encounter.

At my Paris lodging I found a letter from Caserta, signed by a certain Etorre-Lacquanitin, or something like that, asking me to assist him in obtaining a pile of critiques of your works, before and after the Rougon-Macquart [novels]. You probably know this author, who wants to do a critical study of your work.

Alexis, to whom I showed this letter, told me that he had received a similar one, and that he would reply for both of us.

Some minor setbacks have not made my visit to Médan any easier, but I'll come for sure at the end of October. I must leave Pontoise around then, and perhaps I'll go and spend some time in Aix. Before making that trip, when you write to me then, I'll come and spend a few days with you.

Warmest good wishes, and I offer my respects to Madame Zola, and good bathing,

Yours ever,

Paul Cézanne

III · TO ÉMILE ZOLA

Pontoise, 15 October 1881

Mon cher Émile,
The time is drawing near when I must leave for Aix. Before I go I wanted to come and say hello to you. Since the bad weather has set in, I'm writing to you at Médan, guessing that you must be back from Grandcamp. So if you don't see any difficulty, I'll come and see you around the 24th or 25th of this month. If you can drop me a line about this, I'd be grateful.

Please give my greetings to Madame Zola, hoping that you have returned in good health, and warmest good wishes to you.

Your devoted

Paul Cézanne

L'Estaque, 15 February 1882

Mon cher Paul,

I must be well behind in thanking you for sending me your biographical work [*Émile Zola, notes d'un ami*], for I'm in L'Estaque, the land of Sea Urchins. The copy you were kind enough to send me fetched up in Aix, in the unclean hands of my relatives. They took care not to let me know. They took it out of the envelope, cut the pages, went through it in every sense, while I was waiting under the harmonious pine tree. But finally I found out. I asked for it back, and here I am in possession, reading.

I want to thank you most warmly for the good feelings you give me in recalling times gone by. What more can I say. I shan't be telling you anything new if I say what marvellous stuff there is in the beautiful verses of he who wants very much to continue to be our friend. But you know how much it means to me. Don't tell him. He would say that I'm soft in the head. This is between us and not for broadcast.

In consequence, *mon cher* Alexis, allow me to send you compatriotic and friendly greetings.

Vale
Paul Cézanne

---

1 Paul Alexis (1847–1901), writer and boyhood friend. He passed through the Collège Bourbon a few years after Cézanne and Zola , and was known as 'Zola's shadow'. His relations with Cézanne cooled in later life, but he remained almost obsessively loyal to his literary master.

L'Estaque, 28 February 1882

Mon cher Émile,

The day before yesterday I received the volume of literary criticism you were kind enough to send me. So I'm writing to thank you, and at the same time to tell you that, after spending four months in the Midi, I'm going to return to Paris in a week's time. And, as I think that you're at Médan, I'll come and say hello to you in your abode. But first I'll call at the Rue de Boulogne to find out whether you're there.

Greetings to Madame Zola, and warmest wishes to you,
Gratefully yours,

Paul Cézanne

114 • AUGUSTE RENOIR TO VICTOR CHOCQUET¹ [extracts]

[L'Estaque, 2 March 1882]

[…]

I've just been ill and am convalescing. I can't tell you how kind Cézanne has been to me. He was keen to lay everything at my disposal. We're having a grand farewell dinner with his mother, because he is returning to Paris and I must stay somewhere in the Midi: doctor's orders. … At lunch Madame Cézanne gave me a *brandade de morue* [a dish made with cod], I believe it's the nectar of the Gods rediscovered. One must eat it and die.

[…]

1   Auguste Renoir (1841–1919), Cézanne's illustrious contemporary. Renoir was fascinated by Cézanne. He exchanged paintings with him; he made a distinguished-looking pastel portrait of him (which Cézanne copied); he introduced Victor Chocquet to him; he

made a generous selection of his work for the third Impressionist exhibition of 1877; he sought him out to work with him, for short periods in 1882, 1885, 1888 and 1889; he recorded his speech like an anthropologist in a strange tribe; and he was later prepared to say that Cézanne was unique among painters. His wife even had one of Cézanne's recipes, for baked tomatoes. She would tell the cook to be 'a little more generous with the olive oil'.

Renoir had an extravagant admiration for Cézanne's work. It spoke to him of structure and solidity, and of an almost uncanny sense of pictorial order. 'How does he do it?' he asked Maurice Denis. 'He has only to put two strokes of colour on the canvas and it's already something.' On one of several visits to Cézanne's breakthrough exhibition of 1895, he remarked that the paintings bore a certain resemblance to the frescos of Pompeii, a curiously apt comparison, as Pissarro noted at the time. For all that, the relationship did not catch fire. In truth, it was not so much a relationship as a pursuit. Renoir's admiration was tinged with self-interest. He sought out Cézanne for a purpose, to watch and to learn. Cézanne seems to have liked him well enough – he was surprisingly hospitable, on and off the motif – but there is no sense that Renoir really mattered to him. Renoir is usually accorded some respect (though in one outburst of temper Zola was 'a phrasemonger', Monet 'a crook', and Renoir 'a whore'), but he hardly figures in Cézanne's letters or conversation, either as a moral support or as a point of reference.

115 · TO ÉMILE ZOLA

[Paris] 2 September 1882

Mon cher Émile,
Since you told me so in April, I think that you are at your country house. So I'm sending this scrap of letter there. I only have a month left in Paris, then can I come and seek you out in Médan. If you are coming to Paris around the 10th or the 12th, as you did two years ago, please let me know, I'll pop round to say hello. And I'll find out when I see you whether I can set out for your rural residence.

That's all; I hope that my letter finds you in good health.

I close by sending my respects to Madame Zola, and please accept my sincere greetings.

Paul Cézanne

Jas de Bouffan, Tuesday 14 November 1882

Mon cher Émile,

Yesterday I received the volume you sent me and have just written back thanking you for it. Since I got here, I haven't moved from the country [the Jas], and I've met only Gibert, the director of the museum, which I must go and see.

I also met big [Marius] Dauphin, who was at school with us, and little [Isidore] Baille – both lawyers, the latter has the air of a nice little legal crook. But nothing new here, not the least little suicide [a reference to Marguery's suicide the year before].

If you need anything from here, let me know. I should be happy to be at your service. I'm still working a bit, even though I'm doing nothing else.

Please give my respects to Madame Zola, and my mother asks to be remembered to you. My warmest wishes to you,

Ever your

Paul Cézanne

I saw nothing of doughty Alexis; since you can get hold of him more easily, please pass on my greetings.

Jas de Bouffan, 27 November [1882]

Mon cher Émile,

I've decided to make my will, because it appears that I can. The annuities on which I receive interest are in my name. So I'm writing to ask your advice. Could you tell me the form of words to be used when drawing it up? In the event of my death, I wish to leave half of my income to my mother and the other half to the little one. If you know anything of this, would you tell me about it? For if I were to die in the near future, my sisters would inherit from me, and I believe my mother would be deprived, and I think the little one (*being recognized*, when I notified the town hall) would still be entitled to half of my estate, but perhaps not without contestation.[1]

In the event that I can make a holograph will [in his own hand], if it wouldn't be any trouble, I'd like to ask if you could please hold a duplicate of same. Provided that doesn't cause you any inconvenience, because someone could get their hands on said document here.

That's what I wanted to put to you. I salute you and wish you good day, not forgetting to send my respects to Madame Zola.

Yours ever,

Paul Cézanne

1 Cezanne trusted his mother, it seems, but not his sisters. There is no indication that Rose (1854–1909), the younger sister, was especially acquisitive; but if she merely went along with her husband (a lawyer), that would have been enough for Cézanne, who regarded his brother-in-law as mercenary and untrustworthy. Marie (1841–1921), for her part, could be exasperating, with her meddling and her piety. Cézanne was usually prepared to indulge her; he believed she meant well. Marie was a hardy soul, and a spinster, but there were those who had got their hooks into her, as Cézanne would have said. She was in thrall to the Jesuits, and he suspected that they had designs on the estate – most nefariously, on his father's house, the Jas de Bouffan. He talked darkly of 'disarming the Jesuits who insinuated themselves with his elderly sister and coveted the Jas'.

As he saw it, there were good reasons for protecting his interests, and his mother. Conspicuous by her absence from these calculations was Hortense. On the face of it, she was cut out altogether. And yet when Cézanne came into his full inheritance, after his father's death in 1886, he took great pains to make provision for her – generous provision – on an equal footing. To his dying day he was solicitous of her needs and her wellbeing. In later life she was effectively in the care of their son (and a paid female companion); as the years went by, Cézanne entrusted her increasingly to Paul – he who was wise in the ways of the world, as his father liked to think. Doubtless there was an element of convenience to this, but it was also a kind of contract, and an imperishable bond between them. For father and son, and for Cézanne in particular, Hortense was that most precious of beings, a mother. There could be no question of cutting her adrift. She must be looked after.

The story of the will continues in letters 120 and 121.

118 · TO NUMA COSTE

[Aix] 6 January 1883

Mon cher Coste,

I think it's to you that I owe the delivery of the paper *L'Art libre*. I read it with the keenest interest, and for good reason. So I wish to thank you and to tell you how much I appreciate the generous spirit with which you take up the defence of a cause to which I remain far from indifferent.

I am, with gratitude, your compatriot and, if I might be so bold, your colleague.

Paul Cézanne

[Aix] Saturday 10 March 1883

Mon cher Émile,

I'm rather late in thanking you for sending your latest novel [*Au bonheur des dames*]. Here, however, is the extenuating circumstance behind this delay. I got to L'Estaque, where I was going to spend a few days. Renoir, who is supposed to have a show after Monet's, which is on at the moment, had asked me to send him two landscapes that he left with me last year. I sent them off to him on Wednesday; and so here I am in Aix, where the snow fell all day Friday. This morning the countryside had a lovely snowy effect. But it's melting. We're still in the country [at the Jas]. Since October my sister Rose and her husband have been in Aix, where she gave birth to a little girl. All this is not very amusing. I believe that my protestations will result in their not returning to the country this summer. Much to my mother's delight. I shan't be able to get back to Paris for some time, I think I'll spend another five or six months here. So I'm just reminding you of my existence, and ask you to say hello to Alexis for me.

Please give my respectful greetings to Madame Zola, and also my mother's.

With warm thanks, I am yours ever,

Paul Cézanne

[L'Estaque] 19 May 1883

Mon cher Émile,

In December 1882, I think I asked you if I could send you *testamentum meum* [my will]. You said yes. Now I should like to ask if you are at Médan, as is likely, in which case I'll send it to you by registered mail, that's what

I should do, I think. After a good deal of toing and froing, this is what happened. My mother and I went to a solicitor in Marseille, who advised a holograph will, and, if I so desired, my mother as sole legatee. So that is what I did. When I'm back in Paris, if you could come with me to a solicitor I'll make another appointment and redo my will, and then I'll explain to you in person what led me to this.

Now that I've set down the serious matters I had to tell you, I'll conclude my letter by asking you to give my respects to Madame Zola, and best wishes to you, and if hope achieves anything, I hope you're keeping well, for things happen that are not funny.

Paul Cézanne

I almost forgot, here is my address:

Cézanne, Quartier du Château, above the station at L'Estaque (Marseille).

Those last words are prompted by the Manet tragedy [he died a few days after having a leg amputated], otherwise I'm well. So I've finished, and I'm grateful for this further service.

121 · TO ÉMILE ZOLA

[L'Estaque] 24 May 1883

Mon cher Émile,
Now that I know you're at Médan, I'll send you the document in question, of which my mother has a copy. But I fear that all this makes little odds, for these wills are so easily attacked and annulled. A firm agreement before the civil authorities would be better should the need arise.

I shan't be returning to Paris until next year; I've rented a small house with garden in L'Estaque, just above the station and at the foot of the hill, with the rocks and the pines just behind me.

I'm still busy with painting, there are some fine views here, but that doesn't quite make a *motif.* Nevertheless, climbing up high when the sun sets, there's a beautiful panorama down below of Marseille and the islands, all of it wrapped in the evening light to very decorative effect.

I'm saying nothing about you, because I know nothing at all, except that when I buy *Le Figaro* I sometimes light upon a few facts about men I know, thus recently I read a weighty article on the valiant [Marcellin] Desboutins [painter, engraver and playwright]. However, I did learn that Gaut rates your last novel very highly (but no doubt you know that). As for me, I liked it very much, but my assessment is hardly literary. Thank you very much, and don't forget to remember me to Madame Zola, as well as Alexis and anyone else still alive. Sincere good wishes.

Yours ever,

Paul Cézanne

This is pre-dated, because the stamped paper was bought last year.

122 • TO PHILIPPE SOLARI[1]

L'Estaque, 10 July 1883

Mon cher Solari,
I received the letter you wrote to me on the occasion of the marriage of your daughter to Monsieur Mourain. Accordingly, please pass on my warm regards to the young couple and give them our best wishes for their future happiness and prosperity.

I send congratulations to you and also to Madame Solari, and greetings to Baby Émile who must be pleased.

Warmest wishes, your old fellow-walker,

Paul Cézanne

PS My wife joins me in this spirit, and my frightful little brat too.

I Philippe Solari (1840–1906), a sweet-natured sculptor and probably Cézanne's earliest boyhood friend, from the time that they were at primary school together in Aix. In due course Cézanne also became friendly with his son Émile (1873–1961).

123 • TO ÉMILE ZOLA

L'Estaque, 26 November 1883

Mon cher Émile,

I received the book you were kind enough to send me [*Naïs Micoulin*]. But the new circumstance that has delayed my thanking you is that since the beginning of November I've been back in L'Estaque, where I plan to stay until January. Mother has been here for several days now, and last week Rose, who is married to Maxime Conil, lost the baby she had in September or October, I think. The fact is, the poor little thing didn't last long. Otherwise everything goes on as before. If the doughty Alexis is not far away, remember me to him. And then I send good wishes to you and greetings to Madame Zola.

I have the honour to bid you farewell, and to repeat my thanks for kindly remembering me.

Yours ever,

Paul Cézanne

Aix, 23 February 1884

Mon cher Émile,

I received the book that you were kind enough to send me recently, *La Joie de Vivre*, which appeared in *Gil Blas*, because I saw some parts of it in said newspaper. So thank you very much for sending it, and for not forgetting me when I'm so far away. I'd have nothing to tell you, were it not that, finding myself in L'Estaque over the last few days, I received a handwritten letter from doughty Valabrègue, Antony, telling me he was in Aix, whither I hotfooted it straight away, yesterday, and where I had the pleasure of wishing him well this morning, Saturday. We went round the town together. We recalled some of those we had known. But how far apart we are in *sensation*. My head is full of ideas about this region, which seems to me quite extraordinary. And then I've seen Monet and Renoir, who went off vacationing in Genoa in Italy, around the end of December.

Don't forget to remember me to my compatriot Alexis, though I haven't heard anything of him for ages.

All my thanks to you and my respects to Madame Zola, hoping that you're in good health.

Sincere greetings,

Paul Cézanne

[Aix] 27 November 1884

Mon cher Émile,

I've just received two new volumes that you were kind enough to send me. I thank you, and I must tell you that I've nothing much to tell you about the good old town where I first saw the light of day. Except (but doubtless this won't affect you much) art is horribly transforming its outward appearance, dressing up a mean little form, harmony is increasingly revealed in the clashing of the colours themselves, which is even worse than the clashing of tones.

Having moaned about our lot, let us praise the sun, which sheds such a beautiful light.

I can only repeat that I'm ever yours, without neglecting to offer my respects to Madame Zola,

Paul Cézanne

126 · TO ÉMILE ZOLA

[L'Estaque] 11 March 1885

Mon cher Émile,
I received the book you were kind enough to send me ten days or so ago [*Germinal*]. Rather severe neuralgic pains, which allowed me only moments of lucidity, made me forget to thank you. But my headache has eased, and I'm going for walks in the hills, where I see some lovely views. I wish you good health, considering that you lack for nothing else.

Warmest wishes.

Paul Cézanne

[Aix, spring 1885]

I saw you, and you let me kiss you, from that moment I have had no peace from profound turmoil. You will forgive the liberty that a soul tormented by anxiety takes in writing to you. I do not know how to describe to you that liberty that you may find so great, but how could I remain oppressed by this dejection? Is it not better to give expression to an emotion than to conceal it?

Why, I ask myself, be silent about my torment? Is it not a relief from suffering to be permitted to express it? And if physical pain seems to find some relief in the cries of the afflicted, is it not natural, Madame, that psychological suffering should seek some respite in the confession made to the object of adoration?

I quite realize that this letter, sent hastily and prematurely, may appear indiscreet, has nothing to recommend me to you but the goodness of …

1   The draft of this letter is on the back of a landscape. For more on this intriguing episode, see the Introduction.

128 · TO ÉMILE ZOLA

[Aix] Jas de Bouffan, 14 May 1885

Mon cher Émile,

I'm writing to ask if you would be kind enough to answer me. I should be much obliged if you would do me some service, which is I think tiny for you and vast for me. It would be to receive some letters for me, and to forward them by post to the address that I'll send you later. Either I am mad or I am sane, *Trahit sua quemque voluptas!* [Each towed by his own fancy!]¹ I appeal to you and I beg your forgiveness, happy are the wise, don't refuse me this service, I don't know where to turn. My dear friend, warmest wishes,

Paul Cézanne

I am weak and can do you no service; as I shall leave this world before you, I will put in a good word with the Almighty to find you a good place.

| A quotation from Virgil's second *Eclogue*. See the Introduction for what lay behind this agitated letter.

129 • TO ÉMILE ZOLA

La Roche[-Guyon], 15 June 1885

Mon cher Émile,

I arrived at La Roche this morning [where the Cézannes were staying with the Renoirs], so if any letter should come for me, would you please address it to me at

Poste Restante, at La Roche-Guyon, near Bonnières (Seine-and-Oise).

Yesterday evening [when Cézanne and Zola had dined together], I stuffed myself rather too full of good things, please accept my thanks and greetings.

Paul Cézanne

Madame Zola as well, and a speedy recovery.

La Roche-Guyon, 27 June 1885

Mon cher Émile,

It's almost the end of June. When the time comes for your departure for Médan and you are settled in, would you let me know. The need for change is getting on my nerves a little.

Happy are the faithful hearts!

My respects to Madame, and thank you in advance, and for your kindness about my letters from Aix.

I am, with the usual formulas,

Paul Cézanne

La Roche-Guyon, 3 July 1885

Mon cher Émile,

Owing to unforeseen circumstances, my life here is becoming rather difficult. Could you let me know if I could come and visit you.

In the event that you're not yet installed at Médan, be good enough to drop me a line and let me know,

Warmest wishes and many thanks.

Paul Cézanne

La Roche[-Guyon] 6 July 1885

Mon cher Émile,

Please forgive me. I'm a complete idiot. If you can believe it, I forgot to collect your letters from the poste restante. That explains my second [letter], so insistent. A thousand thanks.

Please give my respects to Madame Zola.

As soon as you can, drop me a line:

Grande Rue, Cézanne care of Renoir at La Roche.

Yours ever,

Paul Cézanne

However, should a letter come from Aix, be so kind as to send it to the poste restante and let me know in a note to the house by putting a cross in the corner of the envelope.

[La Roche-Guyon] 11 July 1885

Mon cher Émile,

I'm leaving today for Villennes [near Médan]. I'm going to the inn. I'll come and see you for a moment as soon as I arrive, I'd like to ask you if you'd lend me *Nana* [his boat] for painting, I'll return it to its berth after work.

Doing nothing makes me very bored.

Yours ever,

Paul Cézanne

Don't see anything wrong about my decision, I just felt compelled to move. And then, when you're free, I'll be no more than a step from your place.

134 · TO ÉMILE ZOLA

[Vernon] 13 July 1885

Mon cher ami,
Impossible this holiday week to find a room in Villennes. Not at the Sophora, nor at the Berceau, nor at the Hôtel du Nord. Best wishes to you, I'm at Vernon, Hôtel de Paris. If my canvases for painting are sent to you, please take them in and keep them with you.

Thank you in advance.

Paul Cézanne
Hôtel de Paris
Vernon (Eure)

135 · TO ÉMILE ZOLA

Vernon, 15 July 1885

Mon cher Émile,
As I told you in a note dated the 13th, I'm at Vernon. I can't settle in my current state. I've decided to leave for Aix as soon as possible. I'll come through Médan and drop in on you. I left some papers in your tender care that I'd like to have, if they're in Paris, one day when your servant goes to the Rue de Boulogne could you get him to bring them back.

Farewell and thanks in advance. Excuse me once again for having to call on you in the present circumstances, but to wait another seven or eight days seems very long to me.

Allow me to send you warm wishes,

Paul Cézanne

136 · TO ÉMILE ZOLA

[Vernon] 19 July 1885

Mon cher Émile,
As you say, I'll come to Médan on Wednesday. I'll try to leave in the morning. I should have liked to get on with painting, but I was in a state of the greatest perplexity, for since I must go down to the Midi, I decided that perhaps the sooner the better. On the other hand, perhaps it would be better if I waited a little longer. I'm in a state of indecision. Perhaps I'll get out of it.

A cordial greeting,

Paul Cézanne

[Aix] Jas de Bouffan, 20 August 1885

Mon cher Émile,

I received the news you sent you me about your address last Saturday. I should have replied immediately, but I've been distracted by the molehills under my feet, which are like mountains to me.

Please excuse me. I'm in Aix, and I go to Gardanne every day.[1]

Please give my respects to Madame Zola, and continue to think well of me.

Yours ever,

Paul Cézanne

1   Gardanne was then a picturesque little place, about 12 km (8 miles) away, looking very much like an Italian hilltop village. Cézanne's interest in the pyramidal shape of the settlement and the cubic cast of the houses makes for an unavoidable association with the Cubist landscapes that came twenty years later – not so much landscapes traditionally conceived as variations on the idea of landscape, each element nested in context, but the sense of place increasingly evanescent, or interchangeable.

Jas de Bouffan, 25 August 1885

Mon cher Émile,

The comedy begins. I wrote to La Roche-Guyon the same day that I sent a word to thank you for having thought of me. Since then I've had no news at all; so, for me, complete isolation. The brothel in town, or some other, but that's all. I pay, the word is dirty, but I need some peace, and at this price I ought to get it.

Gardanne, c. 1885. Oil on canvas,
64.8 x 100.3 cm (25½ x 39½ in.).

Gardanne, 1885–86. Oil and conté crayon on canvas,
92.1 x 73.2 cm (36¼ x 28⅞ in.).

Gardanne, 1885–86. Oil on canvas,
80 x 64.1 cm (31½ x 25¼ in.).

So please don't reply, my letter should arrive in due course.

I thank you and beg you to forgive me.

I'm beginning to paint, but [only] because I'm more or less worry-free. I'm going every day to Gardanne, and coming back each evening to the countryside in Aix [to the Jas].

If only I had had an indifferent family, everything would have been for the best.

Warmest wishes to you,

Paul Cézanne

Paris, 31 August 1885

Mon cher Monsieur Sézanne,

I begin by wishing you good day and at the same time inform you of my distress; imagine, my idiot of a landlord has just sent me an order of seizure [a notice of eviction] for the six months' advance rent that I owe him according to our lease, but since it is impossible for me to satisfy him, I turn to you, dear Monsieur Sézanne, to ask you to make every effort to send me a small payment of your account, in this connection I am enclosing the statement for which you asked, which amounts to 4,015.40 francs after deducting your payment of 1,442.50 francs, as detailed below.

I have an IOU for two thousand, one hundred and seventy-four francs 80 centimes (2,174.80) signed by you on 4 March 1878. Thus you should give me an IOU for 1,840.90 for the account of 4,014.40 that you owe. ...

I should be most grateful, *cher Monsieur*, if you could come to my assistance at this critical moment.

[...]

Gardanne, 4 April 1886

Mon cher Émile,
I've just received *L'Œuvre*, which you were kind enough to send me. I thank the author of the Rougon-Macquart for this kind token of remembrance, and ask him to allow me to wish him well, thinking of years gone by.

Ever yours
with the feeling of time passing,

Paul Cézanne

In Gardanne, arrondissement of Aix.

Paris, 28 November 1887

Mon cher Émile,
On returning to Aix I've just received the volume *La Terre* that you were kind enough to address to me. I thank you for sending this new-grown branch of the Rougon-Macquart family tree.

Please accept my thanks and my very best wishes.

Paul Cézanne

When you get back I'll come and see you and say hello.

1 *Publisher's note: letter 140A was discovered after this volume was first published, hence the break in numbering and chronology. The late Alex Danchev translated it himself before his death, and the original footnote has been updated using material he sent to his editor. Letter 140 was long believed to be the last ever to pass between Cézanne and Zola,*

so that *L'Œuvre* was held to be the cause of an abrupt and definitive rupture in their thirty-year relationship. Cézanne's words were combed for any hint of telltale emotion – offence, anger, antagonism, rancour, shock, sorrow, bitterness, or merely coolness – as if the letter might contain the key to the rift, but it seemed well-nigh impossible to infer any fundamental change, let alone unprecedented upheaval.

The newly discovered letter 140A appears equally unremarkable, which is indeed the most remarkable thing about it. In stance and style it echoes many earlier letters, thanking Zola for yet another novel in the same series as *L'Œuvre*, finding an apt figure of speech, employing usual forms of politesse, and in a characteristic postscript adding a pinch of something personal. It is typical, natural, amicable.

This rather ordinary letter implies that the pair's relationship continued on much the same model after *L'Œuvre*. The famous 'rupture' is a misconception, and however their relationship evolved in the years to come, it was not broken by one of Zola's fictions – in itself a rather novelettish notion. As so often, Cézanne spoke true: 'I stopped going to Zola's,' he told Ambroise Vollard later, 'but I could never get used to the idea that our friendship was a thing of the past.' Nor was it.

141 · TO THE PREFECT OF THE SEINE[1] [draft]

[Gardanne, April 1886?]

The undersigned has the honour to request that you be kind enough to legalize the signature of the Mayor of the Fourth Arrondissement, which appears on the birth certificate attached to the present request.

Please, Monsieur le Prefect, accept the respectful greetings of the undersigned,

Paul Cézanne

1 Perhaps in connection with his marriage to Hortense, on 28 April 1886.

Gardanne, 11 May 1886

Monsieur Chocquet,

Touched by your last letter [congratulating Cézanne on his marriage], I wanted to reply at once, but although not busy, on account of failing health or stretches of inclement weather, as always it's put off until tomorrow!

Now, I should not like to weigh too heavily on you, morally I mean, but since Delacroix served as an intermediary between us, I will permit myself to say this: that I should have liked to have your stable outlook, which allows you to reach the desired end with certainty. Your good letter, enclosed with that of Madame Chocquet, testifies to a great balance of human faculties. And so, as I am struck by this requirement, I am discussing it with you. Fate has not endowed me with an equal stability, that is the only regret I have about the things of this earth. As for the rest, I have nothing to complain about. The sky, the bounty of nature, still attract me, and offer me the opportunity to look with pleasure.

When it comes to the realization of wishes for the simplest of things, which ought really to come about by themselves, for example, it would seem that my unhappy lot is for success to be spoiled, for I had a few vines, but untimely frosts came and cut the thread of hope. And my wish would have been, on the contrary, to see them flourish, just as I can only wish you success in what you have planted, and a fine growth of vegetation: green being one of the most cheerful colours, which does the eyes most good. To conclude, I must tell you that I am still occupied with painting and that there are treasures to be carried away from this region, which has not yet found an interpreter to match the nobility of the riches displayed.

Monsieur Chocquet, I should like this letter to find favour with you and by no means bore you, so I shall take the liberty of offering the humble tribute of our greetings and ask you to share them with Madame Chocquet, together with my hope that I have that you will always remain in good health.

As in the past, I am your grateful

Paul Cézanne

The little one is at school and his mother is well.

[Paris] 9 November 1887

Monsieur,

On my return to Paris, after a rather long absence, I find I am lacking in canvases that might be submitted for the delectation of art lovers. Wanting to offer for critical appraisal only those studies that might pass muster, I cannot take part in any exhibition.

Please accept my regrets and my very sincere greetings.

P. Cézanne

Paris, 30 June 1889

Monsieur le Comte,

You have been good enough to give Monsieur Chocquet permission to exhibit *La Maison du pendu* [*The House of the Hanged Man*], which is the name given to a landscape I did in Auvers [in 1874].[1] I have just learned that Monsieur Antonin Proust has accepted it for the exhibition and I therefore ask if you would be so kind as to send this little painting to the Palais des Beaux-Arts for the Exposition Universelle.

Please accept, Monsieur le Comte, along with my thanks, my greetings and my respect.

Paul Cézanne

1 *The House of the Hanged Man* (R202), one of Cézanne's personal favourites, has the habit of stimulating interesting reflections, from everyone from André Breton to Henri Matisse. It was the first work he ever sold to someone he did not know, in 1874, when he was already thirty-five. Fifteen years later, when Victor Chocquet arranged for Cézanne

The House of the Hanged Man, 1874.
Oil on canvas, 55.5 x 66.3 cm (21⅞ x 26⅛ in.).

to be represented at the Exposition Universelle of 1889, they turned to Doria for the loan of that painting. Chocquet was so besotted with it that he persuaded Doria to part with it in exchange for *Snow Melting at Fontainebleau* (R413; see p. 216). No sooner had Chocquet taken delivery than Cézanne was invited by Octave Maus to exhibit with Les XX in Brussels. The good-natured Chocquet agreed to lend it even before the frame was ready. At the Chocquet sale in 1899 it was bought for 6,200 francs (a record for the sale) by Count Isaac Camondo, with Monet's encouragement. 'Well, yes, I bought this painting that isn't accepted yet by everyone!' said Camondo. 'But I'm covered: I have a signed letter from Claude Monet, who has given me his word of honour that this canvas is destined to become famous. If you come to my house one day, I'll show you that letter. I keep it in a little pocket pinned to the back of the canvas, at the disposal of the malicious, who think I am soft in the head with my *House of the Hanged Man*.' In 1908 Camondo left his collection to the French state, on condition that it was exhibited in specially designated rooms in the Louvre for fifty years. Unlike Caillebotte's, Camondo's donation was accepted. *The House of the Hanged Man* has been on view ever since, together with four other Cézannes. Monet knew his onions.

145 • TO ROGER MARX[1]

Paris, 7 July 1889

Monsieur,

I wrote to thank you for going to such trouble on my behalf. I am sorry that the letter did not reach you. Allow me to repeat my thanks most sincerely, and to request that you convey my deep gratitude to Monsieur Antonin Proust.

Yours devotedly,

Paul Cézanne

1   Roger Marx (1859–1913), writer, critic and Inspecteur des Beaux-Arts, and one of Cézanne's earliest influential supporters. See also letter 248.

146 · TO OCTAVE MAUS[1]

Paris, 27 November 1889

Monsieur,

Having absorbed your flattering letter, let me first thank you, and I shall accept with pleasure your kind invitation [to exhibit with Les XX in Brussels].

However, would you permit me to reject the accusation of disdain that you have levelled against me in connection with my refusal to take part in exhibitions?

On this matter I must tell you that the numerous studies to which I devoted myself having produced only negative results, and dreading criticism that is only too justified, I had resolved to work in silence, until the day when I should feel capable of defending theoretically the results of my endeavours.

Faced with the pleasure of finding myself in such good company, I have no hesitation in altering my resolve and ask you, Monsieur, to accept my thanks and confraternal greetings.

Paul Cézanne

1   Secretary of the Belgian avant-garde group Les XX.

Paris, 18 December 1889

Monsieur Chocquet,

I am going to ask for your assistance, provided my idea seems acceptable to you. Invited by the 'Association des Vingt' in Brussels to take part in their exhibition, and finding myself caught unprepared, I venture to ask whether *La Maison du pendu* [*The House of the Hanged Man*] could be sent to them. I am taking the liberty of enclosing with this note the first letter I received from Brussels, which will serve to acquaint you with my position with regard to this Association, when I add that I have acceded to their gracious request.

Please accept my sincerest greetings, and pay my respects to Madame Chocquet.

Mother and child join me in this.
Your grateful

Paul Cézanne

∽∾

Paris, 21 December 1889

Cher monsieur,

I got in touch with Tanguy to find out which of my studies he had sold to Monsieur de Bonnières. He was unable to give me details. So I would ask you to catalogue this canvas: *Étude de paysage* [*Study of Landscape*]. And then, caught unprepared, I got in touch with Monsieur Chocquet, who is not in Paris at the moment, who immediately made available to me *Une Chaumière à Auvers-sur-Oise* [*A Cottage in Auvers-sur-Oise*, also known as *The House of the Hanged Man*]. But that canvas is unframed, as the frame ordered by Monsieur Chocquet (carved wood) is not yet ready. If you should have some old frame for it, you would ease my mind. It's a standard size-15 canvas [55 × 66 cm; 22 × 26 in.]. Lastly, I am sending you a canvas: *Sketch of Bathers*, whose frame I shall have delivered to Monsieur Petit.

Please accept, Monsieur, my most cordial greetings.

P. Cézanne

1890s

Barbizon. 30 septembre 1894.

Mon cher Monet,

Je suis à Barbizon, j'ai
eu le plaisir d'y faire la
connaissance de
Monsieur Radinsky, —
jeune peintre de talent,
plein d'admiration lui-même pour votre
beau talent, pour ne pas
dire plus. Confiant dans
les bonnes relations que vous
avez bien voulu permettre de
se continuer avec vos
anciens confrères, je me
permets de lui confier ces
quelques mots et pour vous
le présenter et pour me
rappeler par là-même

Letter to Monet, 30 September 1894.

Paris, 15 February 1890

Cher Monsieur,

I should like to thank you for sending the catalogue of the exhibition of the XX, especially as I had intended to ask if you would be good enough to send a copy.

Allow me to send you my heartiest congratulations on the picturesque and highly professional appearance you have given this charming pamphlet.

Please accept my sincere thanks and most cordial greetings.

Paul Cézanne

150 · HORTENSE CÉZANNE TO MARIE CHOCQUET[1]

[Emagny] 1 August 1890

Chère Madame et amie,

You must be back from Paris, so I am sending you my letter. We are going to leave on Thursday or Friday for Switzerland where we expect to end the season. It is very good weather and we are hoping that continues.

[Little] Paul and I have already spent ten days in Switzerland and we found the country so beautiful that we came back eager to return. We saw Vevey where Courbet did the lovely painting that you own.

I hope, dear Madame, that you and Monsieur Chocquet and little Marie are well.

You must be very busy with your *hôtel* [in Paris] for it is no small matter to restore and furnish four floors. I hope that it will be finished promptly and that you will be able to settle in soon. I think that you will like it there and that you will not much regret any trouble caused.

We are fine. I feel better than when I left, and I am hoping that my trip to Switzerland will put me right completely. We plan to look for somewhere to stay and to spend the summer there. My husband has been working pretty well; unfortunately he was disturbed by the bad weather that we had until 10 July. Still he continues to apply himself to the landscape with a tenacity deserving of a better fate.

Monsieur Chocquet must be very busy with all his paintings, furniture and lovely bibelots. We hope that next year we shall have the pleasure of seeing you in Switzerland. You will not have the disruption of this year and I can assure you that you will find the country superb; I've never seen anything so beautiful and it is so refreshing in the woods and on the lakes, and it would give us so much pleasure to have you.

My husband and Paul join me in sending you our best wishes and beg you to recall our great friendship for Monsieur Chocquet. We also send a kiss to little Marie, who must be very good, we are sure, and who can read so well.

For you, dear Madame and friend, I embrace you with all my heart and am your affectionate

Hortense Cézanne

PS: My mother-in-law and sister-in-law Marie are reconciled, I am in heaven. Once we are established in Switzerland I will send you our address.

I Hortense Cézanne *née* Fiquet (1850–1922), his companion. Marie Chocquet was the wife of Victor Chocquet, Cézanne's patron and friend (see letter 83). Unusually, the Cézannes and the Chocquets socialized together *en famille*.

Only two letters in Hortense's hand have come down to us. This is the first. It seems to demonstrate that, contrary to popular belief, Hortense was no dumb brunette. She could talk, and she could write. The tone here is perhaps a little stilted, and some of the phrasing over-rehearsed; the preoccupations may appear rather narrow, and the sentiments rather trite. But that is an ungenerous reading. Hortense did not have the benefit of Cézanne's classical education. She was not his intellectual equal; there she was in good company. Her letter-writing lacked polish, but this was evidently not an easy letter to write. It is part bread-and-butter, part cultivation, part gossip. The mix of affection and affectation is carried off reasonably well; and there are flashes of genuine feeling, including the postscript. If Marie Chocquet was not exactly a bosom friend, she was clearly something of a confidante. That was already a considerable achievement. See also letter 254.

151 · TO GUSTAVE GEFFROY[1]

Alfort, 26 March 1894

Monsieur,
Yesterday I read the long article you devoted to shedding light on my efforts at painting. I wanted to express my gratitude for your kindness.

Paul Cézanne

1 Gustave Geffroy (1855–1926), writer and critic, was one of Cézanne's most discerning and convincing advocates. The article in question, in *Le Journal*, was effectively the first profile of the artist; it was widely read. Geffroy had done his homework. He had talked to Monet and Renoir, and doubtless to others. He identified Cézanne as a character at once unknown and famous (a neat encapsulation), a phantom, a truth-seeker, a revelator, a precursor, a kind of gauge; a man who had no desire to cut a figure or seek a role but who had nonetheless achieved a strange renown. In a word, he was fabled. 'Surely this man has lived and lives a fine interior novel,' Geffroy concluded, 'and he is haunted by the demon of art.'

[Melun?] 21 September 1894

Yesterday, the 21st inst., I purchased from you four canvases, three 20s and one 25, the first three at 2 francs 50, the 25 at 2 francs 80. The total therefore should be 10 francs 30 and not 11 francs 50, as I paid by mistake.

I trust that you will bear this in mind on my next visit to Melun.

153 • TO CLAUDE MONET[1]

Barbizon, 30 September 1894

Mon cher Monet,

I'm at Barbizon. Here I had the pleasure of making the acquaintance of Monsieur [Václav] Radinsky [a Czech Impressionist], a talented young painter, full of admiration for your fine talent, to say the least. Confident in the good relations that you have kindly allowed to continue with your old colleagues, I take the liberty of entrusting him to deliver these lines to you and thereby to recall me to your memory.

No doubt I'll have the pleasure of seeing you again in Paris, since I'll be returning there at the beginning of winter, and doing my best to meet up with you.

Please accept, *mon cher Monet*, the homage of my pictorial enthusiasm and warm wishes from your utterly devoted

Paul Cézanne

1 Claude Monet (1840–1926), another illustrious contemporary. Monet was well-disposed towards Cézanne: he admired the work enormously (and bought it freely); he did his best to befriend the man and offer him moral support. In November 1894 he invited Cézanne to Giverny to meet Gustave Geffroy and others. 'I hope that Cézanne will already be here and that he will join us,' Monet wrote to Geffroy, 'but he is so

peculiar, so fearful of seeing new faces, that I am afraid he may let us down, despite his wish to meet you. What a pity that this man has not had more support in his life! He is a true artist who suffers too much self-doubt. He needs to be cheered up: and he much appreciated your article!' Cézanne, for his part, seems to have had a high regard for Monet as a master painter. ('The sky is blue, no? It's Monet who noticed that.') According to Geffroy, Cézanne was very critical of his contemporaries, with the exception of Monet, 'the strongest of us all' – 'Monet! I put him in the Louvre!' There may have been an element of politeness in this – Monet was Geffroy's friend – but there are other reports of similar pronouncements: 'Monet and Pissarro, the two great masters, the only two'. Perhaps the best testimony comes from a young visitor to Cézanne's last studio, the architect Jules Borély: 'Beyond a mass of olives and withered trees, the town of Aix appeared, in the mauve light, framed by the surrounding hills, cerulean, floating. Cézanne stretched out his arm to measure the bell tower of the cathedral between thumb and index finger. "How little it takes to distort this thing," he said, "I try my best and it's quite a struggle. Monet has that abundant talent, he looks and, straight away, draws in proportion. He takes it from here and puts it there; that's what Rubens did." We went up to the studio … . "Unlike Monet," said Cézanne, "Renoir doesn't have a consistent aesthetic; his genius makes it difficult for him to find a way of working. Monet sticks to a single vision of things; he gets where he's going and stays there. Yes, a man like Monet is fortunate; he reaches his beautiful destiny. Woe betide the painter who fights too much with his talent: perhaps one who composed some verses in his youth …"' ('Cézanne à Aix', in *Conversations*, pp. 19–20).

154 • MATILDA LEWIS TO A FRIEND[1] **[extracts]**

[November 1894]

[…]

Monsieur Cézanne is from Provence and is like the man from the Midi whom Daudet describes; when I first saw him I thought he looked like a cutthroat with large red eyeballs standing out from his head in a most ferocious manner, a rather fierce-looking pointed beard, quite grey, and an excited way of talking that positively made the dishes rattle. I found later on that I had misjudged his appearance, for far from being fierce or a cut-throat, he has the gentlest nature possible, *comme un enfant* as he would say. His manners at first rather startled me – he scrapes his soup plate, then lifts it and pours the remaining drops in the spoon; he even takes his chop in his fingers and pulls the meat from the bone. He eats with his knife and accompanies every gesture, every movement of his hand, with that implement, which he grasps firmly when he commences his meal and never puts down until he leaves the table. Yet in spite of the total disregard of the dictionary of manners, he shows a politeness towards us that no other man here would have shown. He will not allow Louise to serve him before us in the usual order of succession at the table; he is even deferential to that stupid maid, and he pulls off the old tam-o'-shanter, which he wears to protect his bald head, when he enters the room. ...

The conversation at lunch and at dinner is principally on art and cooking. Cézanne is one of the most liberal artists I have ever seen. He prefaces every remark with: *Pour moi* it is so and so, but grants that everyone may be as honest and as true to nature from their convictions; he doesn't believe that everyone should see alike.

[…]

1 A portrait drawn from a stay in Giverny, where Monet gave a famous lunch party for Cézanne to meet Gustave Geffroy, together with the radical politician Georges Clemenceau, the writer Octave Mirbeau and the sculptor Auguste Rodin, on 28 November 1894 (see the previous letter). This account was previously ascribed to the American artist Mary Cassatt. The original title of the first of Alphonse Daudet's series of novels, *Barbarin de Tarascon* (1869), seems to be what she had in mind.

[Paris, late December 1894]

Show to … I would ask you to put me in touch with a dealer. Show … if you are intelligent – you will see. Make the reader see what you see. Write for the average intelligence. I don't believe that you are a Huysmans. Never feel that you are his reader.

I was waiting for the new year to recall myself to your esteemed attention, but in view of this recent mark of sympathy you have shown me in *Le Journal*, I can no longer put off thanking you.

I trust I shall have the honour of seeing you again and of being able to show you, in a less ephemeral fashion than by mere words, the gratitude that [illegible] and is called for.

Please offer my respectful homage to Madame Mirbeau and believe me very cordially yours,

Paul Cézanne

1 Octave Mirbeau (1848–1917), writer, critic and a passionate advocate of Cézanne. Mirbeau had been one of the first to write favourably about him: an article on 'Paul Cézanne, the poor unknown of genius' appeared in *L'Écho de Paris* as early as 1891. Cézanne, for his part, considered Mirbeau the foremost writer of the period – and may even have identified with some of his characters. He continued to value Mirbeau's moral support, not to mention his patronage. For Mirbeau, Cézanne was 'le plus peintre des peintres', and his thirteen Cézannes were the pride of his collection. Mirbeau was also friendly with Pissarro, and shared his anarchist convictions. The article in question, 'Le Legs Caillebotte et l'état', in *Le Journal*, 24 December 1894, mocked the hesitant attitude of the state towards the Caillebotte donation, including its five Cézannes. See also letter 226.

Paris, 2 January 1895

Cher Monsieur Geffroy,

I got your kind letter and I'm very happy about the plan you've proposed. I'll have the pleasure of seeing you, then, next Tuesday.

Please give my respects to your mother and to Mademoiselle Geffroy [his sister].

Gratefully and sincerely,

Paul Cézanne

Paris, 31 January 1895

Monsieur,

I have continued my reading of the stories contained in your book *Le Cœur et l'esprit* [1894] in which you were kind enough to write such a nice dedication to me.[1] The more I read, the more I become aware of the honour that you have done me. I hope that in future you will continue to show such kindness, which is precious to me.

Paul Cézanne

1   Cézanne was much taken with this collection of stories. His favourite was 'Le Sentiment de l'impossible' (the title alone would have appealed to him), about a young girl who falls in love with a portrait of a young man, a deceased relative, 'destiny having willed it thus, for him, born too soon, and for her, born too late'. It ends: 'And so it was that, in the fever and the mirage, she came to know the sorrow of the irreparable, the feeling of the impossible.'

Paris, 4 April 1895

Cher Monsieur Geffroy,
The days are getting longer, the weather is turning milder. I am unoccupied every morning until the hour when civilized man sits down at table. I intend to come up to Belleville to say hello and submit to you a plan which I have sometimes embraced, sometimes abandoned, and to which I sometimes revert.[1] Very cordially yours,

Paul Cézanne, painter by inclination[2]

1   The plan was to paint Geffroy's portrait, a project begun and at length abandoned. See letters 161 and 163.

2   One of Cézanne's characteristically playful valedictions – playful, yet difficult to interpret. See the Introduction.

Paris 11 April 1895

Mon cher Monet,
Last Tuesday I went to Gustave Geffroy's, he told me of your return to Giverny.

I'd be happy to come and say hello early next week, if you don't mind.

Please be kind enough to give my respects to Madame Monet, and allow me to call myself, very cordially,

Paul Cézanne

Paris, 9 June 1895

Mon cher Monet,

I've just come from Belleville, where I left Gustave Geffroy, rather tired from his illness, which he contracted at the Calais fair. While he was away for a few days I worked on the still lifes around the model [in his portrait of Geffroy]. And then I ran after Oller, who I suspect was going to the Allier with his friend Doctor Aguiar, his compatriot.[1] So I await his return to take a decision. As soon as I see him, I'll write to forewarn you of the probable day of our visit, if that is not a nuisance.

Allow me to say very cordially to you,

Paul Cézanne

1 Aiguar was a friend of Pissarro's. He was Cuban; Oller was Puerto Rican. In the early 1860s Cézanne and Oller were students together at the Atelier Suisse in Paris. Later they fell out. See letters 162 and 164.

161 · TO GUSTAVE GEFFROY

Paris 12 June 1895

Cher Monsieur Geffroy,

On the point of leaving and unable to bring to a satisfactory conclusion the work that is beyond my powers, and that I was wrong to undertake – I beg you to forgive me and to hand over to the messenger I shall send the things I left in your library.[1]

Please accept the expression of my regret and my esteem.

P. Cézanne

1   So he abandoned the portrait of Geffroy (R791), after two months of intensive sessions. The sitter himself recalled:

> During this period he worked on a painting which is one of his beautiful works, even though it is unfinished. The library, the papers on the table, the little Rodin plaster sculpture, the artificial rose that he brought at the beginning of the sessions, everything is of the first rank, and of course there is also a character in this scene, which is painted with meticulous care, with a richness and an incomparable harmony of tones. He only sketched in the face, however, always saying: 'Perhaps I'll leave that for the end.' Alas, the end never came. One fine day, Cézanne sent for his easel, brushes and paints, writing to me that the project was clearly beyond him, he had been wrong to undertake it, and apologizing for abandoning it. I insisted that he come back, telling him what I thought, that he had started a very fine work and that he should finish it. He came back, and for a week he seemed to work, adding thin films of colour, as only he knew how, always retaining the freshness and sparkle of the painting. But his heart was no longer in it. He left for Aix, once again sending for his painting materials a year later, on 3 April 1896, leaving behind the portrait as he had left so many other paintings, things of wonderful vision and realization. (Gustave Geffroy, *Claude Monet* [1922] (Paris: Macula, 1980), p. 327)

Portrait of Gustave Geffroy, 1885–86.
Oil on canvas, 117 x 89.5 cm (46⅛ x 35¼ in.).

Jas de Bouffan, 5 July 1895

Monsieur,

The officious tone that you have adopted towards me of late and the rather off-hand manner you permitted yourself to use towards me on departure are not calculated to please me.

I have determined not to receive you in my father's house.

The lessons that you take the liberty of giving me have thus borne all of their fruit.

Farewell.

P. Cézanne

1 Francisco Oller (1831–1917), Cézanne's fellow student at the Académie Suisse, was a boyhood friend of Pissarro's. This chilly missive seems to have been precipitated by a series of misunderstandings after Oller invited himself to stay at the Cézanne family home, the Jas de Bouffan ('my father's house'), in Aix. Oller's version is related in a letter from Pissarro to his son Lucien:

> Before leaving Paris I saw friend Oller who told me of some extraordinary things that have happened to him with Cézanne, which indicate that the latter is a bit cracked. ... After a great show of affection in the expansive southern manner, Oller confidently believed that he could follow friend Cézanne to Aix-en-Provence; they are to meet the following morning at the P.L.M. [Paris–Lyon–Marseille] train, in third class, says comrade Cézanne; so that morning Oller is on the platform, straining his eyes, looking in all directions, no Cézanne, trains pass, no one!!! Finally Oller says to himself: 'He's left ... believing I've also left,' makes up his mind, and departs. Arriving in Lyon, at the hotel he is robbed of 500 francs that he had in his wallet; not knowing how to return, he sends a telegram to Cézanne on the off-chance: he [Cézanne] was already at home, having travelled first class!! ... Oller received one of those letters you'd have to read to believe. He

sent him packing, asking if he took him for an imbecile, etc., in short a dreadful letter. My word, it's a variant of what happened to Renoir. It seems he's furious with all of us: 'Pissarro is an old fool, Monet is a wily bird, they've got no guts ... I'm the only one with temperament, I'm the only one who knows how to do a red!!' Aguiar has witnessed scenes of that kind. As a doctor, he assured Oller that [Cézanne] was unwell, that he wasn't responsible for his actions, that [Oller] shouldn't pay any attention. What a shame that a man endowed with such a beautiful temperament should be so lacking in stability! (Pissarro to Lucien Pissarro, 20 January 1896, in Pissarro, *Correspondance*, vol. IV, p. 153)

See also letter 164.

∾

163 · TO CLAUDE MONET

Aix, 6 July 1895

Mon cher Monet,

First of all, please excuse my long delay in replying to you. But I'm in the country, where letters arrive only after a lengthy interval, the rural deliveries being made only once a day. And your letter reached me only yesterday.

I had to leave Paris, since the date set for my trip to Aix had arrived. I am with my mother, who is growing old, and she seems frail and alone.

I had to abandon for the time being the study that I started on of Geffroy, who placed himself so generously at my disposal, and I'm a little embarrassed at the meagre results I obtained, especially after so many sittings, and successive bursts of enthusiasm and discouragement. So I've landed up here [again] in the Midi, which I should perhaps have never left to embark on the chimerical pursuit of art.

To conclude, may I say how happy I was about the moral support that you gave me, which served as a stimulus for my painting. Until my return to Paris, then, where I must go to continue my task, as I promised Geffroy.

With regret at having left without seeing you again, I remain very cordially yours,

Paul Cézanne

Jas de Bouffan, 17 July 1895

Monsieur,

Your rather comical letter came as no surprise to me. But first the matter of settling accounts with you – certain accounts that I had to settle at Monsieur Tanguy's should not have escaped your memory. Let us pass over in silence the unsuccessful attempt at Madame Ch[ocquet]'s. Lastly, I fail to understand how I can be held responsible for the loss of money that you say took place during your stay in Lyon.

You can have your canvas collected from the studio in Rue Bonaparte between now and 15 January next year.

I consider you clear of the money I lent you and of everything else.

I hope that thanks to your change of attitude you will be able to extend your stay with Doctor Aguiar.

Farewell.

P. Cézanne

Aix, 15 April 1896

Cher Monsieur,

I am leaving for Paris tomorrow. Please accept my best regards and sincere greetings.

P. Cézanne

[1] Joachim Gasquet (1873–1921), a poet, was the son of Cézanne's former classmate and lifelong friend Henri Gasquet (1840–1906). Joachim Gasquet had a certain allure. He may have reminded Cézanne of his youth, spent with Zola; they revisited some of his old haunts. He may have conjured a brighter image of Cézanne's son, Paul, now ensconced in Paris. He was twenty-three when they met, two years younger than Paul, but more vivid, more accomplished, more intelligent. He was enthusiastic about the paintings – impulsively, Cézanne gave him one on first acquaintance: the *Mont Sainte-Victoire with Large Pine* (R599), which was later sold for a cool 12,000 francs. And Joachim Gasquet could write. Over the next three years he saw a lot of Cézanne, though not thereafter. Gasquet was a Provençal patriot and evolved into a rightist, a Royalist and, in his own high-flown way, something of a racist. He wrote rapturously of Cézanne's *Old Woman with a Rosary* (R808) as a Provençal racial symbol, and did his best to represent the artist as a kind of penitent Dostoevesky. This effort was doomed to failure. Provençal revivalism had a visceral appeal, and Cézanne was not immune to a little lionizing, but there were limits. Cézanne admired intellectual seriousness (and passion), but any hint of preciousness repelled him. Gasquet was preciousness personified, at once superior and ingratiating. His programme was little more than a glorification of a bygone age, and essentially narcissistic. Cézanne may have lived in the past, as he said, but he was not backward-looking. There was work to be done. After a wave of enthusiasm – 'Vive la Provence!' – Cézanne disengaged. No one would get his hooks into him. He became as wary of Gasquet as he was of Geffroy. In 1896 Cézanne painted portraits of both Henri and Joachim Gasquet (R809 and R810).

Mont Sainte-Victoire with Large Pine, c. 1887.
Oil on canvas, 67 x 92 cm (26⅜ x 36¼ in.).

Portrait of Henri Gasquet, 1896.
Oil on canvas, 56.2 x 47 cm (22⅛ x 18½ in.).

Aix, 30 April 1896

Cher Monsieur Gasquet,

I met you this evening at the bottom of the Cours, you were accompanied by Madame [Marie] Gasquet. If I am not mistaken, you appeared to be extremely angry with me.[1]

If you could but see inside me, the man within, you would not be. You do not see, then, the sad state to which I am reduced. No longer my own master, the man who does not exist. Yet you, who would be a philosopher, want to finish me off? But I curse the Geffroys and the other scoundrels who, for a fifty-franc article, have drawn the attention of the public to me. All my life, I have worked to be able to earn my living, but I thought that one could paint well without attracting attention to one's private life. Certainly an artist wishes to improve himself intellectually as much as possible, but the man should remain obscure. The pleasure must be found in the study. If it had been left to me, I should have stayed in my corner with a few friends from the studio with whom I might go out for the odd drink. I still have a good friend from that time [Emperaire?], well, he has not been successful, which does not prevent him from being a damn sight better painter than those good-for-nothings with their medals and decorations that bring one out in a sweat. Do you expect me to believe in anything at my age? Besides, I am as good as dead. You are young, and I understand that you would like to succeed. But for me, what is there left to do in my situation but keep my head down; and if I were not so fond of the lie of the land, I should not be here.

But I have bored you enough as it is, and now that I have explained my situation I hope that you will no longer look on me as if I had somehow threatened your safety.

Please, *cher Monsieur*, in consideration of my great age, accept my best regards and good wishes.

Paul Cézanne

1   Cézanne may have imagined or overinterpreted some of this, perhaps because his little
    ruse had been rumbled: contrary to his note of 15 April, he had not left Aix for Paris, and
    had no intention of doing so. This letter is a revealing one: see the Introduction.

167 · TO JOACHIM GASQUET

Aix, 21 May 1896

Cher Monsieur Gasquet,
Being obliged to return to town early this evening, I cannot be at the Jas.
I am sorry to be a nuisance.

At five o'clock yesterday evening, I had received neither Geffroy's *Le
Cœur et l'esprit* nor the *Figaro* article.[1] I sent a telegram to Paris about this
matter.

Until tomorrow, Friday, then, if you can, at the usual time [for a sitting
for his portrait].

Very cordially,

P. Cézanne

1   An article by Zola, on 'Painting', in *Le Figaro*, 2 May 1896, which contained the follow-
    ing: 'I had grown up almost in the same cradle as my friend, my brother, Paul Cézanne,
    in whom one begins to realize only today the touches of genius of a great painter come
    to nothing.'

Portrait of Joachim Gasquet, 1896.
Oil on canvas, 65.5 x 54.5 cm (25¾ x 21½ in.).

Vichy, 13 June 1896

Mon cher Gasquet,

You would like to launch a review [*Les Mois dorées*]. I'm afraid you'll have to count me out. Rally to your cause those who have written to Monsieur [José] d'Arbaud in response to your proposal. Their contribution, I should say their support, is necessary – in fact the basis of your review. They have lived; that alone gives them experience. There is nothing belittling about facing facts. You are young, you have vitality, you will give your publication an impetus that only you and your friends who have the future before them can give. It seems to me that's a fine enough role to be proud of and to be immersed in. Take advantage of all the initiatives that have proved their worth. Those who have experienced life and who have reached the summit of existence, whether they know it or not, cannot possibly impede the progress of those who are starting out in life. The path they have trodden is a sign of the road to follow, and not an obstacle in your way.

My son has read your review with the keenest interest. He is young, he cannot but share your dreams.

I landed here in Vichy a week ago. The weather, rainy and gloomy on our arrival, has cleared up. The sun is shining, and hope smiles in the heart. I shall soon be back at work.

If you see my friend Solari, please say hello from me. *Bon courage*, as I'm sure you will. Believe me, I am with you with all my heart, and accept my best wishes.

Paul Cézanne

Vichy, Hôtel Molière (Allier).

Talloires, 21 July 1896

Mon cher Gasquet,

Here I am, far from our Provence for a while. After much toing and froing, my family, in whose hands I find myself for the moment, have persuaded me to stay put in this spot, for the time being. It is a temperate zone. The surrounding hills are fairly high. Narrowed here by two headlands, the lake seems to lend itself to the linear exercises of young misses. It's still nature, certainly, but rather as we have learned to see it in the travel albums of young ladies.

Always hale and hearty, with your magnificent brain power you must be beavering away without undue fatigue. I am too distant from you, in age, and in the knowledge that you acquire every day; nevertheless, I commend myself to you and your kind thoughts, so that the links that keep me attached to that old native soil, so vibrant, so harsh, reflecting the dazzling light, and beguiling the receptacle of *sensations* – so that these links do not snap, detaching me, so to speak, from the land where I have experienced so much, without even knowing it. So it would be truly compassionate and a comfort to me if you would be good enough to continue to send your review, which will remind me of the distant land and of your kind youth, in which I've been lucky enough to play a part. On my last visit to Aix, I was sorry not to be able to see you. But I learned with pleasure that Madame Gasquet and yourself will be presiding over the regional and meridional festivals.

I am so grateful for the good wishes that you were so kind as to express in your letter for my wife. And I must also thank you for sending the second issue of the review, so rich and so full. I dare to hope, therefore, that I shall read more of you and your ardent collaborators.

In closing, please be kind enough to give my respects to the Queen of Provence, remember me to your father and other members of your family, and permit me to remain cordially yours,

Paul Cézanne

Address: Hôtel de l'Abbaye, Talloires near Annecy (Haute Savoie).

It would take Chateau[briand]'s descriptive pen to give you any idea of the old monastery where I'm staying.

170 · TO PHILIPPE SOLARI

Talloires, 23 July 1896

Mon cher Solari,
When I was in Aix, I had the feeling that I'd be better off somewhere else; now that I'm here, I miss Aix. For me life is becoming deadly tedious. I was in Aix three weeks ago, I saw the elder Gasquet [Henri], his son being in Nîmes. In June I spent a month in Vichy, one can eat well there. Here one doesn't do badly either. I'm staying in the Hôtel de l'Abbaye. What a superb relic of ancient times; a flight of steps five metres wide, a staggering entrance, an interior courtyard with columns forming a gallery all round; you go up the grand staircase, the rooms open onto an immense corridor, the whole thing very monastic. No doubt your son [Émile] will soon be in Aix. Remember me to him, recall our walks to Peirières and [Mont] Sainte-Victoire, and if you see Gasquet, who must be revelling in the joys of fatherhood regained, give him my best.

Remember me to your father and give him my respects.

To relieve my boredom, I'm painting. It's not much fun, but the lake is very good with the big hills all around, 2,000 metres, I'm told, not much in our country, though truth to tell it's fine. But when you're born down there [in Provence], that's it, there's nothing more to be said. One must eat well, drink well – do you remember Pierre's "the vine is the mother of the wine"? – and by the way I'll be getting back to Paris at the end of August. When shall I see you again? If your son should be passing through Annecy on his way back, let me know.

Best wishes.
Your old

Paul Cézanne

Lake Annecy, 1896. Oil on canvas, 64 x 79 cm (25¼ x 31⅛ in.).

Jo [Gasquet] sent me the second issue of the review around the end of June, when I was still in Vichy. *Mon cher*, it does you good to get news of down there.

My address here is: Hôtel de l'Abbaye, Talloires near Annecy (Haute-Savoie).

Gasquet told me that you'd done some very good things – good for you.

171 • TO JOACHIM GASQUET

Paris, 29 September 1896

Mon cher Gasquet,

Here I am, very late in confirming receipt of the last two issues of *Les Mois dorés* you were kind enough to send me. But on returning to Paris, after leaving Talloires, I spent a good deal of time finding a studio for the winter. I am very much afraid that circumstances will keep me for a while in Montmartre where my work is. I'm a stone's throw from the Sacré-Cœur, whose campaniles and belfries soar into the sky.

At the moment I'm rereading Flaubert, and at the same time going through the review. I'm in danger of repeating myself often: it embalms Provence. I revisit you in reading you, and with a calmer head I think of the brotherly sympathy you have shown me. I won't say that I envy your youth, that's impossible, but your drive, your inexhaustible vitality

So I thank you warmly for not forgetting me now that I'm far away.

Please remember me to your father, my old schoolmate, and give my respects to the Queen who presides so magnificently over the artistic renewal that is dawning in Provence.

For you, my best wishes and hopes for your continued success. Yours ever,

Paul Cézanne

PS Unfortunately, however, I must inform you of Vollard's lack of success in placing Monsieur [Gustave] Heiriès's drawings. He says that he has made several attempts, all fruitless, on account of the difficulty of finding an outlet, so little demand is there for illustrations for books. I'll retrieve the drawings, with great regret, and send them on to you.

172 · TO ÉMILE SOLARI

Paris, 30 November 1896

Mon cher Solari,

I was extremely sorry not to be at the Rue des Dames when you came. There's only one way to make up for it, that is to fix a rendezvous, for tomorrow, for example. A particular place, a precise time, which I leave to you to choose. I'm free from four in the afternoon. So please drop me a line, and believe me to be yours very cordially.

Paul Cézanne

173 · TO ANTOINE GUILLEMET

Paris, 13 January 1897

Mon cher Guillemet,

Having been confined to my room for a fortnight with a persistent attack of influenza, only the day before yesterday did I receive your letter making an appointment and the card confirming your kind visit. So I must tell you how sorry I am that I couldn't be at my studio when you came to see me, and how upset I am by this annoying occurrence, which prevented me from letting you know about the condition I was in and that I could not get to the studio.

Please accept my apologies in this matter, and believe me yours cordially,

P. Cézanne

174 · TO PHILIPPE SOLARI

Paris, 30 January 1897

Mon cher Solari,

I've just received your kind letter. Needless to say, I didn't receive the one you say you wrote at the end of December. I haven't seen Émile [Solari's son] since the end of last month, and for good reason. Since the 31st, I've been confined to barracks by the flu; Paul [Cézanne's son] took care of my move from Montmartre. And it's not over yet, though it's getting better. As soon as I can, I'll drop Émile a line to arrange a meeting.

Now, let's come to Gasquet. His request touches me deeply, pass on to him my wish to present the two canvases in question to Monsieur [Georges] Dumesnil [Professor of Philosophy at the University of Aix].[1] To this end, please get in touch with Gasquet and go to my sister [Marie] at 8 Rue de la Monnaie, and ask her to take you to the Jas, where the above-mentioned canvases are. I'm going to write to my sister about it.

Except for a slight depression inherent in my situation, it's not going too badly, though if I'd been able to organize my life to live down there [in Provence] that would have suited me better. But a family entails a good many concessions.

A big hug for you, and my greetings to your entire circle of friends.

Cordially yours,

Paul Cézanne

You'll find my sister at home either around 11 o'clock in the morning, her lunch time, or around 6 o'clock in the evening, her dinner time.

1 Cézanne gave Dumesnil *Rocks at L'Estaque* (R442) and *Quarry at Bibémus* (R836). In 1910 Dumesnil sold them to Bernheim-Jeune for 12,000 francs, 'to buy an estate with pines'.

Rocks at L'Estaque, 1882–85.
Oil on canvas, 73 x 91 cm (28¾ x 35⅞ in.).

Quarry at Bibémus, c. 1898–1900.
Oil on canvas, 64.8 x 81.3 cm (25½ x 32 in.).

Paris, 30 January 1897

Mon cher Gasquet,

Solari has just told me about your plan. May I ask you to employ all the circumlocutions necessary in the circumstances to present the two canvases in question to Monsieur Dumesnil? I should be very happy if the Professor of Philosophy at the Faculty of Aix would deign to accept my homage. I can put forward as an argument the fact that in my home town I'm more of a friend of art than a producer of paintings, and that at the same time I should be honoured to learn that two of my studies had found a welcome in a good place, etc., etc. Please fill out these arguments with a few flourishes of your own, for I know that you are a marvel at that.

So that's settled. And thank you for the honour I've been given through your mediation.

Please give my respects to Madame Gasquet – I mean the Queen – and my best wishes to your father, and believe me your grateful

Paul Cézanne

Thanks for the last big issue of the review.
And long live Provence!

Mennecy, 24 May 1897

Mon cher Solari,

I shall have to leave soon for Aix. In all probability this departure will take place during the night of Monday 31 May–1 June, God willing. On Saturday 29th inst. I'll be going to Paris; if you're free, and would like us to get together again before my departure, please be at 73 Rue Saint-Lazare, at the agreed time.

Very cordially,

Paul Cézanne

Hôtel Belle Étoile – Mennecy, near Corbeil (Seine-et-Oise).

‿∽‿

177 • TO JOACHIM GASQUET

Tholonet, 18 July 1897

Mon cher Gasquet,
Owing to great fatigue, I am overcome with such weariness that I cannot accept your kind invitation. I feel that I have no strength left, and ask you to excuse me and to make my excuses to your family. I ought to have more sense and to understand that at my age, illusions are no longer possible and will always be my ruin.

Please give my respects and regrets to Madame Gasquet, Madame and Monsieur Girard [Marie Gasquet's parents] and believe me, very cordially,

Paul Cézanne

‿∽‿

178 • TO PHILIPPE SOLARI

[Tholonet, late August 1897]

Mon cher Solari,
On Sunday, if you're free and would like to, come and have lunch in Tholonet, at the Restaurant Berne. If you come in the morning, you'll find

me around 8 o'clock at the [Bibémus] quarry where you did a study when you came the time before last.

Very cordially,

Paul Cézanne

179 · TO ÉMILE SOLARI

Tholonet, 2 September 1897

Mon cher Solari,
I received your letter of 28 August. I didn't reply at once. You told me that you were sending me a review that held out the enticing prospect of some of your poems. I waited several days, but no review.

I've just reread your letter and I realize that I misunderstood it, and that what you were promising was a report of the festivities in Orange.

In what you wrote you call it the *unknown* review. Is that really what it's called, the title under which I should claim it at the post office, since I haven't received it?

Otherwise, you are really very kind in the midst of your Parisian occupations and preoccupations to remember the all-too-short hours you spent in Provence; it is true that the great magician, I mean the sun, was involved. But your youth, your experiences must have played some part in making you see our region in a favourable light. Last Sunday your father came to spend the day with me – the poor man, I soaked him in theories about painting. He must have a forbearing nature to have put up with it. But I notice that I'm going on a bit and I send you a warm greeting in wishing you good luck and farewell.

Paul Cézanne

Tholonet, 8 September 1897

Mon cher Solari,
I've just received *L'Avenir artistique et littéraire,* which you were kind enough to send me. Thank you.

Your father is coming to eat a duck with me next Sunday. Done in olives (the duck, of course). If only you could be with us. Remember me kindly in future years, and allow me to call myself very cordially,

P. Cézanne

Tholonet, 26 September 1897

Mon cher Gasquet,
To my great regret I cannot accept your excellent invitation. But having left Aix at 5 o'clock this morning, I cannot get back until the end of the day. I'm having supper with my mother, and the state of weariness in which I find myself at the end of the day doesn't allow me to present myself in a suitable manner in company. So please excuse me.

Art is a harmony parallel to nature – what can those imbeciles be thinking who say that the artist always falls short of nature?

Very cordially yours, and I promise to come and say hello soon.

P. Cézanne

Jas de Bouffan, 2 November 1897

Mon cher Solari,

I received your letter telling me of your forthcoming marriage. I have no doubt that in your future companion you will find the support indispensable to every man who has a long and often arduous career ahead of him. My best wishes for the realization of your well-founded hopes.

You also tell me of the difficulties you are having in finding an opening to get your plays produced on stage. Thinking about it, I have to admit that I fully appreciate the difficulties you are facing. What can I add, other than that I sympathize with your troubles, and urge you to be brave, for you have to be in order to succeed.

By the time these few words reach you, you'll have heard of the death of my poor mother.[1]

Urging you yet again to be strong and to work hard, I remain very cordially,

Paul Cézanne

A few days ago I had the pleasure of seeing your father, who promised me he would come out to the Jas.

---

1 After abandoning the portrait of Geffroy and returning to Aix, in July 1895, Cézanne wrote to Monet: 'I am with my mother who is growing old, and she seems frail and alone.' He spoke no more than the truth. His mother was a shadow of her former self. In 1895 she turned eighty-one. She seemed to have shrunk; she could hardly walk; she was increasingly isolated. Cézanne adjusted his routine accordingly. He would work at Bibémus or the Château Noir by day, setting off at the crack of dawn, coming back in the evening to have supper with his mother at her house in the Cours Mirabeau. He organized outings for her by horse-drawn carriage; he would take her to sit in the sun at the Jas, or to watch the world go by along the 'petite route' to Le Tholonet. Their coachman, Baptistin Curnier, remembered him picking her up, delicately, carrying her from the house to the carriage, and from the carriage to her chair. He ministered to her with great patience, keeping her amused with a fund of little stories. He made a tender drawing of her sleeping peacefully in an armchair, with a suggestion of his

father's papal throne, attended by apples. She died on 25 October 1897. The death-bed portrait was done by Villevieille. Two days later the funeral service was held at the church of Saint-Jean-de-Malte. Cézanne was not present for the interment. He had returned to the solitude of his *motif*. 'That pierced me like an arrow,' confessed Rilke, 'like a flaming arrow.'

183 · TO LOUIS LE BAIL[1]

Montgeroult, Monday evening [1898]

Cher Monsieur,

I have just woken up, and I remember that, in a similar circumstance to that which I faced recently, I returned a visit that someone had been kind enough to make. I am much vexed by the false position in which I have placed myself. Although I have not had the honour of knowing you for very long, I take the liberty of asking for your assistance in making amends for my blunder. I should be most grateful if you would tell me what I should do.

Please accept my best wishes.

P. Cézanne

1   Louis Le Bail was a young painter who got to know Cézanne through Pissarro. Cézanne's discomposure arose from a recent encounter. While he was painting outdoors at Montgeroult, Cézanne was accosted by Baron Denys Cochin, who was out riding. Not realizing who he was, Cézanne was rather curt with him. In fact Cochin was a great admirer and collector; twenty-one Cézannes are said to have passed through his hands. It was Le Bail who explained to Cézanne who he was. Recounting the story to Le Bail a little later, Cochin said of Cézanne: 'C'est un sauvage!'

Marines [1898]

Cher Monsieur,

The rather cavalier way in which you take the liberty of appearing at my home is not calculated to please. You would be well advised to have yourself announced in future.[1]

   Please return the glass and the canvas that are still in your studio to the person who will come for them.

Yours sincerely,

Paul Cézanne

1   Cézanne had asked Le Bail to call on him every day after his nap, around 3 pm. Le Bail had taken him at his word: after knocking on the door, to no avail, he went into Cézanne's bedroom, to find him still asleep. Relating this to John Rewald, long afterwards, Le Bail added that the real reason for Cézanne's annoyance was quite different, but that was another story ...

Paris, 17 May 1898

Cher Monsieur Geffroy,

I am happy to join in the subscription that you kindly told me about, and I subscribe for 40 francs to the list of admirers of Rodin's genius.[1]

Regretting that, owing to accidental circumstances beyond my control, I cannot accept your kind invitation, I send you my best wishes,

Paul Cézanne

1   This was for the monument to Balzac. According to Vollard, Cézanne subscribed in order to show that Rodin's admirers were not all Dreyfusards. That seems very unlikely.

Cézanne was not given to gesture politics; he himself admired artists (and writers) of all political persuasions, including the notorious Communard Courbet. Moreover, Rodin's subscribers show no discernible pattern: Renoir (anti-Dreyfusard) subscribed for 100 francs; Monet and Mirbeau (Dreyfusard) subscribed for 500 francs; Degas (anti-Dreyfusard) did not subscribe at all; neither did Vollard himself. In the event, in order to put an end to controversy, Rodin cancelled the subscription and refunded the subscribers.

Cézanne was on the wrong side in the Dreyfus affair. But not all anti-Dreyfusards were dolts or bigots. And not all were reflexively anti-Semitic. At a time when piping nationalism and shameless anti-Semitism were sweeping the land, and Degas and Renoir were shunning 'the Jew' Pissarro in the street, Cézanne appeared in an exhibition catalogue as a 'pupil of Pissarro' and recorded a magnificent tribute to that 'humble and colossal' figure (see letter 253).

186 • TO EUGÈNE MONTFORT[1]

Paris 11 June 1898

Cher Monsieur,
I am in possession of the literary work that you have been kind enough to send me via Joachim Gasquet. Becoming acquainted with it gives me the greatest pleasure, and when there is a suitable occasion perhaps you will be kind enough to allow me to speak with you about Art things, which interest us so much.

Please accept my best wishes,

Paul Cézanne

<table>
<tr><td>1</td><td>Eugène Montfort (1877–1936) was a writer and co-founder of the naturist movement. In 1898 he published Sylvie, ou Les émois passionnés; Chair [Flesh]; and Exposé du naturisme.</td></tr>
</table>

Paris, 22 June 1898

Mon cher Gasquet,

Having read your superb lines in praise of the Provençal blood, I cannot remain silent, as if I had the misfortune to be faced with a vulgar Geffroy.[1]

It remains to add that the finished work is unequal to your praise of it. But for you that's normal, and you see things through such a prism that any word of thanks must pale.

Please be so good as to tell Paul [Cézanne's son] when I may see you again?

In sending my most heartfelt thanks, I would ask you to give my respects to Madame Gasquet.

Paul Cézanne

1   Cézanne is referring to Gasquet's 'Le sang provençal', in *Les Mois dorés* – a review of *La Société provençale à la fin du Moyen-âge*, by the Aixois historian Charles de Ribbe.

188 • TO HENRI GASQUET

Paris, 23 December 1898

Mon cher Henri,

I've just received the kind memoir you were good enough to send me. I can only thank you warmly. For me it's an evocation of more than forty years ago. Can I say that it was providence that introduced me to you? If I were younger, I would say that it's a support and comfort for me. Someone so steadfast – that's astonishing. Please thank your son as well, getting to know him is a heaven-sent gift, and his friendship is very precious to me.

I hope I shall see him again soon, either when I come down to the Midi or if his studies and literary interests bring him back here. He, Madame Gasquet and their friends have their future before them. I wholeheartedly support the artistic movement that they are establishing and making their own. You have no idea how invigorating it is to find yourself surrounded by young people gracious enough not to bury you on the spot, so I can only extend my most sincere wishes for their success.

I shan't dwell on this any longer here; it's better to talk face-to-face – one always explains oneself and makes oneself better understood that way.

In closing, please remember me to your mother, who, in your house, is the mother of the wisdom that you have. I know that she cherishes the memory of the Rue Suffren that was our cradle. It's impossible to be unmoved when we recall those bygone days, and that atmosphere we breathed unawares, which is no doubt the source of our outlook today.

Mon cher Henri, in sending my warmest greetings to your family, allow me to embrace you with all my heart.

Your old comrade,

Paul Cézanne

189 · TO ÉMILE SOLARI

Paris, 25 February [1899?]

Mon cher Émile,
Two sittings a day with the model are more than enough to wear me out. And that is how it has been for several weeks [working on his portrait of Vollard]. Tomorrow, Sunday, rest.

Would you like to come and see me in the studio during the afternoon? I'll be there from 2.00 till 4.00.

Yours very cordially.

Paul Cézanne

Portrait of Ambroise Vollard, 1899.
Oil on canvas, 100 x 81 cm (39⅜ x 31⅞ in.).

Paris, 3 April 1899

Mon cher Monet,

I am entirely with you in the action that you have taken, and I shall do my best not to be too inferior to the works of the artists with whom I am going to appear [at a sale for the benefit of Alfred Sisley's children].

At a convenient moment I will send the canvases that I am planning to contribute to Georges Petit.

Please accept my thanks, *mon cher Monet,* for the opportunity that you have given me to be in such good company, and believe me yours very cordially,

Paul Cézanne

Forgive the delay in my reply. I have only just received your letter dated 27th last.

Paris, 16 May 1899

Ma chère nièce,

Yesterday I received your letter inviting us to attend your first communion. Aunt Hortense, your cousin Paul and myself are very touched by your kind invitation. To our great regret, however, the great distance between us and Marseille prevents us from being with you at that beautiful ceremony.

At present I am detained in Paris by a fairly lengthy piece of work [a portrait of Vollard, R811], but I hope to come down to the Midi sometime next month.

So I shall soon have the pleasure of giving you a hug. Remember me in your prayers, for once we have begun to grow old, we can find no greater support and consolation than in religion.

With thanks for your kind thought, I send greetings from Aunt Hortense, cousin Paul, and a big kiss from your old uncle.

Paul Cézanne

Please say hello to your sisters Paulette and Cécile.

1 Marthe Conil (1882–1969), eldest child of Rose Cézanne and Maxime Conil.

192 • TO EGISTO FABBRI[1]

Paris, 31 May 1899

Monsieur,

The number of my studies to which you have given hospitality is proof of the great artistic sympathy you have shown me.

I could not possibly resist your most flattering desire to make my acquaintance. The anxiety of falling short of what is expected of a person assumed to be on top of every situation is doubtless the excuse for choosing to live in seclusion.

Monsieur, please accept my respects.

Paul Cézanne
15 Rue Hégésippe Moreau
Villa des Arts

1 Egisto Fabbri (1866–1933) was born in New York to an Italian father and American mother. In 1885 he moved to his ancestral home in Florence. He painted with Pissarro, and began buying Cézannes at a time when most people would not have given them houseroom. By 1899 he had sixteen; he went on to amass a total of thirty-three. He wrote to Cézanne of their 'aristocratic and austere beauty – for me, they represent what is most noble in modern art', and requested an audience in order to tell the artist in person something of the feelings the works inspired in him.

Paris, 3 June 1899

Mon cher Henri,

Last month I received an issue of *Le Mémorial d'Aix*, which published as its leading article a splendid piece by Joachim on the ancient rights of our region. I was touched by his recollection and I'd be grateful if you would pass on to him the feelings that he has awakened in me, your old classmate at the St Joseph school, for we are not forever numb to the vibrations of those *sensations* activated by that lovely Provençal sun, our old childhood memories, those horizons, those landscapes, those unbelievable lines that have left such a deep impression on us.

When I come down to Aix I'll come and give you a hug. For the time being I continue to seek to express those confused *sensations* that we bring with us into the world. If I die, it will all be over, but no matter. If I come to Aix first or if you should come to Paris beforehand, please think of me; let me know and we'll get together.

Please give my respects and good wishes to Madame Gasquet your mother, and my best regards to your son and his wife, and for yourself, in the hope of seeing you soon, the fond memory of your old comrade,

Paul Cézanne

1900

194 • 10 July 1900
195 • early August 1900
196 • 11 August 1900

1901

197 • 4 January 1901
198 • 5 June 1901
199 • 17 June 1901
200 • 22 July 1901
201 • October 1901
202 • 20 November 1901
203 • *c.* 1901?

1902

204 • 16 January 1902
205 • 23 January 1902
206 • 28 January 1902
207 • 3 February 1902
208 • 3 February 1902
209 • 10 March 1902
210 • 11 March 1902
211 • 17 March 1902
212 • 17 March 1902
213 • March 1902
214 • 2 April 1902
215 • 10 May 1902
216 • 12 May 1902
217 • 17 May 1902
218 • 8 July 1902
219 • 16 July 1902
220 • 1 September 1902
221 • 22 November 1902

1903

222 • 9 January 1903
223 • 22 February 1903
224 • March 1903
225 • 25 June 1903
226 • 11 July 1903
227 • 5 September 1903
228 • 13 September 1903
229 • 25 September 1903

1904

230 • 17 January 1904
231 • 25 January 1904
232 • 29 January 1904
233 • 15 April 1904
234 • 12 May 1904
235 • 26 May 1904
236 • 27 June 1904
237 • 25 July 1904
238 • 27 July 1904
239 • 24 September 1904
240 • 11 October 1904
241 • 11 November 1904
242 • 9 December 1904
243 • 23 December 1904
244 • 1904

1905

245 • 5 January 1905
246 • 7 January 1905
247 • 10 January 1905
248 • 23 January 1905
249 • 23 March 1905

250 • 20 April 1905
251 • 6 July 1905
252 • 14 July 1905
253 • Friday 1905
254 • 10 September 1905
255 • 23 October 1905

1906

256 • 22 February 1906
257 • *c.* 1906?
258 • 16 March 1906
259 • 20 July 1906
260 • 24 July 1906
261 • 25 July 1906
262 • 3 August 1906
263 • 12 August 1906
264 • 14 August 1906
265 • 26 August 1906
266 • 2 September 1906
267 • 8 September 1906
268 • 13 September 1906
269 • 21 September 1906
270 • 22 September 1906
271 • 26 September 1906
272 • 28 September 1906
273 • 8 October 1906
274 • 13 October 1906
275 • 15 October 1906
276 • 17 October 1906
277 • 20 October 1906
278 • 22 October 1906

1900s

Aix, 11 8bre, 1904.

Cher Monsieur,

ma réponse est tardive
J'aurais tenu à...
des marques d'estime et
d'intérêt... il y a aux de
votre lettre
Je me demande
pas mieux que de
répondre favorablement
à votre désir, si
tout cela dit la bonne
pour moi à vous faire
l'expression de mes

Letter to Gaston Bernheim-Jeune, 11 October 1904.

Aix, 10 July 1900

Monsieur,

I have the honour to send you the information you were kind enough to request [for the Exposition Centennale].

Born in Aix-en-Provence in 1839.

Yours faithfully,

Paul Cézanne

Aix, Sunday [early] August 1900

Mon cher Gasquet,

I am returning the article you lent me, which I read with great pleasure. It admirably sets off the verses you devoted to the picture of rustic life in your fine poems. And now that you are *master of the expression* of your feelings, I too think that, offering work of this quality, you will receive public recognition of your talent.

Please accept my best regards and my hopes for your future success.

Paul Cézanne

196 · TO JOACHIM GASQUET

Aix, 11 August 1900

Mon cher Gasquet,
I am ill and cannot come and thank you as I should have liked to do. I shall come and say hello as soon as possible.

Very cordially,

Paul Cézanne

197 · TO JOACHIM GASQUET

Aix, 4 January 1901

Mon cher Gasquet,
I thank you for the kind letter you wrote to me. It proves to me that you have not dropped me. If isolation causes the strong to falter, it is a real stumbling-block to the waverers. I confess that it is always dispiriting to give up life while we are on earth. Morally in solidarity with you, I shall hold out to the bitter end.

P. Cézanne

Aix, 5 June 1901

Monsieur,
Through the press I learned of the demonstration of your artistic sympathy towards me, exhibited at the Salon of the Société Nationale des Beaux-Arts.

Please accept this expression of my deepest gratitude and be good enough to convey it to the artists who joined with you on this occasion.

P. Cézanne

Still Life with Compotier, 1879–80.
Oil on canvas, 46.4 x 54.6 cm (18¼ x 21½ in.).

Maurice Denis, *Homage to Cézanne*, 1901.
Oil on canvas, 182 x 243.5 cm (71⅝ x 95⅞ in.).

1 Maurice Denis (1870–1943), who had exhibited his *Homage to Cézanne*. The painting is
   set in the shop of Ambroise Vollard, Cézanne's dealer at this point (see letter 200).
   Cézanne's *Still Life with Compotier* (R418) is on the easel. Gathered round it are Odilon
   Redon, Édouard Vuillard, André Mellerio, Vollard, Denis himself, Paul Sérusier, Paul
   Ranson, Ker-Xavier Roussel and Pierre Bonnard. Sérusier is holding forth; Redon is
   cleaning his glasses, the better to see his point. In a corner Marthe Denis, the painter's
   wife, looks out knowingly from behind a veil. Vollard, head and shoulders above the
   rest, seems almost to ascend the upright of the easel; his ever-present cat, Ambroise,
   crouches at its base, a malevolent look in his eye, as if about to pounce on Sérusier's
   foot to quiet him.

Aix, 17 June 1901

Mon cher Gasquet,

I received *L'Ombre et les vents,* which you sent me. How kind of you to have thought of the recipient. I shall read it carefully, but already, in leafing through it, exquisite and heady aromas have been emitted.

I have no doubt that you will have the great success that you deserve.

Yesterday, Sunday, I saw your father and his mother who ask you not to forget them.

Please give my regards to Madame Gasquet, and I hope that your success will be followed by many more.

Very cordially yours,

Paul Cézanne

200 • TO AMBROISE VOLLARD[1]

Aix, 22 July 1901

Cher Monsieur Vollard,

I have forwarded you today by road the canvases and the pastel. You or Paul [Cézanne's son] put me on the track of the maker, who is none other than Guillaumin (Paul has just written to me).

Very cordially, you are in my thoughts, and warm thanks,

Paul Cézanne

So it is a false attribution.

1   Ambroise Vollard (1865–1939), latterly Cézanne's dealer, and the organizer of his first one-man show in 1895. 'Cézanne was the great romance of Vollard's life,' as Gertrude

Stein said. Tanguy had introduced them from beyond the grave. Vollard bought his first Cézannes at the Tanguy sale in 1894, at absurdly low prices (between 95 and 215 francs). He sold them within a year, turning a profit of 1,000 francs. In the early days he operated as a kind of privateer, cruising and pillaging as the opportunity arose, rarely holding onto any of his plunder for very long. Soon he could stockpile with impunity. For about a decade, coinciding with the last ten years of Cézanne's life (1896–1906), Vollard acquired an effective monopoly on his work. According to the catalogue raisonné of Cézanne's paintings, no fewer than 678, more than two-thirds of his lifetime production, passed through Vollard's hands – almost certainly a significant underestimate, given the prevalence of off-the-record transactions and the impenetrable character of the dealer's books. Vollard seized his chance. He emptied the artist's studio of a huge cache of oil paintings and watercolours, snapped up any unconsidered trifles, propositioned every Cézanne owner, and established a remarkably close relationship first with Cézanne's son, and then with Cézanne himself – a relationship never broken. In time, this relationship made Vollard's fortune and Cézanne's reputation. The fortune came first. At his death in 1939, Ambroise Vollard must have been one of the richest men on earth.

201 · **TO LOUIS AURENCHE**[1]

[Café Clément, Aix, October 1901]

Cher Monsieur Aurenche,

If I were not under the powerful sway of the poet [Léo] Larguier, I would let drop some well-turned phrases. But I'm only a poor painter and doubtless the brush is what heaven has put into my hands as a means of expression instead. So having ideas and developing them is not my province. I shall be brief – I hope that your trials will soon come to an end, and that your liberation will permit us a warm and friendly greeting.

He who entered the career of life before you wishes you the best of luck.

Paul Cézanne

1 Louis Aurenche (1877–1952), a young writer who was absorbed for a while into Joachim Gasquet's circle and later wrote a memoir of Cézanne, published in John Rewald's *Cézanne, Geffroy et Gasquet* (1960).

202 · TO LOUIS AURENCHE

Aix, 20 November 1901

Cher Monsieur Aurenche,

My pen is clogged up – please excuse the handwriting, which I hope will still allow a glimpse of the pleasure that reading your letter has given me.

Yesterday evening, the 19th inst., Léo Larguier and the undersigned dined together. We talked about all manner of things; as you can well imagine, you were not forgotten in our conversation, quite the contrary. Since we are well aware of your profoundly human feelings, we could not but sympathize with you. *Homo sum: nihil humani a me*, etc.[1]

I had the pleasure of making the acquaintance of Monsieur [Pierre] Léris [a young friend of Aurenche's], who has all the appeal of his years and the exquisite qualities with which a benevolent nature has endowed him.

You refer in your letter to Monsieur de Taxis. He is, I believe, an excellent man whose acquaintance should be cultivated; reason, that clarity which allows us to see into the issues with which we are faced, seems to me to be his guide in life and in his social studies. As you say, we will not be far apart, and neither you nor I will forget each other.

Yesterday evening I received news of my rascal of a son, who is gliding through life waiting to become a sober citizen. He is leaving [Paris] a week on Friday, that is the 29th, to land in Aix on the 30th of this month. If you can send me a note with the date of your arrival, we shall arrange it so that we can all dine together here in Aix.

I hope that this letter finds you in good spirits; have courage and we shall try to spend some more pleasant evenings together philosophizing at length. *Les Jo* [the Gasquets] seem to have moderated their arrogance somewhat (*nescio cur*) [I don't know why], though it hardly signifies.

Very cordially yours. One who preceded you in life and who – plodding along – will very probably precede you out of it, your old

Paul Cézanne

ı   Strictly, 'Homo sum: humani nil a me alienum puto': 'I am a man: I count nothing human foreign to me'. The quotation is from *The Self-Tormentor* by the Roman playwright Terence.

203 · TO GUSTAVE HEIRIÈS¹ [?] [incomplete]

[Aix, *c.* 1901?]

[…]

I have perhaps come too soon. I was the painter of your generation more than my own. You are young, you have vitality, you will imbue your art with a force that only those with emotion can give. As for me, I'm getting old. I won't have time to express myself. … Let's get to work.

[…]

The reading of the model and its realization are sometimes very slow in coming.

ı   One of Joachim Gasquet's circle.

Aix, 16 January 1902

Mon cher Monet,

Thank you for taking the trouble to forewarn me of the imminent arrival in the good city of Aix of that enlightened friend of the Arts [unknown]. I shall receive him with the consideration and proprieties due to a person driven by such magnificent intentions. The opportunity that you have given me to hear your news touched me deeply, and I shall take advantage of it to thank you with a good slap on the back – you the promoter of the Impressionist movement.

My best regards, *mon cher Monet,* and good wishes from one of those you have not forgotten,
Very cordially yours,

Paul Cézanne

Aix, 23 January 1902

Cher Monsieur Vollard,

A few days ago we received the case of wine you were kind enough to send us. Since then your last letter has reached me. I am still working on the bouquet of flowers, which will probably take me until 15 or 20 February.[1] I will have it carefully packed and sent to you at Rue Laffitte. When it arrives, please be so good as to have it framed and entered [for the Salon].

The weather is very changeable; sometimes beautiful sunshine, followed unexpectedly by heavy slate-grey days, which complicates landscape work.

Paul and my wife join me in thanking you, and for my part warm thanks for the magnificent gift you have made me of the work of the great Master.[2]

Please accept my best regards.

Paul Cézanne

1   This bouquet of flowers (R893) was not finished in time for the 1902 Salon (see letter 214); it was abandoned one year later (see letter 222).

2   Another *Bouquet of Flowers* (1848–50), a watercolour by Delacroix, bought by Vollard at the Chocquet sale in 1899 for 1,325 francs after a tip-off from Cézanne. It was copied by Cézanne sometime during the period 1902–04 (R894).

206 · TO CHARLES CAMOIN[1]

Aix, 28 January 1902

Cher Monsieur Camoin,

Many days have passed since I had the pleasure of a letter from you. I have little to tell you; indeed, we can talk more, and perhaps better, about painting when *sur le motif* rather than devising purely speculative theories, in which we often get lost. I have often thought of you during my long hours of solitude. Monsieur Aurenche has been appointed tax collector in Pierrelatte in the Dauphiné. Monsieur Larguier, whom I see fairly often, especially on Sundays, gave me your letter. He yearns for his release [from military service], which will come in six or seven months. My son, who is here, has made his acquaintance, and they often go out and spend the evening together; they chat about literature and the future of art. When his army service is over, Monsieur Larguier will probably return to Paris to continue his studies (moral and political science) in the Rue Saint-Guillaume, where Monsieur Hanoteaux in particular teaches, without giving up poetry,

Eugène Delacroix, *Bouquet of Flowers*, c. 1849.
Watercolour, gouache and pastel on paper, 65 x 64 cm (25⅝ x 25¼ in.).

Bouquet of Flowers, after Delacroix, 1902–04.
Oil on canvas, 77 x 64 cm (30⅜ x 25¼ in.).

Vase of Flowers, 1900–03. Oil on canvas,
101 x 81.9 cm (39¾ x 32¼ in.).

of course. My son will go back, too, so he will have the pleasure of making your acquaintance when you return to the capital.

Vollard passed through Aix some two weeks ago. I've had news of Monet, and a card from Louis Leydet, the son of the senator from the Aix district. The latter is a painter, he is currently in Paris and has the same ideas as you and I. So you see a new artistic era is coming, as you foretold; continue to study unwaveringly, God will do the rest. I close wishing you good luck; good studies, and success will not fail to crown your efforts.

Believe me most sincerely with you, and long live our native land, our common mother and land of hope, and please accept my heartfelt thanks for your good wishes.

Your devoted,

Paul Cézanne

1   Charles Camoin (1879–1965) was a pupil in Gustave Moreau's studio in 1898, where he met Albert Marquet, who introduced him to Matisse. He was recommended to Cézanne by Vollard. Like the young poet Léo Larguier, Camoin did his military service in Aix. Cézanne was very fond of them both.

207 · TO CHARLES CAMOIN

Aix, 3 February 1902

Cher Monsieur Camoin,
I received your last letter only on Saturday. I sent my reply to Avignon. Today, the 3rd, I find in my letterbox your letter of 2 February from Paris. Larguier was ill last week and kept in hospital, which explains the delay in forwarding your letter.

Since you're in Paris and the masters of the Louvre appeal to you, do studies from the great decorative masters Veronese and Rubens, but as you would from nature – which I myself have never quite succeeded in doing.

But above all you should really study from nature. From what I've seen of you, you'll make rapid progress. I'm glad to hear that you like Vollard, who is at once sincere and serious. I am truly happy that you are with your mother, who will be the surest moral support for you in moments of sadness and dejection, and the most vital source of renewed courage to work at your art, which one must strive to achieve, not weakly and half-heartedly, but rather calmly and consistently, which will surely lead to a state of clear-sightedness very useful for guiding one firmly through life.[1]

Thank you for the very brotherly way in which you view my attempts to express myself lucidly in painting.[2]

In the hope that I shall have the pleasure of seeing you again one day, I send you warm and affectionate wishes.

Your old colleague.

Paul Cézanne

1 Cézanne had definite ideas about the moral purpose of mothers. He was very close to his own mother; more unexpectedly, perhaps, he found support in his reading. Thomas Couture's handbook of advice for artists, *Méthode et entretiens d'atelier* (1867), emphasizes the role of the mother. 'Yes, in women, above all in your mother, you will find your best counsellor.'

2 Camoin had suggested that Baudelaire's 'Les Phares' ('The Beacons') now had a verse missing. The poem is a paean to Rubens, Leonardo, Puget, Watteau, Goya and Delacroix – artists esteemed by Cézanne. Coincidentally or otherwise, the verse on his idol Delacroix yokes the name of the painter with that of his favourite composer:

> Delacroix, lake of blood, the evil angels' haunts,
> Shaded within a wood of fir trees always green;
> Under a gloomy sky, strange fanfares pass away
> And disappear, like one of Weber's smothered sighs.

Aix, 3 February 1902

Cher Monsieur Aurenche,

I received your kind letter a few days ago and it made me very happy. All the good memories you evoke come back to me. I was extremely sorry to see you go, however life is nothing but a continual journey. And being with you perked me up; it was selfishness, finding new friends in the steppes of good old Aix. I haven't been able to feel close to anyone here. Today, with the sky full of overhanging grey clouds, I see things in an even darker light.

I see Léris very rarely; my son, who goes out often, meets him frequently. Larguier, who is a very well-balanced fellow, does me the honour of dining here at the house on Sunday evenings, with my wife and Paul. We miss you.

Larguier has been promoted to Corporal. I received a long letter from Camoin and I replied in paternal vein, as befits my age. The painting plods along. Sometimes I have flights of enthusiasm, more often painful disappointments. Such is life.

I'm very pleased by the news you give me of the presence of Madier de Montjau [the former conductor of the Paris Opéra] in Pierrelatte. I don't doubt that he is a deeply serious artist, not only in his talent, but also in his heart. In my youth (we were then in the sixth grade, with Père Brémond, nicknamed 'Pupille' [orphan]) there was also Edgard de Julienne d'Arc who was killed at Gravelotte [in 1870]. He was already a virtuoso. Please pass on to him [Madier] my gratitude for having remembered our time at the Collège Bourbon.

Paul, my son, who was sorry to see you go, and my wife join me in sending you greetings. I would be very happy if you were to come to Aix next April. Léo [Larguier] will still be here and I invite you to stay with me here at 23 Rue Boulegon, if you are free.

My best wishes. When you are sad, think of old friends and do not give up art altogether; it is the most intimate expression of ourselves.

Thank you for your kind thoughts, and very cordially yours.

P. Cézanne

Aix, 10 March 1902

Cher Monsieur Aurenche,

I am very late in replying to your last letter. The cause is the *brain trouble* from which *I suffer* and which permits me to be guided only by the model in painting.

Here, then, is what I propose. Can you delay your arrival in Aix until May; for otherwise I could not offer you hospitality at home since my son will be using his room at that time. In May, he's returning to Paris with his mother, who is not very well.

Larguier has been in hospital for a fortnight with eye trouble called *conjunctivitis.* I have not set eye on the Gasquets of either sex. They have acquired a château in Eguilles, a hamlet ten kilometres from Aix. Château life is going full swing; Abbé Tardif is going to buy a car, a luxury model, to get out there. They say he's a distinguished preacher.

As for me, I'm painfully pursuing my painting studies. If I were young, it might have produced some *cash.* But old age is man's great enemy.

Walking along the main road to Marseille, I had the honour to meet Madame de Taxis. I had the honour of saluting her and all the usual courtesies.

Very cordially yours.

Paul Cézanne

[Who is] obliged to concede that he is not one of the most wretched of the earth. A little confidence in yourself, and work. Never forget your art, *sic itur ad astra* [thus one reaches the stars].[1]

I   More Virgil, from the *Aeneid*, 9.641. Aeneas gives heart to his son, Ascanius: 'Macte nova virtute, puer; sic itur ad astra': 'Blessings on your young courage, boy; thus one reaches the stars.'

Aix, 11 March 1902

Cher Monsieur Camoin,
On the first question, I must tell you that I know Monsieur Louis Leydet, the senator's son, only as a painter, he is a charming fellow and I believe you can go and see him, mentioning my name. I am sorry that he has not come to Aix at all, I think we would have been able to strengthen the bonds of artistic comradeship already established between us. He lives with his father the senator at 85 Boulevard Saint-Michel [Paris].

On the second question, I would reply: I believe absolutely in Vollard as an honest man. Since your departure, the Bernheims [Josse and Gaston Bernheim-Jeune] and another dealer have been to see me. But I remain faithful to Vollard, and am only sorry that my son has left him with the impression that I might take my canvases elsewhere.

I am having a studio built on a piece of land that I acquired for the purpose, and Vollard will certainly continue to be my intermediary with the public. He's a man of tremendous flair, good bearing and sense of propriety.

Please believe me yours cordially,

P. Cézanne

Aix, 17 March 1902

Cher Monsieur Vollard,
I have received a letter from Maurice Denis saying that he regards my abstaining from taking part in the Indépendants exhibition as tantamount to desertion.

I am replying to Maurice Denis telling him that I am asking you to put at his disposal the canvases that you can lend him and to choose those that will do the least harm.

Please believe me yours very cordially.

P. Cézanne

I seem to find it difficult to dissociate myself from young people who have shown such sympathy towards me, and I do not think that exhibiting will compromise my studies in any way.

P. Cézanne

If this causes you any inconvenience, please let me know.

212 · TO MAURICE DENIS

Aix, 17 March 1902

Monsieur et confrère,
On receipt of your letter of the 15th, by which I was very touched, I wrote immediately to Vollard so that he should put at your disposal the canvases you judge suitable for showing at the Indépendants.

Please believe me very cordially yours,

P. Cézanne

[Aix] March 1902

Cher Monsieur Aurenche,

I have a lot of work to do; that is what happens to everyone who is someone [serious]. Thus I cannot allow myself to be disturbed this year. I strongly urge you to work intellectually; that is the only true recourse we have here on earth to take our mind off the worries that hound us.

Very cordially yours.

Paul Cézanne

214 • TO AMBROISE VOLLARD

Aix, 2 April 1902

Cher Monsieur Vollard,

I am obliged to put off sending the canvas of your *Roses* [*Bouquet of Flowers*] to a later date. Although I should have liked very much to send something to the 1902 Salon, I am postponing that project again this year. I am not satisfied with the outcome thus far. On the other hand I am not giving up the pursuit of my study, which involves making efforts that will not be fruitless, I like to think. I have had a studio built on a little plot that I bought with that in mind.

So I'm pursuing my researches, and will keep you apprised of the results as soon as my work offers me a trace of satisfaction.

Please believe me very cordially yours

Paul Cézanne

Aix, 10 May 1902

Cher Monsieur Vollard,
De Montigny, distinguished member of the Société des Amis des Arts d'Aix, Chevalier of the Légion d'Honneur, has just invited me to show something with them.

I should therefore like to ask you to send something that would not look too bad, frame it at my expense, of course, and send it posthaste to the Société des Amis des Arts d'Aix-en-Provence, Bouches-du-Rhône, 2 Avenue Victor-Hugo.

Aix, 12 May 1902

Mon cher Gasquet,
Invited by Monsieur de Montigny to show at the Société des Amis des Arts, I find I have nothing ready. The aforementioned distinguished colleague has just been to see me *iterum* [again] and asks if you would be so good as to lend them the head of the old woman [*Old Woman with a Rosary*, R808], the former maid of Marie [Joseph] Demolins, major contributor to the review you direct.

Please accept this expression of my deep feelings of co-citizenship,

P. Cézanne

If it does not have a frame, please let me know, and I will do the necessary.

Old Woman with a Rosary, c. 1895–96. Oil on canvas,
80.6 x 65.5 cm (31¾ x 25¾ in.).

Aix, 17 May 1902

Mon cher Gasquet,

Thank you for the salutary advice you were kind enough to give me. I shall make use of it.

I believe you made a wise move isolating yourself in the country. You should be able to work marvellously well there.

As soon as I have recovered from these latest upheavals, I shall come and say hello.

Thank you, very cordially yours.

P. Cézanne

Aix, 8 July 1902

Mon cher Gasquet,

Solari came to the house yesterday. I was out. According to the tale told by my housekeeper, I gather that you are unable to understand why I broke my word with regard to my planned stay at Font Laure [Gasquet's 'château' in the country].

I am pursuing success through work. I despise all living painters, except Monet and Renoir, and I want to succeed through work.

As soon as an opportune moment arises, I shall come and say hello.

You have to have the stomach for it, and after that there's nothing but work.

Very cordially yours.

Paul Cézanne

I did have a study, begun two years ago; I had hoped to pursue it. The weather has eventually turned fine.

219 · TO LOUIS AURENCHE

Aix, 16 July 1902

Cher Monsieur Aurenche,

I have just received your good news. I shall certainly be in Aix on 24, 25 and 26 July. I shall therefore have the pleasure of seeing you again, and, hoping that the Tutelary Gods of Work and Intelligence look kindly upon you.

Please accept my best regards.

Please give my respectful greetings to Madame Aurenche.

Paul Cézanne

220 · TO PAULE CONIL[1]

Aix, 1 September 1902

Ma chère filleule,

I received your nice letter on Thursday 28 August. Thank you very much for thinking of your old uncle; your remembering touches me and at the same time reminds me that I am still in the world, which might not have been so.

I well remember Establon and the once so picturesque shores of L'Estaque. Unfortunately, what we call progress is nothing but the invasion of bipeds, who won't stop until they have transformed everything into hideous streets with gas lamps and – even worse – electric light. What times we live in!

The sky that looked set for a storm has cooled the air a little, and I fear that, not being so warm, the sea won't make swimming so much fun, if indeed it permits that hygienic distraction at all.

On Thursday I went to Aunt Marie's where I stayed for dinner in the evening. There I met Thérèse Valentin, to whom I conveyed your letter, as well as to my sister.

All is in order here. Little Marie has cleaned my studio, which is finished, and I'm settling in little by little. I enjoy the thought that you might grace it with a visit when you return.

Say hello from me to your sisters and also to little Louis. A big kiss,

Your uncle

Paul Cézanne

1 Paule Conil (1885–1978), daughter of Rose, Cézanne's younger sister, and Maxime Conil.

221 · TO OCTAVE MIRBEAU

Aix, 22 November 1902

Cher Maître,
During the two years of [military] service he has spent in Aix, I have made the acquaintance of a young Cévenol with a more brilliant future [Léo Larguier, from the Cévennes]. Your kindly sympathy for all those who are struggling, of which I myself have a fond memory, allows me to hope that you will be good enough to forgive the liberty I am taking in giving him a word of introduction to you, which he will deliver in person.

I recently received personal news of *Monet*. I trust I do not appear too indiscreet?

Please accept my deepest gratitude for the good memory you have retained of our meeting at the home of the master of Giverny [Monet].

Very cordially yours,

Paul Cézanne

Aix, 9 January 1903

Cher Monsieur Vollard,

Geffroy wrote a volume, *Le Cœur et l'esprit*, where there are very fine things, among others 'Le Sentiment de l'impossible'. How has such a distinguished critic reached such a complete castration of feeling? He's become a businessman.

I work tenaciously, I glimpse the Promised Land. Will I be like the great leader of the Hebrews, or will I be able to enter?

If I am ready at the end of February I'll send you my canvas for framing and shipping to some hospitable port. I had to abandon your flowers, with which I'm not very happy. I have a big studio in the country, I'm working, I'm better off there than in town.

I've made some progress. Why so late and so laboriously? Is Art really a priesthood that requires the pure in heart, who completely surrender themselves to it? I regret the distance that separates us, for more than once I would have turned to you for moral support. I live alone, the Gasquets, the Demolins are priceless, the clan of intellectuals, good God, they're all the same. If I'm still alive we'll talk about all this again. Thank you for thinking of me.

Paul and his mother are fine, they will soon return to Paris, and they send you their best wishes.

Very cordially yours,

Paul Cézanne

Aix, 22 February 1903

Cher Monsieur Camoin,
Very tired, *64 years of age*, I beg you to forgive the long delay in answering you. It will be brief. My son, now in Paris, is a *great philosopher*. By that I don't mean the equal or the emulator of Diderot, Voltaire or Rousseau. Would you like to honour him with a visit, 31 Rue Ballu, near the Place Clichy, near the statue of General Moncey. When I write to him, I'll tell him a little about you; he is rather touchy, *incurious*, but a good boy. As a go-between he will ease the difficulty I have in coping with life.

Warmest thanks for your last letter. But I must work. Everything, *art above all*, is theory developed and applied through contact with nature. Let us talk about all this again when I next have the pleasure of seeing you.

This is the truest letter I've written to you so far.

Credo.

Very cordially yours.

P. Cézanne

When I see you, I'll talk to you more truly than *anyone* about painting. *In art* I have nothing to hide.

There is nothing but primary force, *id est temperament* [that is temperament], that can carry someone forward to the goal that he must reach.

P. Cézanne

[Aix, March 1903]

[…]

Pointless sending it to me, every day I find one under my door, not to mention copies of *L'Intransigeant* that arrive in the post.[1]

[…]

1   A poisonous attack by Henri Rochefort, the revolutionary tribune turned reactionary zealot, in *L'Intransigeant*, 9 March 1903, on Zola and his art. He described it as spearheaded by 'an ultra-Impressionist named Cézanne' and insinuated that 'Dreyfusard' painting was not only laughable, but treasonable: 'We have often stated that there were Dreyfusards long before the Dreyfus affair. All the sick minds, the perverted souls, the twisters, the distorters, are ready for the coming of the Messiah of Treason. When you see nature as interpreted by Zola and his ordinary painters, it is quite simply that patriotism and honour appear to you in the form of an officer handing over to the enemy the plans for the country's defence. The love of physical and moral ugliness is a passion like any other.' Copies of this article were distributed all over Aix; evidently there were some who took some pleasure in it. Thereafter, Cézanne's housekeeper remembered his hands trembling slightly as he opened the papers from Paris.

225 • TO JOACHIM GASQUET

Aix, 25 June 1903

Mon cher Gasquet,
I didn't have your address, which explains the delay in thanking you for what you very kindly sent me. Your father saw to its delivery. So far I've only managed to leaf through your poem.

   You have acquired the title of young master: by young I mean burdened with few years and ready for the good fight that is about to be joined.

The artistic movement that Louis Bertrand described so well in his fine preface to [Gasquet's] *Chants séculaires* is under way. March on and you will continue to clear a new way for Art leading to the Capitol.

Your very devoted compatriot and admirer.

P. Cézanne

226 • TO OCTAVE MIRBEAU

Aix, 11 July 1903

Mon cher Mirbeau,

I've just received a letter from my son, who has alerted me to the interest you have taken in me. Your moral support is so precious to me that I can't thank you enough.

I continue to seek to develop through design and colour the idea of art according to my beliefs.

Despite my advanced years, it will no doubt be given to me to see you again, and it will be a great pleasure to be able to talk with you about that artistic gift that exercises so many fine minds.

Please accept my very cordial greetings,

Paul Cézanne

Aix, 5 September 1903

Mon cher Gasquet,

I've just learned that you did me the honour of visiting Rue Boulegon. Let me explain my situation: I have six months' more work to do on the canvas I've begun; it will go and meet the fate for which it is destined at the Salon des Artistes Français. Meanwhile, I'll find a day to come and say hello. If there is some delay, the cause is the inextricable position from which I long to escape. I need either 10,000 or nothing, or, like Bourdelet and the idiots he does business with, I'll be inspecting the streets, to find out who is the wretch who has had a child before going to the Town Hall [that is, an illegitimate child], and you know that nice intellectual level.

My respects to Madame Gasquet, and warm wishes to you.

P. Cézanne,
Bête noire de Roujon.[1]

---

1 Octave Mirbeau had taken it upon himself to raise with the Director of the Beaux-Arts, Henri Roujon, the question of a decoration for Cézanne: the Legion of Honour. This was the same Roujon who was responsible for the selection of two out of five Cézannes from the Caillebotte bequest (and, later, the rejection of Cézanne's murals from the Jas de Bouffan). On his own testimony, Mirbeau broached the matter of a decoration with the utmost discretion, but to no avail. Roujon became apoplectic: 'Cézanne? You said Cézanne?' 'Yes indeed. What do you think?' 'What do I think? What do I think?'

> M. Henri Roujon, who would not manage to recover from such a dreadful shock, got up, banged his desk – a magnificent Louis XIV desk – and marched uncontrollably around the room, as if on the point of an epileptic fit, repeating: 'What do I think? You ask what do I think? Well, I think … what I would prefer … you understand … yes, what I would prefer … would be to decorate the assassin of Bourg-la-Reine [a certain Soleilland, condemned to death] … if I had known him. And how I regret at this moment not knowing him! Cézanne! Ah! Ah! Ah! Cézanne! Come on, out with it! Don't be embarrassed! You mean burning the Louvre, don't you?'

Aix, 13 September 1903

Cher Monsieur Camoin,

I was glad to get your news, and I congratulate you on being free to devote yourself entirely to your studies.

I think I mentioned to you in passing that Monet lived in Giverny; I hope that the artistic influence the Master cannot help but exert on his more or less immediate circle will make itself felt in precisely the measure that it can and should on any young artist willing to work. [Thomas] Couture used to tell his pupils: keep good company, that is, go to the Louvre.[1] But, after seeing the great masters who repose there, one must hasten to leave and, through contact with nature, revive in oneself the artistic instincts and sensations that reside within us. I regret not being able to be with you. Age wouldn't matter, if other considerations didn't prevent me leaving Aix. I hope, nevertheless, that I'll have the pleasure of seeing you again one day. Larguier is in Paris. My son is in Fontainebleau with his mother.

What can I wish you but good studies in Nature's presence, that's the best thing there is.

If you should meet the Master we both admire [Monet], remember me to him.

I believe he doesn't take very kindly to being disturbed, but realizing your sincerity he may perhaps soften a little.

Believe me very cordially yours.

Paul Cézanne

---

1 Unlike Manet, who spent a full six years with Couture, Cézanne missed out on the traditional artistic apprenticeship with an established master. He never experienced the servitude and grandeur of the studio. Thomas Couture (1815–1879) was a master to be reckoned with. He cut a figure. His *Roman Orgy*, otherwise known as *Romans of the Decadence* (or *Nero at the Circus*, as Zola had it in *L'Œuvre*), caused a sensation when it was unveiled at the Salon of 1847, and another shiver when it appeared at the 1855 World's Fair. He also had a considerable reputation as a teacher. The story was told of an exchange between preceptor and pupil, in front of a model who had been instructed

to adopt a natural pose – clothed. 'Do you pay Gilbert not to be nude?' enquired Couture delicately. 'Who is responsible for this foolishness?' 'I am,' said Manet. 'Off with you, my poor boy,' came the rejoinder, 'you will never be anything more than the Daumier of your day.' Couture was a true *maître*. 'As for me,' Cézanne would lament in later life, 'if only I'd had a master! People have no idea what Manet owed to Couture.'

Aix, 25 September 1903

Cher Monsieur Aurenche,
I am very happy to hear of the birth of your son, you will soon come to understand what a difference he will make to your life.

Paul, who is in Fontainebleau, will undertake to give my compliments in person on his return, I can't say when that will be; however, I am working tenaciously, and if the Austerlitz sun of painting shines for me we'll come as a chorus and say hello.[1]

Please give Madame Aurenche my congratulations and most respectful greetings.

Paul Cézanne

---

1 Austerlitz was the decisive battle of the War of the Third Coalition. Napoleon routed the Austrians and the Russians on 2 December 1805 under a brilliant winter sun.

[Aix] 17 January 1904

Mon cher confrère,

I received your remembrance and I thank you. If I can get up to Paris in the spring, I will come and say hello.

What I would wish you, in full artistic sympathy, is to be able to give sufficient form to the sensations we experience through contact with beautiful nature – man, woman, still life – and that the conditions should be favourable for you. Your old

P. Cézanne

Aix, 25 January 1904

Mon cher Monsieur Aurenche,

Thank you very much for the New Year's wishes sent to me by you and yours.

Please accept mine in return, and extend them to your family.

In your letter you speak to me of my *réalisation* in art. I believe I attain it more each day, if a little laboriously. For if the keen sensation of nature – and I certainly have that – is the necessary basis for all artistic conception, on which rests the grandeur and beauty of future work, knowledge of the means of expressing our emotion is no less essential, and is acquired only through very long experience.

The approval of others is a stimulant, but sometimes one needs to beware. The feeling of its strength leads to modesty.

I'm pleased by the success of our friend Larguier. Gasquet, who lives entirely in the country, I haven't seen for a long time.

Monsieur Aurenche, I am very truly yours.

Paul Cézanne

Aix, 29 January 1904

Cher Monsieur Aurenche,

I am greatly touched by your concern. At the moment I am well enough. If I did not reply to your first letter sooner, the reason is simple. After a whole day spent wrestling with the difficulties of *réalisation* in front of nature, when evening comes I feel the need to rest a little, and so I don't have the freedom of mind one needs for writing.

I don't know when I'll have the opportunity to get up to Paris. If it presents itself, I shan't forget that friends await me in Pierrelatte.

If you were to come to Marseille, I believe I would be more sure of having the pleasure of seeing you.

Monsieur Aurenche, my very best wishes.

P. Cézanne

Aix, 15 April 1904

Cher Monsieur Bernard,

When you receive this you will very probably have received a letter coming from Belgium, I believe, and addressed to you at Rue Boulegon [Cézanne's apartment]. The testimony of artistic sympathy that you are kind enough to send me by writing to me made me happy.

Allow me to repeat what I told you here: to treat nature in terms of the cylinder, the sphere and the cone, everything put in perspective, so that each side of an object, of a plane, leads to a central point. Lines parallel to the horizon give breadth, be it a section of nature or, if you prefer, the spectacle that Pater Omnipotens Oeterne Deus spreads before our eyes.[2] Lines perpendicular to this horizon give depth. Now, we men experience nature more in terms of depth than surface, whence the need to introduce into our vibrations of light, represented by reds and yellows, a sufficient quantity of blue tones, to give a sense of atmosphere.

Allow me to tell you that I've had another look at the study you did from the ground floor of the studio. It's good. I believe you need only to continue along that path. You know what should be done, and you'll soon be able to turn your back on the Gauguins and Gogs [Goghs].

Please thank Madame Bernard for the kind remembrance of the undersigned, a big kiss from Père Goriot for the children, all my respects to your good family.[3]

I   This is the first of an important series of letters addressed to the young painter Émile Bernard (1868–1941), whose unfeigned admiration and determined cultivation provoked Cézanne to some of his most intriguing reflections on art, life and self. Spiced with this first-hand evidence, Bernard's early writings are foundational texts: 'Paul Cézanne' (1904), about which they corresponded, and 'Memories of Paul Cézanne' (1907), which appeared a year after Cézanne's death, at the same time as the revelatory retrospective of his work at the 1907 Salon d'Automne. As Cézanne complained, Bernard had a penchant for theorizing. He also had form: he had already admired, cultivated and corresponded with Gauguin and Van Gogh. It is not often remarked that Cézanne (nine letters in 1904–06) and Van Gogh (twenty-two letters in 1887–89) had Bernard in common, and indeed other minor characters such as the amateur Dr Gachet and the colour merchant Père Tanguy. The comparison between those two habitual letter-writers and fabled temperaments is an interesting one – as Bernard himself must have realized, for he staged a fictitious encounter between them, in Tanguy's paint shop. Van Gogh is supposed to have shown Cézanne his work and asked for his opinion. 'After inspecting it all, Cézanne, whose character was timid but violent, said to him: "Truly, you paint like a madman!"' The invention is instructive. Bernard's testimony has the ring of authenticity, yet it is not completely reliable.

2   When the young Allen Ginsberg discovered Cézanne, as a student in 1948–49, he became an avid reader of the letters. He was especially taken with this expression, which later found its way into his homage to the artist in *Howl* (1956):

> Who dreamt and made incarnate gaps in Time & Space through
> images juxtaposed, and trapped the archangel of the soul
> between 2 visual images and joined the elemental verbs and
> set the noun and dash of consciousness together jumping
> with sensation of Pater Omnipotens Aeterna Deus.

According to his neighbour in Aix, Cyril Rougier, Cézanne would sometimes remark on how a man or a woman resembled a cylinder. Evidently he said something similar to Maurice Denis and Ker-Xavier Roussel when they visited him in 1906. He may well have found some support for this conception in his reading. As on other subjects, Cézanne was more widely read in the theoretical literature than is often supposed. His annotated copy of the 1891 edition of Jean-Pierre Thénot's *Les Règles de la perspective pratique* (1839) has only recently come to light. Thénot's *Morphologie, ou l'art de répresenter ... des corps solides* (1838) mentions the cylinder, the cone and the sphere (in that order). In *Règles du paysage* (1841) he emphasizes the value of grey, as did Cézanne.

3   Cézanne was a lifelong devotee of Balzac. He kept a battered copy of the *Études philosophiques* (1837), containing among other things *Le Chef-d'œuvre inconnu* (1831), by his bed. He advised Léo Larguier to reread Balzac, in particular the *Comédie humaine*, and talked to him of Rastignac, the protagonist of *Père Goriot* (1835). With Bernard's

children he seems to have identified himself as Goriot. The novel feasts on death obsession, and Cézanne's allusion to it has been interpreted as reinforcing the artist's own preoccupation with death. Cézanne was acutely aware of mortality and of his failing health, but here the identification seems more playful. Among other things, Goriot was a vermicelli-maker, which would have appealed to Cézanne's sense of humour, in connection with his fictional alter ego Claude Lantier in *L'Œuvre*. See letter 77.

Aix, 12 May 1904

Mon cher Bernard,

My commitment to work and my advanced age will explain well enough the delay in replying to you.

Moreover, you wrote to me about such a variety of things in your last letter, though all of them relate to art, that I cannot follow all of your argument.

As I have told you, I much admire [Odilon] Redon's talent, and I share his feeling and admiration for Delacroix. I don't know whether my precarious health will ever allow me to realize my dream of painting his apotheosis.[1]

I am proceeding very slowly. Nature appears to me very complex, and the improvements to be made are never-ending. One must see one's model clearly and feel it exactly right, and then express oneself with distinction and force.

Taste is the best judge. It is rare. Art speaks only to an excessively small group of people.

The artist should scorn all opinion not based on the intelligent observation of character. He should be wary of the mind of the *littérateur*, who so often diverts the painter from his true path, the concrete study of nature, to waste too much time in abstract speculation.

The Louvre is a good book to consult, but it should be only a means. The real, prodigious study to undertake is the diversity of the scene offered by nature.

Thank you very much for sending your book; I look forward to reading it in a restful frame of mind.

If you think it is a good idea, you can send Vollard what he asked for.

Please give Madame Bernard my respectful greetings, and a kiss for Antoine and Irène from their adoptive father.

Cordially yours,

P. Cézanne

1   The project was never fully realized. On the back of an earlier sketch for an apotheosis of Delacroix, Bernard stumbled upon another of Cézanne's verses. The original drawing has been dated to the late 1870s; Cézanne took it up again twenty years later and added some watercolour (RWC68). If the verse is contemporaneous with the sketch, then it appears that he continued to fight his talent, as he said, for longer than is generally thought – or else that the poetaster made an unscheduled return.

> Here is the young woman with the curvaceous buttocks.
> How well she flaunts herself in the setting of the meadow,
> Her supple form, splendid blossoming;
> No serpent has greater suppleness
> And the sun obligingly shines
> Some golden rays on that flesh.

The Apotheosis of Delacroix, 1878–80. Pencil, pen, ink and watercolour,
20 x 22 cm (7⅞ x 8¾ in.).

Aix, 26 May 1904

Mon cher Bernard,

I approve for the most part the ideas that you are going to develop in your forthcoming article for *L'Occident*. But I always come back to this: the painter should devote himself completely to the study of nature, and try to produce paintings that will be an education. Talking about art is virtually useless. Work that leads to progress in one's own *métier* is sufficient recompense for not being understood by imbeciles.

The *littérateur* expresses himself in abstractions while the painter gives concrete expression to his *sensations*, his perceptions, by means of line and colour. One cannot be too scrupulous, too sincere, or too submissive to nature; but one is more or less master of one's model, and above all of one's means of expression. Fathom what you have in front of you, and make every effort to express yourself as logically as possible.

Please give my respectful greetings to Madame Bernard, a warm hello to you, and remember me to the children.

Pictor P. Cézanne

Aix, 27 June 1904

Mon cher Bernard,

I received your esteemed letter of [blank], which I left in the country. If I delayed replying, it's because I've been in the grip of brain trouble, which prevented me from moving about freely. I remain in the grip of *sensations*, and, despite my age, set on painting.

The weather is fine, I'm taking advantage of it to work, I must do ten good ones, and sell them dear, since *amateurs* are speculating on them.

A letter arrived here yesterday addressed to my son, which Madame [Marie] Brémond guessed is from you, I had her forward it to 16 Rue Duperré, Paris IX arrond[issement].

It seems that Vollard had a dinner dance a few days ago, at which everyone stuffed themselves. All the younger set were there, it seems. Maurice Denis, [Édouard] Vuillard, etc., Paul met Joachim Gasquet there. I believe that the best thing is to work hard. You are young, *réalisez* and sell.

Do you remember the beautiful pastel by Chardin, equipped with a pair of spectacles with a visor shading his eyes?[1] He's a crafty one, that painter. Have you noticed how, by allowing a plane of light to cross his nose at a slight angle, the values adapt much better to the eye? Take a close look and tell me if I'm not right.

Very cordially yours, and please give my respects to Madame Bernard and remember me to Antoine and Irène.

P. Cézanne

I think Paul wrote that they had rented something in Fontainebleau for a couple of months.

I must tell you that, because of the great heat, I have lunch brought to me in the country.

1 *Self-Portrait Wearing an Eyeshade* (1775) was a late work, as Cézanne would have known, painted four years before his death. It was acquired by the Louvre in 1839.

Jean-Siméon Chardin, *Self-Portrait Wearing an Eyeshade*, 1775.
Pastel, 46 x 38 cm (18⅛ x 15 in.).

Aix, 25 July 1904

Mon cher Bernard,

I've received *La Revue occidentale* [*L'Occident*]. I can only thank you for what you have written about me.

I am sorry that we cannot be side by side, because I don't want to be right in theory, but in nature. Despite his *estyle* (Aixois pronunciation) and his admirers, Ingres is only a very minor painter. The greatest, you know them better than I, the Venetians and the Spaniards.

In order to make progress in realization, there is only nature, and an eye educated by contact with it. It becomes concentric by dint of looking and working. I mean that in an orange, an apple, a ball, a head, there is a culminating point, and this point is always the closest to our eye, the edges of objects recede towards a centre placed at eye level.[1] With only a little temperament one can be a lot of painter. One can do good things without being either a great harmonist or a great colourist. All you need is an artistic sensibility. And doubtless this sensibility horrifies the bourgeois. So institutes, pensions and honours are only for cretins, jokers and rascals. Don't be an art critic, paint. Therein lies salvation.

Warm good wishes, your old comrade,

P. Cézanne

All my respects to Madame Bernard, and remember me to the children.

[Added in the margin near 'the edges of objects':]
   despite the terrible effect, light and shade
[And near 'a little temperament':]
   sensations colorantes

---

1   It may be that the listing here, 'an orange, an apple, a ball, a head', is what Giacometti had in mind when he explained to an interviewer in 1957 the lesson he took from Cézanne:

Cézanne revolutionized the representation of the exterior world. Until then, one valid conception reigned, since the Renaissance, since Giotto, to be precise. Since that time, there had been no fundamental alteration in the way of seeing a head, for example. The change between Giotto and the Byzantines was greater than that between Giotto and the Renaissance. After all, Ingres' way of seeing was almost a continuation. Cézanne blew sky high that way of seeing by painting a head as an object. He said as much: 'I paint a head like a door, like anything else.' As he painted the left ear, he established a greater rapport between the ear and the background than between the left ear and the right ear, a greater rapport between the colour of the hair and the colour of the sweater than between the ear and the structure of the skull – and because what he himself wanted was still to achieve a whole head, he completely shattered the idea that we had before of the whole, the unity of the head. He completely shattered the bloc, so completely that first of all we pretended that the head had become a pretext, and that, in consequence, painting had become abstract. Today, every representation that seeks to return to the previous way of seeing, that is to say the Renaissance way of seeing, is no longer believable. A head whose integrity would have to be respected would no longer be a head. It would be a museum piece. (Giacometti interviewed by Georges Charbonnier, 16 April 1957, in *Le Monologue du peintre* [1959] (Paris: Durier, 1980), pp. 186–87)

The remark about the head as object testified to one of Cézanne's lessons for his successors: no hierarchy of genre or subject or patch of paint. 'Equality of all things,' as the director Robert Bresson put it in his famous *Notes on the Cinematographer* (1975): 'Cézanne painting with the same eye and the same soul a fruit dish, his son, the Mont Sainte-Victoire'.

Aix, 27 July 1904

Mon cher Gasquet,

I can't tell you how touched I was by your excellent remembrance. Shaking off my torpor, I come out of my shell and will make every effort to respond to your invitation.

I went to the [Cercle?] Musical in order to get some information from my friend, your father, about the projected journey. Please tell him to give me some idea of the trains' departure times and the place we might settle on to meet.

Very cordially yours and my respects to your family.

P. Cézanne

I read the review of your fine work in *La Provence nouvelle.*

[Aix] Friday 24 September [1904]

Mon cher Solari,

I'd like to have a sitting on Sunday morning.[1] Would you come and have lunch with me at Madame [Rosa] Berne's [restaurant] at eleven o'clock? From there we could go up to your place – see if this arrangement suits you, if not I'll try and come to you by asking directions; yours ever

P. Cézanne

1   Solari was working on a life-size bust of Cézanne in plaster.

Aix, 11 October 1904

Cher Monsieur,

My reply is late, no doubt my frail state of my health will seem sufficient excuse.

I was very touched by the marks of esteem and laudatory terms of your letter.

I should be only too pleased to respond favourably to your request [to meet], if all I have to do is to expound my theories and explain to you the goal I've been striving for all my life.

Please accept, *cher Monsieur*, the expression of my artistic sympathy.

P. Cézanne

1   Gaston Bernheim-Jeune (1870–1953), one-half of the celebrated Bernheim-Jeune deal-ership, and also an amateur painter. The Bernheim-Jeunes dealt in Cézannes whenever they could; no doubt they would have liked to supplant Vollard and deal in more. If they cultivated Cézanne's son with that in mind, they reckoned without the artist himself, who remained steadfastly loyal to Vollard (see letter 210). On this occasion, Gaston appears to have made a point of writing as a fellow artist and not as a dealer, a point underlined in Cézanne's response.

241 · PAUL CÉZANNE *FILS* TO AMBROISE VOLLARD

Aix, 11 November 1904

Cher Monsieur Vollard,

A little tardily, I acknowledge receipt of your transfer of two thousand francs, and I enclose herewith two signatures. My father is delighted with the success of the Salon d'Automne and he is most grateful to you for the care you have taken with his exhibition. He will be very happy to see the four walls of the room that was graciously devoted to him. I await the first batch of photographs that you are about to send. I will do my best to catalogue them according to date, place and type of subject, as you request. My return to Paris will be in early December. Then I will bring you the finished product of this small task.

My father is as keen as ever on his art, as you can imagine. The canvas of the bathers is making progress. The portrait of the old poacher who models for him is going well. He has started three or four landscapes, which he plans to pursue next year. He is also doing a few watercolours. The weather is favourable, for it is very fine.

My father and mother send you their best wishes.
Cordially,

Paul Cézanne f.

242 · TO CHARLES CAMOIN

Aix, 9 December 1904

Mon cher Camoin,
I received your good letter from Martigues. Come whenever you like; you will always find me at work; you can come with me to the *motif*, if you like. Let me know the day of your arrival, for if you come to the studio on the hill of Les Lauves, I'll have lunch brought up for two. I eat at eleven o'clock and after that I set off for the *motif*, unless it's raining. I have a baggage store 20 minutes from the studio.

The reading of the model and its *réalisation* is sometimes very slow in coming for the artist. Whichever master you prefer, he must be only a guide for you. Otherwise you will be nothing but a *pasticheur*. With a feeling for nature, whatever it may be, and a modicum of talent – which you have – you should be able to stand out; someone else's advice or method shouldn't make you change your way of feeling. Even if you give way momentarily to someone older than you, as soon as you become aware of it, be assured that your own emotion will emerge and find its place in the sun – *embrace it*, confidence! – you must gain possession of a good method of *construction*. Drawing is merely the configuration of what you see.

Michelangelo is a constructor, and Raphael *an artist*, who, great as he may be, is always restricted by the model. Whenever he turns reflective, he falls below the level of his great rival.

Very cordially yours,

P. Cézanne

243 · TO ÉMILE BERNARD

Aix, 23 December 1904

Mon cher Bernard,

I received your good letter sent from Naples. With you I won't dwell on aesthetic considerations. Yes, I approve of your admiration for the greatest of the Venetians, let us celebrate Tintoretto. Your need to find a moral and intellectual support in works that will certainly never be surpassed keeps you constantly on the alert, always searching for sure means that will lead you to experience before nature your [own] means of expression, and when you find them you may be sure that you will effortlessly rediscover before nature the means employed by the four or five great Venetians.

Undoubtedly – I am categorical – a *sensation optique* is produced in our visual organ that allows us to classify as highlight, half-tone and quarter-tone the planes represented by *sensations colorantes*. Light does not exist, therefore, for the painter. As long as you [we] pass inevitably from black to white, the first of these abstractions being a support for the eye as much as the brain, we flounder, we cannot achieve mastery, *self-possession*. During this period (inevitably I repeat myself), we turn to the admirable works handed down to us through the ages, where we find comfort and support, like the plank for the bather.

Everything you say in your letter is very true.

I am happy to learn that Madame Bernard, you and the children are well. My wife and son are in Paris at the moment. I hope that we will soon be together again.

I've tried to respond as fully as possible to the main points in your good letter, and I ask you please to convey my respectful greetings to Madame Bernard, to give a big kiss to Antoine and Irène, and to you, my dear colleague, with my best wishes for a happy new year, a warm hello.

P. Cézanne

244 · TO JEAN ROYÈRE [fragment]

[Aix, 1904]

[…]

[Responding to his *Poèmes eurythmiques*:]

I wanted to penetrate straightaway that keen vision that makes them stand out so clearly. Unfortunately, the great age I've reached makes it difficult for me to appreciate new artistic formulas. … At first, therefore, I was not prepared to relish the full savour of your coloured rhythms. That, in a word, explains my delay in replying …

[…]

245 · TO CHARLES CAMOIN

Aix, 5 January 1905

Mon cher Camoin,

In answer to your last letter, I can tell you that, after making inquiries, Madame Brémond says that there are rooms to let at the Crémerie d'Orléans, 16 Rue Matheron. They are on the first, second and third floor; the food is also quite good.

Very cordially yours,

P. Cézanne

246 · TO AMBROISE VOLLARD

Aix, Saturday 7 January 1905

Cher Monsieur Vollard,

I am very happy to have received your good letter, and I would be glad if you put your plan into action.

Monsieur Gasquet, known as Jo, and Monsieur Dumesnil are the most courageous protagonists of the art movement that so deeply engages the Mediterranean people and others.[1]

Please accept my best wishes for the new year,

P. Cézanne

1   Compare letters 222 and 267.

Aix, 10 January 1905

I'm sorry I won't have the pleasure of seeing you again this year. But I too send you my good wishes.

I'm still working, and without worrying about criticism and critics, as a true artist should. The work must prove me right.

I have no news of Gasquet, who is in Paris at the moment, I believe.

My best regards to you, and my respects to Madame Aurenche.

Paul Cézanne

Aix, 23 January 1905

Monsieur le Rédacteur,

I read with interest the lines you were kind enough to devote to me in the two articles in the *Gazette des Beaux-Arts*. Thank you for the favourable opinions you express in them about me.

My age and my health will never allow me to realize the artistic dream I have pursued all my life. But I shall always be grateful to the audience of intelligent art lovers who have sensed what I was trying to do to renew my art, in spite of my halting attempts.

In my opinion, one does not replace the past, one only adds a new link. With a painter's temperament and an artistic ideal, that is to say a conception of nature, there should be sufficient means of expression to be intelligible to the general public and to occupy a suitable rank in the history of art.

Please accept this expression of my keen artistic fellow feeling.

P. Cézanne

249 · TO A COLOUR MERCHANT[1]

Aix, 23 March 1905

[Cézanne writes that he is *un peu souffrant* and cannot deal with the return of some cinnabar green that he has been sent. He requests five tubes of Prussian blue and a bottle of Harlem Siccative, which he needs urgently.]

1 This letter is known only from the account given by John Rewald (*Letters*, p. 314).

250 · PAUL CÉZANNE *FILS* TO AMBROISE VOLLARD

Aix, 20 April 1905

Cher Monsieur Vollard,
The case with the five photograph albums arrived three days ago in good condition. I have not acknowledged receipt sooner, being troubled by a little rheumatism in the right shoulder.

I have just heard from my friend [Louis] Guillaume that you have collected from the framer the watercolours and drawings that you are planning to include in the forthcoming exhibition. I have been asked to send you the enclosed list of a collection of good pictures, more or less authentic, all for sale, very reasonable!!!

Please put to one side until further notice the still lifes you have on consignment, my father is not at all sure that he wants to part with them for the moment.

My father and mother say hello, and warm wishes from me.

Paul Cézanne f.

Fontainebleau, 6 July 1905

Yesterday I was pleased to take delivery of the canvases and paints that I had ordered from you, but I am awaiting impatiently the box that I had asked you to have mended for me by adding a palette with a hole big enough for my thumb.

Please send these items as soon as possible.

Regards.

P. Cézanne
8 Rue de la Coudre
(Fontainebleau)

Please add one bright yellow
and one chrome yellow No. 2.

Fontainebleau, 14 July 1905

Monsieur,
I have received your various deliveries and now request you to send me

5 burnt lake [no.] 7 (Maison Chabot)
5 Veronese green [no.] 7 or 8 from [Maison] Bourgeois –
and 5 cobalt from the same house, *same number.*

Regards,

P. Cézanne

[Aix] Friday [1905]

Mon cher Bernard,

A succinct reply to some of the paragraphs in your last letter. As you write, I do believe I've made some more very slow progress in the latest studies that you saw here. Yet it is distressing to record that the growth of one's understanding of nature, from the point of view of painting and the development of means of expression, should be accompanied by age and frailty.

If the official Salons remain so inferior, it is because they employ only more or less commonplace procedures. It would be better to introduce more personal feeling, observation and character.

The Louvre is the book from which we learn to read. However, we should not be content with holding onto the beautiful formulas of our illustrious predecessors. Let us go out to study beautiful nature, let us try to capture its spirit, let us seek to express ourselves according to our individual temperaments.

Time and reflection modify our vision, moreover, and at last we reach understanding.

In this rainy weather it is impossible to put these theories into practice outdoors, be they ever so sound. But perseverance leads us to understand interiors just like everything else. Only old residues block our intelligence, which needs spurring on.

Very cordially yours and all my respects to Madame Bernard, best regards to the children.

P. Cézanne

You will understand me better when we meet again; study so modifies our vision that the humble and colossal Pissarro seems justified in his anarchist theories.

Draw, but it is the reflection that creates the enveloping atmosphere. Light through the overall play of reflections is the enveloping atmosphere.

P.C.

[Paris?] 10 September 1905

Cher Monsieur Bernard,

I enclose the requested authorization. I hope that it is in the desired form? But my husband says that you have absolutely no need for it in Holland. One can reproduce whatever one wants, there is no law for the protection of artworks – nor books – no one can make any complaint on that subject. And since my husband is a doctor of law (he did his studies before becoming a painter) he should know!

Nevertheless, I am writing this evening to the 'Wereldbibliotheek' [publishing house in Amsterdam], which has the folios, to send us an authorization. However, if they do not do it, do not worry – it is an indication that you do not need one. ...

You saw from my previous letter that the drawings are at [illegible]. I hope those 25 drawings are enough for you? With the others that makes a reasonable total and, as I said, I can *categorically* promise the others. The choice is yours – that is all I can do. You have no idea how much trouble this causes me all the time. Now they are asking me for more exhibitions for November. I had only two months' rest this summer and I really needed them because I am worn out! In any event good luck with your book. I shall be very glad to have a copy of your South of France!

All the best to you.

MHC

Regards from my husband and son ...

1 This letter offers a striking corrective to the usual image of Hortense, and of her relationship with Cézanne. Here she is transacting business on his behalf. It has been assumed that the business, like the art, was not her province – that she was rigorously excluded, or that she effectively excluded herself, on grounds almost of diminished responsibility. Towards the end of his life Cézanne used his son as an intermediary with dealers, with Vollard in particular. That his wife may have played an active part in his affairs comes as a surprise. Yet it seems to be so. And the signs are that it was a continuing one, at

least on a relatively small scale. They appear to have discussed this matter together. What is more, the business is transacted with some aplomb, and even with a dash of wit (Cézanne as doctor of law is a nice touch). The letter as reproduced here omits one or two details of the publishers. See also letter 150, written by Hortense.

255 · TO ÉMILE BERNARD

Aix, 23 October 1905

Mon cher Bernard,

Your letters are doubly precious, in the first place purely selfishly, since their arrival relieves the monotony created by the ceaseless pursuit of the one and only goal, which in moments of physical fatigue brings on a kind of intellectual exhaustion, and secondly because they allow me to reiterate, perhaps a little too much, the stubbornness with which I pursue the *réalisation* of that part of nature that falls before our eyes and gives us the picture. So, the thesis to be expounded – whatever our temperament or strength in the presence of nature – is to give the image of what we see, forgetting everything that has appeared before us. This, I think, should allow the artist to give his whole personality, big or small.

So, old as I am, around seventy [actually sixty-six], the *sensations colorantes* that create light are the cause of abstractions that do not allow me to cover my canvas, nor to pursue the delimitation of objects when their points of contact are subtle, delicate; the result of which is that my image or painting is incomplete. On the other hand, the planes fall on top of one another, from which comes the neo-Impressionism that outlines [everything] in black, a defect that must be resisted with all one's might. But consulting nature gives us the means of achieving this goal.

I did remember that you were in Tonnerre, but the problems of moving have made me totally dependent on my family, who make use of this for their own convenience while rather forgetting me.

That's life, at my age I should have more experience, and use it for the general good.

I owe you the truth in painting and I shall tell it to you.

Please give all my respects to Madame Bernard, I must send love to the children, Saint Vincent de Paul being the one to whom I should most commend myself.

Your old

Paul Cézanne

Best wishes and courage.

Optical experience that we develop through study teaches us to see.

256 • TO KER-XAVIER ROUSSEL[1]

Aix, 22 February 1906

Cher Monsieur Roussel,

I've just received *Le Journal de Delacroix* [three volumes published in 1893–95], I accept with the greatest of pleasure, for reading it will reconfirm once again, I hope, the feeling I have about the truth of certain of my researches in nature.

I thank you very much for your kind sympathy; for me, precious testimony to the fact that my efforts towards the *réalisation* of art, to which I have always devoted myself, are not altogether in vain since I find in the young an approval that is as disinterested as it is flattering.

Best regards in artistic confraternity,

Paul Cézanne

1 Ker-Xavier Roussel (1867–1944), a young painter and ardent admirer. Roussel featured in the *Homage to Cézanne* (1901) by Maurice Denis (see p. 303). In 1906 he and Denis made the pilgrimage to Aix. They went first to the Jas de Bouffan, but it was a Sunday, and Cézanne was at mass at the cathedral of Saint-Sauveur. They arrived just as he was coming out, clad in a grey-green coat and a paint-spattered suit, his hands dirty, his head bare. They introduced themselves. Denis was pleased to find that Cézanne remembered writing to him (to thank him for the *Homage*). They wanted to give some coins to a beggar. '*Satis!* [Enough!],' exclaimed Cézanne. 'He's a drunkard. Drunkenness has its merits, but one shouldn't overdo it.' Having had his weekly helping of the Middle Ages, he was evidently in the mood to talk:

> 'Ah! The Middle Ages. Cathedrals have everything. I too liked Veronese and Zurbarán, but the seventeenth century, that's perfection! You were at the Jas de Bouffan. It's not much, but in the end it's painting. ...
>
> 'I look for the light – the cylinder and the sphere; I want to make black and white with colour, to recapture the confusion of sensations. *La sensation* above all. ...
>
> 'For the painter, pride is everything. Even [Flaubert's] Mathô in *Salammbô* and the others don't compare. You have to have pride and not let it show too much, you have to be decent. But Gauguin had too much, he amazed me. Ah! Renoir? He's too stiff. ...
>
> 'You have to have a method. My father, who was a fine man, people attacked him! My father would say: you have to play games. That's what I look for in painting. ...
>
> 'I am a milestone, others will come who ... . At my age, you dream of eternity.' (Maurice Denis's diary, 26 January 1906, in *Conversations*, p. 93–94)

[*c*. 1906?]

Don't think that our most high and noble art is taught or learned in schools or academies: what you discover there will be reworked as soon as you're able to observe forms and colours with love. Don't set so much store by the pontiffs, who live the errors they teach, as by the errors themselves: sometimes they're nothing but the distortion of an ancient truth that would appear magnificent if only we cleared away the dross that covers it and hides it.

Don't set store either by those who spout my name or argue over my wretched corpse, after my death, but rather by the worst, the most imperfect of my works. Always, after the battle, in the auspicious night, jackals and hyenas will roam.

If they give me an ovation, don't believe it; if they try to found a school in my name, tell them they never understood, never liked what I did.

---

1 This letter is known only from a book of reminiscences by Léo Larguier, *Cézanne, ou La Lutte avec l'ange de la peinture* (1947), set among Cézanne's correspondence with young artists in his last years. In the context of his late letters, this passage is rather high-flown but not impossible. Rouault (1871–1958) for his part was surely alert to Cézanne. In the early 1890s he was a fellow student of Matisse and Marquet at the École des Beaux-Arts. He commenced with religious subjects (Cézanne's letter plays on religious language). Around 1898 he underwent a psychological crisis. He began a long association with Vollard in 1906.

Aix, 16 March 1906

Cher Monsieur Vollard,

Your letter arrived this morning; but I received the notice from Crédit Lyonnais yesterday afternoon. I went there today to collect the six thousand francs that you sent me for my father's two still lifes, which you have had since 2 March 1905, for which we had set a price of three thousand francs each.

Thank you for your kind offer of assistance for the exhibition [of Provençal artists] about which I wrote to you. But since the agent has not yet written to you, I hope that he will now have the good sense to leave us in peace.

My father's state of health is not too bad at the moment. But he lost a good month of work in the snow and the winds, and then because of a bout of flu. He has resumed his studies. I will probably not return to Paris before the end of May. I hope to bring my father with me.

My parents send a friendly greeting, and I my warm regards.

Paul Cézanne f.

[Aix] Friday [20] July 1906

Mon cher Paul,

This morning, my head being fairly clear, I am replying to your two letters, which gave me great pleasure as usual.

At four-thirty in the morning – at eight the temperature will be unbearable – I continue with my studies. One needs to be young, and do a lot of them. The atmosphere is sometimes rather hazy and the tones deplorable. It's fine only at certain moments.

Thank you for the news you sent me, I'm plodding along in the same old way.

Hello to maman and to everyone who still remembers me. Hello to Madame Pissarro, how far away it all seems already and yet how near.[1]

Your father, who sends you both a hug.

Paul Cézanne

I haven't seen your aunt yet, I sent her your first letter.
Do you know where the little sketch of the Bathers is?

| Pissarro died in 1903. Cézanne's devotion to him never wavered, though they met only once (by accident) over the last twenty years of their lives. Neither of them appears to have considered this cause for remark. Proximity was not necessary for Cézanne's conduct of relationships.

260 • TO HIS SON

Aix, 24 July 1906

Mon cher Paul,
Yesterday the ghastly Abbé Gustave Roux got a carriage and came to see me once more at Jourdan's.[1] He's a leech. I promised to go and see him at the Catholic college. I won't go, you have time to send me a reply and give me your advice.

A hug for you and maman. It's very hot.

Your old father,

Paul Cézanne

| Jourdan's Cabanon (R947) may be Cézanne's last landscape.

Jourdan's Cabanon, 1906. Oil on canvas,
65 x 81 cm (25⅝ x 31⅞ in.).

Aix, 25 July 1906

Mon cher Paul,

Yesterday I received your kind letter with your news, I can only deplore the state your mother is in, care for her as much as you can, try for comfort and coolness, and appropriate distractions. Yesterday, Thursday, I was supposed to go and see the soutaned Roux. I didn't go, and that's how it will be until the end, that's still the best thing to do. He's a leech. As for Marthe [Conil, Paul's cousin?], I went to see your Aunt Marie. That's another sore point, at my age it's better to live alone and paint.

Vallier massages me, the kidneys are a bit better, Madame Brémond says the foot is better. I'm following Boissy's treatment, it's horrible.[1] It's very hot. By eight o'clock, the weather is unbearable. The two canvases of which you sent me photographs are not mine.

I embrace you both with all my heart,
Your old father,

Paul Cézanne

Say hello to Monsieur and Madame Legoupil. I'm touched by their remembering me, and they are so kind to your poor mother.

1 These afflictions relate to his diabetes, diagnosed around 1890. In the absence of medical records it is difficult to determine what exactly this meant for him – conceivably diabetic neuropathy or nerve damage; diabetic nephropathy or nephritis (inflammation of the kidneys); and diabetic retinopathy, which can lead to various forms of colour blindness (notably blue-green), blurred or double vision, and even partial or complete blindness. Contemporary physicians also described impotence as a common symptom, often the presenting one.

Aix, 3 August 1906

Mon cher Paul,

I received your kind letters of various dates quite close together. If I didn't reply immediately, it's because of the oppressive heat we're having. It fairly saps the brain and stops me from thinking.

I get up early and it's only really between five and eight that I can lead my own life. By that time the heat becomes stupefying, and saps the brain so much that I can't even think of painting. I've had to call Doctor Guillaumont, having caught bronchitis, I've abandoned homeopathy for old-fashioned mixed syrups. I coughed a good deal, Mother Brémond applied some cotton wool in iodine, and that helped. I regret my advanced age, because of my *sensations colorantes*. I'm pleased to hear that you see Monsieur and Madame Legoupil, who are very steady, and should bring some calm into your life. I'm happy to hear of the good relationship you have with the artistic intermediaries to the public, who I hope will persist in being favourably disposed towards me.

It's a shame that I can't give many demonstrations of my ideas and *sensations*, long live the Goncourts, Pissarro, and all those who have a propensity for colour, which represents light and air. I know that with the terrible heat you and maman will be tired; so it's a good thing that you were both able to get back to Paris in time to find yourselves in a less burning atmosphere. As for my foot, it's not doing too badly at the moment. I'm very touched by the kind remembrance of [Jean-Louis] Forain and Léon Dierx, whom I've known for quite a long time. Forain, in the Louvre in 75, and Léon Dierx at Nina de Villars's in the Rue des Moines in 77.

I must have told you that when I used to dine at the Rue des Moines, the guests included Paul Alexis, Franck Lami [Franc-Lamy], Marast, Ernest d'Hervilly, [Villiers de] L'Isle Adam, and many hearty trenchermen, the late lamented Cabaner.[1] Alas, such memories, engulfed in the abyss of years. I think I've answered almost everything you asked me. Now I must remind you not to forget the slippers, the ones I have are just about giving up on me.

I embrace you and maman with all my heart,
Your old father,

Paul Cézanne

1 At the salons of Nina de Villars, 'the princess of Bohemia', artists, writers and musicians
   would dine, surrounded by her cats, dogs, parrots, squirrel and monkey. These soirées
   are evoked in Paul Alexis's novel *Madame Meuriot* (1890), featuring the hostess Eva de
   Pommeuse and thinly veiled portraits of Manet, Mallarmé and 'Kabaner' (Cabaner).
   Cézanne appears as Poldex (Paul d'Aix) – 'a kind of colossus, gauche and bald, an old
   child, naïf, inspired, at once timid and violent, the only one who really understood
   Kabaner'. Alexis highlighted Poldex's temperament, his awkwardness and his struggle:
   'Engrossed in the problems of his art, everything he could never capture, the miseries
   of the métier, banging his fist on the wall, he repeated endlessly, *Nom de Dieu! Nom
   de Dieu!*'

263 · TO HIS SON

Aix, 12 August 1906

Mon cher Paul,
It's been unbearably hot for days; today, this morning in particular, it was
fine from five o'clock, when I got up, to about eight. The pain I feel gets
so exasperating that I can't keep it under control any longer, and it drives
me to live a withdrawn life, which is the best thing for me. At Saint-
Sauveur [the cathedral], the old choirmaster Poncet has been succeeded by
an idiot of a abbot who takes charge of the organ and plays out of tune.
So much so, that I can't even go to mass, his way of playing makes me feel
positively ill.

I think that to be a Catholic one must be devoid of all sense of justice,
but have an eye to the main chance.

Two days ago Sire Rolland came to see me; he engaged me in conversation about painting. He offered to pose for me as a bather on the banks of the Arc. That quite appealed to me, but I'm afraid that gentleman only wants to get his hands on my study; however, I'm almost tempted to try something with him. I demolished Gasquet and his Mardrus for him; he told me he was reading the *Thousand and One Nights* in Galland's translation.[1] He seems to understand that influence can help us get ahead, but that in the long run the public becomes aware of what one is up to. I hope that the heat will pass as soon as possible and above all that you and your mother aren't suffering too much.

You must have received Aunt Marie's letter.

When you get the chance, say hello to our friends there. I've had no further news of Émile Bernard, I fear that he's not overwhelmed with commissions.

A bohemian gent from Lyon came to borrow a few sous, he seemed to be in a frightful mess.[2]

I embrace you both with all my heart.
Your old father,

Paul Cézanne

The heat is getting stultifying again.
I remind you about the slippers.

1 Another jibe at Gasquet. Cézanne favoured the translation of the *Thousand and One Nights* by Antoine Galland, from 1704–17. A new translation by J. C. Mardrus appeared in 1898–1904. Accordingly to Larguier, Mardrus was no fan of Cézanne.

2 Rewald speculated that this gent was the poet-tramp Germain Nouveau (1851–1920), Cézanne's former classmate at the Collège Bourbon. Cézanne gave generously to Nouveau outside after mass at the cathedral on Sundays (and admonished his nieces for making fun of 'the beggar'). But Nouveau was not from Lyon, and in the circumstances Cézanne would perhaps have said a little more to his son about the man's past history.

Aix, 14 August 1906

Mon cher Paul,

It's two in the afternoon. I'm in my room, it's turned hot again, it's dreadful. I'm waiting until four when the carriage will pick me up and take me to the river, at the Trois-Sautets bridge. It's a bit cooler there, I felt very well there yesterday. I began a watercolour like those I was doing at Fontainebleau, it seems more harmonious to me, the thing is to convey as much *rapport* as possible.[1]

In the evening I went to wish your Aunt Marie happy birthday; I found Marthe there, you know better than I what I think of the situation, so it's up to you to manage our affairs. My right foot is getting better. But how hot it is, the air smells nauseating.

I received the slippers, I put them on, they fit very well, it's a success.

At the river a poor little mite, very lively, dressed in rags, came up to me and asked me if I was rich, and another, older, told him that one didn't ask such questions. When I got back into the carriage to return to town, he followed me, when we got to the bridge I threw him two sous, if you could have seen how he thanked me.

Mon cher Paul, the only thing I have left is painting, I embrace you with all my heart, you and maman, your old father,

Paul Cézanne

1   *Bathers by a Bridge* (RWC601), perhaps, or *The Trois-Sautets Bridge* (RWC644).

Bathers by a Bridge, 1900–06. Watercolour and pencil,
21 x 27.2 cm (8¼ x 10¾ in.).

The Trois-Sautets Bridge, c. 1906. Watercolour and pencil,
40.8 x 54.3 cm (16⅛ x 21⅜ in.).

Aix, Sunday [26] August 1906

Mon cher Paul,
When I forget to write to you, it's because I lose track of time a little. It's been terribly [hot], and in addition my nervous system must be much weakened. I live as if in a dream. Painting is the best thing for me. I'm very irritated at the gall of my compatriots who liken themselves to me as artists, and who want to get their hands on my studies. You should see the mess they make. I go to the river by carriage every day. It's nice enough there, but my weakness is getting me down. Yesterday I met the soutaned Roux, he disgusts me.

I'm going to go up to the studio, I got up late, after five. I'm still working happily, and yet sometimes the light is so bad that nature seems ugly to me. So one has to choose. My pen is hardly moving. I embrace you both with all my heart, and remember me to all the friends who still think of me across time and space.

A big hug for you and maman. Hello to Monsieur and Madame Legoupil, your old father,

Paul Cézanne

Aix, 2 September [1906]

Mon cher Paul,
It's nearly four, there isn't a breath of air. The weather is still stifling. I'm waiting for the carriage to take me to the river. I spend a few pleasant hours there. There are tall trees, they form a vault over the water. I go to the place known as Gour de Martelly, it's on the little Chemin des Milles, which leads to Montbriant. Towards evening they bring cows along to graze. There's

plenty to study and make lots of pictures of. Sheep also come there to drink, but they disappear a bit too quickly. Some house-painters came up to me and said that they'd like to do the same kind of painting, but they aren't taught it at the school of art; I said that [Auguste-Henri] Pontier [the director] was a foul oaf, they seemed to agree. As you can see, there's nothing new. It's still hot, there's no rain, and it looks as though there will be none for some time. I don't know what else to tell you, other than that four or five days ago I met Demolins [Gasquet's associate] and he seemed to me a complete fake. Our judgment must be much influenced by our mood.

I embrace you and maman with all my heart,
Your father,

Paul Cézanne

267 • TO HIS SON

Aix, 8 September 1906

Mon cher Paul,
Today (it's nearly eleven) a new heat wave. The air is overheated, not a hint of a breeze. The only thing such a temperature is good for is to expand metals, encourage the sale of drinks, make beer merchants happy, an industry that seems to be attaining respectable proportions in Aix, and swell the pretentions of the intellectuals of my country, a load of old sods, idiots and fools.

The exceptions, and there may be some, keep their heads down. Modesty always conceals itself. Finally, I must tell you that as a painter I'm becoming more clear-sighted in front of nature, but the *réalisation* of my *sensations* is still very laboured. I can't achieve the intensity that builds in my senses, I don't have that magnificent richness of colour that enlivens nature. Here on the riverbank the *motifs* multiply, the same subject from a different angle provides a fascinating subject for study, and so varied that I think I could occupy myself for months without moving, leaning now more to the right, now more to the left.

Mon cher Paul, in closing let me tell you that I have the greatest confidence in your *sensations*, which give your mind the direction it needs in looking after our interests, in other words I have the utmost confidence in your management of our affairs.

I learn with great patriotic satisfaction that the venerable statesman who presides over the political destinies of France [President Armand Fallières] is going to honour our country with a visit; for the people of southern France, their cup runneth over. Jo [Gasquet], where are you now? Is it the artificial and conventional things in the course of life on earth that lead to the surest success, or is it a series of happy coincidences that brings our efforts to fruition?[1]

Your father, who embraces you and maman,

Paul Cézanne

1 Evidently Cézanne's expressions of 'patriotic satisfaction' are not always to be taken straight.

268 · TO HIS SON

Aix, 13 September 1906

Mon cher Paul,
I'm sending you a letter I've just received from Emilio Bernardinos [Émile Bernard], most distinguished aesthete, whom I'm sorry not to have under my thumb in order to inculcate in him the sane, comforting and sole correct idea, of art developing in contact with nature. I can hardly read his letter, though I believe it is right; yet the good fellow turns his back completely on the things he expounds in his writings, and in his drawings he produces nothing but old-fashioned rubbish that smacks of the dreams

of art prompted not by excitement at nature but by what he has seen in museums, and even more by a philosophical turn of mind that comes from knowing too well the masters he admires. Let me know if I'm wrong. Even so, I am still sorry about the annoying accident he has had. I cannot come to Paris this year, as you know. I wrote to you that I go every day by carriage to the riverbank. Because of fatigue and constipation, I've had to give up going to the studio. This morning I took a little walk, I came back around ten or eleven, I had lunch, and at three thirty I left for the banks of the Arc, as I told you earlier.

I'm very interested in my research. Perhaps I could have made a true believer of Bernard. Clearly one must experience things for oneself and express oneself as best one can. I'm always going over the same thing, but arranged in this way my life allows me to isolate myself from the hoi polloi.

I embrace you and your mother with all my heart,
Your old father,

Paul Cézanne

One who is strong is Baudelaire, his *Art romantique* is amazing, and he is never mistaken about the artists he likes.[1]

If you want to reply to his [Bernard's] letter, send it to me and I'll copy it. Don't mislay the above-mentioned letter.

1 *L'Art romantique* (1868) was one of Cézanne's favourite books. It contained the celebrated essay on 'The Painter of Modern Life' (first published in instalments in *Le Figaro* in 1863). For Cézanne, the highlight was Baudelaire's tribute to 'The Life and Work of Eugène Delacroix' (first published in *L'Opinion nationale* in 1863), which he read and reread all his life.

Aix, 21 September 1906

Mon cher Bernard,

I find myself in such a state of brain trouble, trouble so great that I fear my feeble reason may desert me at any moment. After the terrible heat we've been enduring, a more clement temperature has brought a little calm to our spirits, and not a moment too soon; now it seems to me that I'm seeing better and thinking more clearly about the direction of my studies. Will I reach the goal I've sought so hard and pursued for so long? I hope so, but while it remains unattained a vague unease persists, which will disappear only once I've reached the harbour, in other words when I've realized something that develops better than in the past, and thus becomes proof of theories that, of themselves, are always easy; it is only providing proof of one's ideas that presents serious obstacles. So I continue my studies – but I've just reread your letter and I see that I always reply off the point. Please excuse me, as I've said, the reason is my constant preoccupation with the goal to be attained.

I always study from nature, and it seems to me that I'm making slow progress. I should have liked you beside me, for the loneliness always weighs on me a little. But I am old, and ill, and I have vowed to die painting rather than sink into the degrading senility that threatens old people who let themselves be ruled by passions that dull the senses.

If I have the pleasure of being with you again one day, we'll be able to explain ourselves better face-to-face. You'll forgive me for always coming back to the same point, but I believe in the logical development of what we see and feel through the study of nature, never mind about the techniques [*les procédés*]. Techniques are merely the means of making the public feel what we ourselves feel, and of making us acceptable. The greats whom we admire must have done the same thing.

Warm regards from the pig-headed old macrobite who sends you cordial greetings.

P. Cézanne

Aix, 22 September 1906

Mon cher Paul,

I sent a long letter in reply to Émile Bernard, a letter filled with my concerns, as I told him, but since I see a bit better than him, and since my way of imparting my thoughts cannot offend him in the slightest, even though I don't share his temperament or his way of feeling, well, in the end I've come to believe that we can do nothing for others. It is true that, with Bernard, one could go on theorizing indefinitely, for he has the temperament of a logician.

I go out into the landscape every day, the *motifs* are beautiful and I spend my days more agreeably than anywhere else.

I embrace you and maman with all my heart, your devoted father,

Paul Cézanne

Mon cher Paul, I've told you before that I suffer from brain trouble, my letter reflects that; besides, I tend to look on the dark side, so increasingly I feel compelled to rely on you, and to take my bearings from you.

Aix, 26 September 1906

Mon cher Paul,

I've had a letter from the Salon d'Automne, signed Lapigie, doubtless one of the main organizers and sherpas of the exhibition, from which I gather that I have eight canvases in it. Yesterday I saw the valiant Marseillais Carlos [Charles] Camoin, who came to show me a bundle of canvases and ask my opinion; what he does is good, he'll make rapid progress, he's coming to spend a few days in Aix to work on the little Chemin du Tholonet. He showed me a photograph of a figure by poor Émile Bernard, we're agreed that he's an intellectual, blocked by the memories of museums, who doesn't look at nature enough, and this is the main point, to get away from any and every school. So Pissarro was not mistaken; he went a bit far, however, when he said that all the artistic necropolises should be burned down.

You could certainly make up a strange menagerie of all those art professionals and their like. The Secretary-General himself is an artist. In this case, in the light of his position, in the Salon d'Automne of course, he should be the equal of a member of the Institute. So there you have a building that rises proudly, not to say victoriously, opposite the shack on the Quai Conti, whose library was founded by the one Sainte-Beuve calls 'the artful Italian' [Cardinal Mazarin]. I'm still going *sur nature*, on the bank of the Arc, leaving my gear with a man called Bossy, who offered it houseroom. I embrace you and maman with all my heart, your father, Paul Cézanne.

272 · TO HIS SON

Aix, 28 September [1906]

Mon cher Paul,

I must ask you to send me some no. 4 restorative pills. I only have two or three left in the last box. I told you that I had to return to Vignol three out of five tubes of fine lake, the other two I mislaid moving out of the studio in Rue Boulegon or in the country. I don't believe the good man is capable of running his business. The weather is magnificent, the countryside superb. Carlos Camoin is here, he comes to see me from time to time. I'm reading Baudelaire's treatments of the work of Delacroix. As for me, I must remain alone. People are so crafty, there's no escaping them, their thieving, their self-importance, their conceit, their violations, their hands on your work, and yet nature is very beautiful. I still see Vallier, but I'm so slow in *réalisation* that it makes me very sad.[1] Only you can comfort me in my sad state.

The Gardener Vallier, c. 1906. Watercolour and pencil,
48 x 31.5 cm (18⅞ x 12⅜ in.).

The Gardener Vallier, 1905–06. Oil on canvas,
65.4 x 54.9 cm (25¾ x 21⅝ in.).

The Gardener Vallier, 1902–06. Oil on canvas,
107.4 x 74.5 cm (42¼ x 29⅜ in.)

So I commend myself to you, I embrace you and maman with all my heart. Your old father,

Paul Cézanne

1 'Seeing Vallier' meant only one thing. Cézanne painted six oil portraits of *The Gardener Vallier* (R948–51, 953, 954), plus three large watercolours (RWC639–41), the culmination of the late work. There is Vallier in summer and Vallier in winter: he is a man for all seasons. One of those portraits was the last oil painting he ever worked on (R954). Lawrence Gowing found that 'the gardener in profile has not only a look of Cézanne himself but the look of a Michelangelesque Moses', and it may well be that these works are in some sense self-portraits. Vallier was Cézanne's secret sharer.

273 · TO HIS SON

Aix, 8 October 1906

Mon cher Paul,

I'm sending you the card you asked for [admission to the Salon d'Automne]. I'm terribly sorry for the nervous state I'm in, which prevents me from writing at greater length, the weather is fine, I go to the *motif* in the afternoons. Emery raised the price of the carriage to 3 francs return, when I used to go to the Château Noir for 5 francs. I've let him go. I made the acquaintance of Monsieur Roublard, who has married money in the person of Mademoiselle Fabry. When you're here you'll see what he's up to. He's a young man, well set up in town, he organizes concerts, spiritual and highly artistic.

I won't go on any longer today. Yesterday evening I spent about three hours before dinner with [Alexis-Ernest] Capdeville, [Barthélémy] Niol[l]on, Fernand Bouteille, etc., at the Café des Deux Garçons.

Your father, who tenderly embraces you and maman,

Paul Cézanne

Aix, 13 October 1906

Mon cher Paul,

Today, after a thunderstorm in the night and as it was still raining this morning, I stayed at home. As you remind me, I did indeed forget to mention the wine to you, Madame Brémond tells me that we must get some in. If you see Bergot at the same time, you could order some white for yourself and your mother. It's rained a lot and I think that this time the heat is over. The banks of the river have become a little cool, so I've abandoned them and am going up around Beauregard, where the path is steep, very picturesque but very exposed to the mistral. At the moment I'm going on foot with just a bag of watercolours, leaving oil painting until after I've found somewhere to leave my gear, in the old days you could do that for thirty francs a year. I feel exploitation everywhere. I'll wait for you before taking a decision. The weather is stormy and very changeable. Nervous system much weakened. Only oil painting keeps me going. So I must *realize* after nature. Sketches, canvases, if I were to do any, would only be constructions after [nature], based on the methods, *sensations* and developments suggested by the model, but I'm always saying the same thing. Could you get me a small quantity of almond thins?

I embrace you and maman with all my heart,
Your father,

Paul Cézanne

Mon cher Paul, I found Émile Bernard's letter. I hope he pulls through, but I fear the contrary.

Ever your

Paul Cézanne

Aix, 15 October 1906

Mon cher Paul,
It poured with rain on Saturday and Sunday, it's much cooler now. In fact it's not hot at all. You're quite right to say that here we're deep in the provinces. I continue to work with difficulty, but finally there is something. That's the important thing, I think. Since *sensations* are my stock-in-trade, I believe I'm impervious. So I'll let the wretch (you know who) imitate me as much as he likes, he's not much of a threat.

When you have a chance, say hello to Monsieur and Madame Legoupil, who are so kind as to remember me. And don't forget Louis [Guillaume] and his family, and old Guillaume [the cobbler]. Everything goes by with frightening speed, I'm not doing too badly. I look after myself, I eat well.

Would you be kind enough to order me two dozen mongoose-hair brushes, like those we ordered last year.

Mon cher Paul, to give you the satisfactory news you want, I would have to be twenty years younger. I repeat, I eat well, and a little boost to morale would do me a power of good, but only work can give me that. All my compatriots are arseholes [*culs*] beside me.[1] I should have told you that I received the cocoa.

I embrace you, you and maman, your old father,

Paul Cézanne

I think the young painters are much more intelligent than the others, the old can only see me as a disastrous rival.[2] Ever your father

P. Cézanne

I'll say it again, Émile Bernard seems to me deserving of deep compassion, since he has to tend souls.[3]

1 Not quite the sweeping denunciation it might seem: 'compatriots' in Cézanne's language meant people of the Midi or, more narrowly, Provence.

2 Possibly a comment on the survey conducted by the prestigious *Mercure de France* the previous year, on 'Current Trends in the Plastic Arts'. See the Introduction.

3 Perhaps a reference to Bernard's two small children, Antoine and Irène.

276 · TO A COLOUR MERCHANT

Aix, 17 October 1906

Monsieur,
A week has gone by since I asked you for ten burnt lakes no. 7, and I have had no reply. What is going on?

A reply, and a speedy one, I beg you.

Yours faithfully,

Paul Cézanne

Aix, 20 October 1906

Mon cher Paul,
Your father has been ill since Monday [15 October]; Dr Guillaumont does not think that he is in danger, but Madame Brémond cannot look after him alone. You must come as soon as possible. At times he is so weak that a woman cannot lift him by herself; with your help that would be possible. The doctor said to get a male nurse; your father would not hear of it. I think your presence is required in order for him to be as well cared for as possible.

He was out in the rain for several hours on Monday; they brought him back on a laundry cart and it needed two men to carry him up to bed. The next day, as soon as it was light, he went to the garden [of his studio at Les Lauves] to work on a portrait of Vallier under the linden tree; he came back at death's door. You know what your father is like; it's a long story. I repeat: I feel your presence is required.

Madame Brémond particularly wishes me to tell you that your father is using your mother's dressing room as his studio, and that he doesn't intend to move out of it for the present; she wants your mother to know this detail, and since the two of you were not expected back here for another month, your mother can remain in Paris for some time longer; by then perhaps your father will have changed studio.

There, my dear child, is what I think it my duty to tell you; it is for you to decide.

I hope to see you soon, I embrace you affectionately.

Your devoted aunt,

M. Cézanne

1 Cézanne's wife and son were then in Paris. This letter from Cézanne's sister was the first notification of his collapse five days earlier. It was addressed to his son alone. Marie, who passed much of her life in devout disapproval, strongly disapproved of Hortense. Here, she is concerned to convey the message that Paul's presence is absolutely

The Gardener Vallier, 1906. Oil on canvas,
65 x 54 cm (25⅝ x 21¼ in.).

necessary, but that Hortense's is not required. This is an important part of the story of Cézanne's end. See the telegram that immediately follows.

Aix, 10.20 am, 22 October 1906

COME IMMEDIATELY BOTH OF YOU FATHER VERY ILL

BRÉMOND

1 This telegram did not arrive in time. Cézanne died in the early hours of the morning of 23 October. He is variously said to have contracted pleurisy or congestion of the lung; the death certificate provides no details. Madame Brémond alone was present. She called his friend and neighbour, Cyril Rougier, who came over and closed his eyes. His wife and son arrived just in time for the funeral. Their late arrival has been the source of malicious gossip ever since. Its target is Hortense, and it can be traced back to Jean de Beucken, *Un Portrait de Cézanne* (1955), who wrote of Madame Brémond's telegram: 'It was Hortense who received it, but not wanting to postpone a fitting at her dress-maker's, she hid it in a drawer – where probably her son discovered it.' This story was given currency by John Rewald ('Gossip had it …'). It became an essential part of the martyrology – and a stick with which to beat Hortense, faithless or feckless, according to taste.

The story is not entirely believable. It is too neat. It takes no account of the letter sent (too late) by Marie Cézanne to Paul two days earlier. It accepts Jean de Beucken's account at face value, despite his rather novelistic, sometimes novelettish approach. (Towards the end he was close to Paul, who died in 1947, and may have heard things that were common currency, at least in the Cézanne family.) Most importantly, it assumes a good deal about Hortense, and about the nature of the relationship between Cézanne and his wife. Many of these assumptions are unwarranted.

Acknowledgments

I am grateful to the following for moral support (as Cézanne might have said):
Wayne Andersen, Ruth Butler, Denis Coutagne, Elizabeth Cowling, André
Dombrowski, John Elderfield, Bruno Ely, Walter Feilchenfeldt, Jack Flam,
the late John Golding, the late John House, Pavel Machotka, Joachim Pissarro,
Elisabeth Reissner, Richard Shiff, Paul Smith and Jayne Warman.

Among curators, archivists and librarians, I should like to thank in particular
Christine Ekelhart at the Albertina, Vienna; Colin Harrison and his colleagues
at the Ashmolean Museum, Oxford; Stephanie Buck and her colleagues at
the Courtauld Institute, London; Bernard Terlay and his colleagues at the
Musée Granet, Aix-en-Provence; Philippe Ferrand and his colleagues at the
Bibliothèque Méjanes, Aix-en-Provence; Elisa Bourdonnay and her colleagues
at the Musée des Lettres et Manuscrits in Paris; Jean Henry and her colleagues
at the National Gallery of Art, Washington, DC; the staff of the archives
of the Musée d'Orsay, Paris; the staff of the Pavillon de Vendôme, Aix-en-
Provence; the staff of the Harry Ransom Research Center for the Humanities,
Austin, Texas; and Françoise Antiquario at the Centre d'Études sur Zola et
le Naturalisme, Paris.

Research assistance from Caroline Girard in Paris helped to get this project
under way.

I have relied throughout on the wise counsel of Andrew Gordon at David
Higham Associates. At Thames & Hudson, I much appreciate the sympathetic
engagement of Jamie Camplin, the picture research of Pauline Hubner and
the careful editing of Sam Wythe.

The translations were supervised by my friend Paul Edson, a professional
translator, who improved them considerably and taught me a good deal
along the way. I need hardly say that the responsibility for the finished product
is mine alone.

Sources of illustrations

1 Private collection. Courtesy Musée des Lettres et Manuscrits, Paris; 2–3 Private collection. Courtesy Musée des Lettres et Manuscrits, Paris; 6 Bridgestone Museum of Art, Ishibashi Foundation, Tokyo; 10 Photographer unknown; 15 Collection Harold Gershinowitz, Paris; 16 Roger-Viollet/TopFoto; 19 Art Institute of Chicago; 20 Private collection. Courtesy Musée des Lettres et Manuscrits, Paris; 26 Private collection/Bridgeman Art Library; 29 Photographer unknown; 31 Bibliothèque Nationale de France, Paris; 32 Gift of Mr and Mrs Frederick Deknatel, Fogg Museum (1961.152)/Harvard Art Museums, Cambridge, MA; 35 Private collection; 37 The Granger Collection/TopFoto; 38 Collection of Mr and Mrs Paul Mellon, in Honor of the 50th Anniversary of the National Gallery of Art, Washington, DC; 45 Private collection. Courtesy Musée des Lettres et Manuscrits, Paris; 53 Private collection; 65 Private collection; 77 Private collection; 81 Private collection; 85 Private collection; 97 Private collection. Courtesy Musée des Lettres et Manuscrits, Paris; 115 Private collection, Cambridge, MA; 123 Private collection; 124 Private collection; 130 Gift of Paul Mellon, National Gallery of Art, Washington, DC; 131 Musée d'Orsay, Paris (on deposit at the Musée Granet, Aix-en-Provence); 132 State Hermitage Museum, St Petersburg; 139 Private collection. Courtesy Musée des Lettres et Manuscrits, Paris; 141 Musée d'Orsay, Paris; 142 *Album Stock*, 1870; 145 Museu de Arte de São Paulo Assis Chateaubriand; 150a Musée d'Orsay, Paris; 150b Musée d'Orsay, Paris; 157 Fondation Rau pour le Tiers-Monde, Zurich; 159 Gift of Justin K. Thannhauser, Thannhauser Collection, Solomon R. Guggenheim Museum, New York; 167 Private collection/Giraudon/Bridgeman Art Library; 168 National Gallery, London (on loan from Graff Diamonds Ltd); 184 Musée d'Orsay, Paris; 185 Musée d'Orsay, Paris; 186 Arthur Gordon Tompkins Fund, Tompkins Collection, Museum of Fine Arts, Boston; 187 Chester Dale Collection, National Gallery of Art, Washington, DC; 188 Barnes Foundation, Philadelphia; 192 Private collection, Paris; 203 Private collection. Courtesy Musée des Lettres et Manuscrits, Paris; 216 Gift of André Meyer, Museum of Modern Art, New York; 240a Barnes Foundation, Philadelphia; 240b Brooklyn Museum, New York; 241 Gift of Dr and Mrs Franz H. Hirschland, 1957, Metropolitan Museum of Art, New York; 247 Musée d'Orsay; 253 Private collection. Courtesy Musée des Lettres et Manuscrits, Paris; 265 Musée d'Orsay, Paris; 270 Samuel Courtauld Trust, Courtauld Gallery, London; 271 McNay Art Museum/Art Resource, NY/Scala, Florence; 274 Národní Galerie, Prague; 278 Samuel Courtauld Trust, Courtauld Gallery, London; 282 Museu de Arte de Sao Paulo Assis Chateaubriand; 283 Cone Collection, Baltimore Museum of Art; 294 Petit Palais, Musée des Beaux Arts de la Ville de Paris; 299 Private collection. Courtesy Musée des Lettres et Manuscrits, Paris; 302 Fractional gift of Mr and Mrs David Rockefeller, Museum of Modern Art, New York; 303 Musée d'Orsay, Paris; 310 Musée du Louvre, Paris/Giraudon/Bridgeman Art Library; 311 Pushkin Museum, Moscow/Bridgeman Art Library; 312 Gift of Eugene and Agnes Ernst Meyer, National Gallery of Art, Washington, DC; 321 National Gallery, London; 338 Private collection, London; 341 Musée du Louvre, Paris; 361 Galleria Nazionale d'Arte Moderna, Rome; 367 Maria DeWitt Jesup Fund, 1951 (acquired from The Museum of Modern Art, Lillie P. Bliss Collection), Metropolitan Museum of Art, New York; 368 Gift of John J. Emery, Cincinnati Art Museum, OH; 376 Museum Berggruen, Nationalgalerie, Staatliche Museen zu Berlin; 377 Tate Gallery, London; 378 Gift of Eugene and Agnes E. Meyer, National Gallery of Art, Washington, DC; 384 Private collection.

Index